B+T 17.40

Southern Literary Studies
Louis D. Rubin, Editor

# Eudora Welty's Achievement of Order

Michael Kreyling

Louisiana State University Press
*Baton Rouge and London*

Designer: Patricia Douglas Crowder

Typeface: VIP Goudy Old Style

Typesetter: G&S Typesetters, Inc.

Printer: Thomson Shore, Inc.

Binder: John Dekker & Sons

Grateful acknowledgment is made to: Russell & Volkening, Inc., literary representatives, for permission to quote from the published and unpublished works of Eudora Welty; Random House, Inc., and Alfred A. Knopf, Inc., for permission to quote from the copyrighted works of Eudora Welty and Elizabeth Bowen—"The Optimist's Daughter" was originally published in the *New Yorker*, March 15, 1969; the Humanities Research Center, University of Texas at Austin, for permission to quote from Eudora Welty manuscripts held by them; State of Mississippi Department of Archives and History, for permission to quote from the papers of Eudora Welty. Excerpts from Eudora Welty's *The Robber Bridegroom*, *The Bride of the Innisfallen and Other Stories*, *A Curtain of Green and Other Stories*, *Delta Wedding*, *The Golden Apples*, *The Ponder Heart*, *The Wide Net and Other Stories* reprinted by permission of Harcourt Brace Jovanovich, Inc.; copyright © 1941, 1942, 1943, 1946, 1949, 1953, 1954, 1955, 1969, 1970, 1974, 1977 by Harcourt Brace Jovanovich, Inc. Excerpts from T. S. Eliot's "Burnt Norton" and "The Love Song of J. Alfred Prufrock," in *Collected Poems 1909–1962*, reprinted by permission of Harcourt Brace Jovanovich, Inc., and Faber and Faber, Ltd. Excerpts from William Butler Yeats's "The Stolen Child," from *Collected Poems of William Butler Yeats*, copyright 1906 by Macmillan Publishing Co., Inc., renewed 1934 by William Butler Yeats, reprinted by permission of the publisher and M. B. Yeats and Anne Yeats. Chapter IX herein was originally published, in slightly different form, as "Life with People: Virginia Woolf, Eudora Welty and *The Optimist's Daughter*," in *Southern Review*, n.s., XIII (Spring, 1977), 250–71. Chapter VIII herein was originally published, in slightly different form, in *Mississippi Quarterly*, XXVI (Fall, 1973), 639–49. Chapter III herein was originally read as a paper at the Eudora Welty Symposium held at the University of Mississippi in November, 1977, and is published in the volume containing the proceedings of that symposium, *Eudora Welty: A Form of Thanks*.

LIBRARY OF CONGRESS CATALOGING IN PUBLICATION DATA

Kreyling, Michael, 1948–
   Eudora Welty's achievement of order.
   (Southern literary studies)
   Based on the author's thesis, Cornell.
   Bibliography: p.
   Includes index.
   1. Welty, Eudora, 1909–    —Criticism and interpretation. I. Title. II. Series.
PS3545.E6Z75    813'.5'2    79–13121
ISBN 0–8071–0553–8

*For Chris*

# Contents

# Acknowledgments

This book has been a long time in the making. Along the way it has collected a lot of help. It began as my doctoral dissertation at Cornell University. Even though it is a much different work now, the advice and help of those who guided the dissertation have remained forceful and positive. Professor James McConkey directed the dissertation; his deep admiration for Eudora Welty's fiction has always been a demanding presence. Professors Robert Elias and Walter Slatoff also read and helped to direct the dissertation. I have tried to follow not only their specific comments and recommendations but also the example set by their own work.

Professors Noel Polk, University of Southern Mississippi, and Ruth M. Vande Kieft, Queens College of City College of New York, read parts of the manuscript when it was a dissertation and helped me to break up a few jams. Professor Vande Kieft also helped me with revisions in the manuscript.

Among the people in the Department of Rare Books, Cornell University Libraries, who have generously assisted me are Professor Donald D. Eddy, rare books librarian, who purchased several limited and first editions of Welty's works and has since added a large collection of newspaper reviews of her work; his secretary, Mrs. Jane Woolston, who typed my dissertation during her breaks and lunch hours; and Dr. James Tyler, who helped me to identify several of the reviews of Welty's fiction and went to a good deal of trouble to see that I got the most use out of the collection.

The director and staff of the State of Mississippi Department of Archives and History and the director and staff of the Humanities Research Center at the University of Texas at Austin have been kind and helpful. Professors E. O. Hawkins, Jr., Peyton W. Williams, Jr., and Robert L. Phillips, of the Department of English, Mississippi State University, provided necessary encouragement.

I would like to thank Mr. Timothy Seldes, president of Russell & Volkening, Inc., Miss Welty's literary representatives, whose decision to grant me permission to quote from her work, published and unpublished, has helped both dissertation and book tremendously.

Reynolds Price, who stole time from his own work to read and criticize this manuscript, deserves special thanks. If there are weaknesses in the book, it is because I was too stubborn to heed his advice.

Christine M. Kreyling, my wife, adamantly refused to type a single word of the manuscript. But she read the whole thing and fought with me over it, always to make it better. The truth is that she frequently knew what I should write and read before I did. Her suggestions have been more than helpful; they have been right.

The only way I can thank Eudora Welty herself is to write the best book I can. I once thought, vainly, that this book itself would be fitting thanks. But knowing her and her work has presented me with a permanent obligation.

# Introduction

This is not primarily a book about southern literature. It is a book about the work of a novelist and short story writer who lives in Jackson, Mississippi, where she has put down strong roots. Her writing, having retained its hardy and delicate uniqueness, has taken a place among the work of writers outside the American South. Thus, it has exhibited the simultaneous nature of all good writing: it is rooted in a specific time and place while comprehending more than just one time and one place. This volume is aimed at discovering how Eudora Welty's fiction has come to embrace so much more than its local materials and local color.

Previous attempts to discuss Welty's fiction have assumed various forms. Reviews, limited by preparation time and column space, generally mention a few significant points about the plot and some of the major characters, remind the reader of the author's reputation or promise, and assign to her labels such as "regionalist," "stylist," and "local colorist." Welty's early short stories, in which many reviewers saw the "promise" of a novel, were very often explicated individually in longer, more reflective articles, essays, and notes. The frequency of patterns of myth and other imagery has given the early stories the reputation of being flawless performances. Katherine Anne Porter called them "almost perfect stories" in her introduction to A *Curtain of Green* (1941).[1] Articles on Welty's

1. Katherine Anne Porter, introduction to *Selected Stories of Eudora Welty* (New York, 1954),

work have appeared steadily since then; some follow Porter's lead and others take the opposing side, terming the fiction "obscurantist."[2] Dissertations too have been written about her work—a positive indication of respect and popularity.

A few writers have attempted to discuss the whole of Welty's work, her vision. Robert Penn Warren was the first to recognize that her writing merited such an appraisal; his "The Love and Separateness in Miss Welty" remains one of the indispensable views of her work. More recent essays that have not yet become established but should, are Ruth Vande Kieft's "The Vision of Eudora Welty" and John A. Allen's "Eudora Welty: The Three Moments."[3] Vande Kieft's essay captures the range and depth of Welty's sensitivity to her world, and Allen's makes some very good observations on the special nature of Welty's concept of heroism.

Of the two book-length studies of Welty's writing, Ruth Vande Kieft's *Eudora Welty*, published in 1962, deals with all of the fiction published to that time. Vande Kieft's book is the established, influential critical work in this area and deserves to be. Her readings and insights into the fiction of Eudora Welty have not only endured but grown. Some of her suggestions for further critical approaches have been rewarding. Alfred Appel, Jr.'s *A Season of Dreams: The Fiction of Eudora Welty*, published in 1965 and now out of print, arranges a discussion of the fiction around certain topics. J. A. Bryant, Jr., and Neil D. Isaacs have written pamphlet introductions to Welty's fiction—not an easy task, considering the restricted range of such pamphlets.[4] Zelma Turner Howard's *The Rhetoric of Eudora Welty's Short Stories* makes use of a set of rhetorical terms (derived from Wayne Booth's *The Rhetoric of Fiction*) in her approach to the stories in *A Curtain of Green*, *The Wide Net*, and *The Golden Apples*. Marie-Antoinette Manz-Kunz, in her *Eudora Welty:*

xviii. The Modern Library volume reprints the complete contents of *A Curtain of Green* (Garden City, N.Y.: Doubleday, Doran, 1941), and *The Wide Net* (New York: Harcourt, Brace, 1943).

2. Victor H. Thompson, "'Life's Impact is Oblique': A Study of Obscurantism in the Writings of Eudora Welty" (Ph.D. dissertation, Rutgers University, 1972).

3. Robert Penn Warren, "The Love and Separateness in Miss Welty," *Kenyon Review*, VI (Spring, 1944), 246–59; Ruth M. Vande Kieft, "The Vision of Eudora Welty," *Mississippi Quarterly*, XXVI (Fall, 1973), 517–42; John A. Allen, "Eudora Welty: The Three Moments," *Virginia Quarterly Review*, LI (Autumn, 1975), 605–27.

4. J. A. Bryant, Jr., *Eudora Welty* (Minneapolis, 1968); Neil D. Isaacs, *Eudora Welty* (Austin, Tex., 1969).

*Aspects of Reality in Her Short Fiction*, examines the theme of the need for humans to belong to a community and finds in the short fiction many instances in which its expression takes symbolic, allusive, or even human form. But no full-length study includes *Losing Battles* and *The Optimist's Daughter*, published in 1970 and 1972 respectively—novels that have enhanced the critical reputation of Welty appreciably.

Since the previous critical studies were written, the State of Mississippi Department of Archives and History, in Jackson, and the Humanities Research Center at the University of Texas at Austin have acquired significant collections of original materials such as manuscripts, unpublished stories, letters, and other items. New insights into the making of the stories and the novels are now possible for the first time. Welty's revisions are especially interesting to one curious about the *how* of her fiction. Stories once considered so flawless and effortlessly made are seen to be the work of a careful craftsman, not the work of the "natural writer" (such was F. Scott Fitzgerald's onus).

In recently published interviews and articles, Welty herself has given her readers more reasons to read her again. She has discussed the reading that has influenced her and has commented upon her own feelings and thoughts about literature and the themes she considers important. These new statements have made the topic of influence, always elusive and enticing, more than an educated shot in the dark.

Scholars and critics in other fields of literature must also be mentioned, for there is more than one critical approach in this study. Lewis Simpson's *The Man of Letters in New England and the South* suggested to me that the moral dilemma of *The Robber Bridegroom* might be compared with dilemma faced by Coverdale in Hawthorne's *The Blithedale Romance*. Welty has herself implicitly suggested an approach through the comparison of her work with Elizabeth Bowen's.[5] There is certainly an affinity in subject and style in their works. Ruth Vande Kieft has suggested that there is much to be gained in an appreciation of Welty from such a comparison.[6] Welty's work has also been compared, in other essays of long-standing, with that of the "moderns" Yeats, Joyce, and

5. Eudora Welty, review of Elizabeth Bowen's *Pictures and Conversations*, in *New York Times Book Review*, January 5, 1975, pp. 4, 20.
6. Vande Kieft, Ruth M., *Eudora Welty* (New York, 1962), Chap. 8. See also Rebecca Smith Wild, "Studies in the Shorter Fiction of Elizabeth Bowen and Eudora Welty" (Ph.D. dissertation, University of Michigan, 1965).

Eliot for her use of epiphany and symbol. With the aid of some reappraisals of the modern writers, I have used this approach. *The Optimist's Daughter* has illuminated Welty's fiction through the similarities with Virginia Woolf's *To the Lighthouse.* And the publication of *The Eye of the Story: Selected Essays and Reviews* has reminded us of a strong aspect of Welty's achievement—her literary criticism.

This study approaches Welty's fiction from many of these directions. Each approach attempts to locate the elusive, irreducible voice of the fiction—the "prophecy," E. M. Forster would call it. Earlier work has guided me away from some errors; but, to get at what I think should be said, I have sometimes had to retrace the steps of others. What is the focus of this variety of angles? A creative process in which a self senses its physical world, struggles to express this sense of the joining up of things and people, and achieves a finished work of art which, if it is successful, embodies not only this world but the vital principle of seeing, and goes on living and affecting those who read. This unity occurs, according to Forster, in "a region which can only be implied and to which fiction [or the criticism of fiction] is perhaps the wrong approach."[7] Other critics have entered where Forster feared to tread and have given this "region" a map. One, Mark Schorer, writes about technique in search of unity. "For technique is the means by which the writer's experience, which is his subject matter, compels him to attend to it; technique is the only means he has of discovering, exploring, developing his subject, of conveying its meaning, and, finally, of evaluating it."[8] The thesis of Schorer's "Technique as Discovery" is that technique is not solely the conscious organization and selection of the given. It is also the discovery of the resources of language and of vision that become the "achieved content" through the artistic process. The reader's responsibility in this activity is great because he must free himself to discover as the author does, must be prepared to recognize the moment of unity when it emerges separate from its parts.

I am interested in this discovering, since the impression of unity has always accompanied my reading of Welty. I want to find out how it comes about, which entails a study of technique. Hugh Kenner, writing

7. E. M. Forster, *Aspects of the Novel* (New York, 1955), 134.
8. Mark Schorer, "Technique as Discovery," in James Calderwood and Harold Toliver (eds.), *Perspectives on Fiction* (New York, 1968), 200.

about Faulkner's technique, has aided my reading of Welty. "The symbolist work, avoiding symbols, prolongs what it cannot find a way to state with concision, prolongs it until, ringed and riddled with nuance, it is virtually camouflaged by patterns of circumstance. (You cannot skim a Faulkner story.) With good will, an identifiable world emerges, which, seeing the lavish trouble the writer has taken, we are apt to try to 'interpret.' This is usually a mistake."[9] Kenner's admonition against overly ardent attempts to specify an exclusive meaning must be kept in mind. Welty's own critical writings maintain this reserve and invariably skirt explicit interpretation in search of the writer's sensibility, vision, or prophetic voice. Analytical or argumentative criticism—any approach that is dogmatic—seems inappropriate to her work. It is not that Welty's prose is muddled or murky (the argument that her style is obscure is easily countered), and not that the readers are muddled and murky either. But the fiction, taken as individual works or as a corpus, is so integral that taking it piece by piece, moment by moment, cannot duplicate the sense of wholeness one continues to enjoy in reading it. It would be as well to direct the reader back to *Delta Wedding* or to "A Worn Path."

The label *southern* obviously does not contain the elusive quality in Welty's fiction. It is not a quality that any single critical approach alone can describe. There is a "press of meaning upon structure . . . varying ways in which the inner themes . . . unfold, with their adaptation of existing kinds of discourse."[10] This appears as integrity, style reflecting meaning and vice versa, climaxing in a moment in which the two merge. Welty's fiction is more lyrical than narrative; one must read it with "an ear for song."[11] Sometimes the fiction is symbolist in the sense in which Kenner uses the word; sometimes it is more easily divisible into stanzas than into chapters or plot and subplot.

A special version of the "historical sources" approach helps to illuminate the technique of *The Robber Bridegroom*. The legends and history of the Natchez Trace make a counterpoint for the rollicking fairy tale aspect of the novella. The interplay of legend and comic tone also entitles *The Robber Bridegroom* to be read in the wider and older tradition of

9. Hugh Kenner, *A Homemade World: The American Modernist Writers* (New York, 1975), 205.

10. Laurence Stapleton, *The Elected Circle: Studies in the Art of Prose* (Princeton, N.J., 1973), 5.

11. Forster, *Aspects of the Novel*, 128.

ironical American treatments of the self-contradictory pastoral myth and our pursuit of it. Welty has called her first novella "my historical novel."[12] Little Harp, for example, is modeled after a real, savage killer of the Old Southwest. The Natchez Indians are resurrected from historical extermination to play a part in the novella, as is the town of Rodney. Salome's dream mansion is modeled on a real ruin. But this is not, Welty amends, "a *historical* historical novel." The special way in which *The Robber Bridegroom* is a historical novel and, at the same time, is not, is a manifestation of the unique prophecy in the novelist's voice.

Welty's early stories, collected in *A Curtain of Green* and *The Wide Net*, benefit from the realism and the eye and ear for detail for which Welty's fiction is justly praised and remembered; but they also reveal the beginnings of the technical explorations and discoveries adumbrated in *The Robber Bridegroom*. In mythological allusion and other patterned imagery and symbol used in these early stories, Welty shows her desire to reach through reality for the still moment in the flux, for some resolution in but also beyond the plot. In many of these stories the climax is a moment of discovery, of seeing (not just with the physical eye), that requires a leap beyond the plot, a passage away from the parts and into the whole, into a state in which the connections are more significant than what is connected.

*Delta Wedding*, Welty's first novel, is also the major discovery of the technique that has sustained her as a novelist. *Delta Wedding* evolved from an unpublished short story, "The Delta Cousins," in which themes of innocence, of family love and individual freedom, and of the mystery of the world are taken up in the consciousness of an individual not yet tempered by love and susceptibility, a lonely nine-year-old girl. The change into novel begins with the distribution of the point of view among several female characters. The artistic distance thus gained clarifies the themes, in fact discovers the full scope and complexity of them. This novel is a vivid example of what Schorer says about point of view in his essay on technique; in *Delta Wedding* the point of view is not a means of limitation, but of definition of the theme.[13] The reviewers who first commented on the novel did not pay close attention to any technique except that of realism. Not surprisingly, they gave *Delta Wedding* a rough time.

12. Eudora Welty, *Fairy Tale of the Natchez Trace* (Jackson, Miss., 1975), 7.
13. Schorer, "Technique as Discovery," 201.

The Golden Apples has long been considered the most successful example of Welty's technique in the coordination of the fictional elements
of theme, character, and plot with a mythological pattern that gives
them resonance and depth. Each of the seven stories was published independently prior to being collected. Comparing the uncollected with
the collected versions helps to show the shaping of the parts into the
whole. The Golden Apples, if not a novel (Welty has said that it is not),
is not a mere assembly of seven short stories either.[14]

The mythological pattern alone, on which there has been abundant
and rewarding critical commentary, does not unify the collection. There
is a prior, more fundamental unifier—technique in the service of a strong
and intense creative vision that includes, but is not defined by, mythology. Meaning emerges in a network of mundane, or "homemade," images
of stance, posture, rooms, looks, gaits, and "each other" (the multiplicity of selves). The Golden Apples, in a way Welty's favorite among her
books, is filled with nuance.[15] It is the finest example of overtly allusive
technique wedded to the gradually emerging sensitivity, which, at about
this time (Short Stories, 1949), Welty began to identify with technique.
A stage of artistic self-awareness or maturity is attained in The Golden
Apples.

Walls, division, the languishing of the wish to live lie behind the
wacky comedy of The Ponder Heart also. There are two stories here. One,
the foreground farce of Daniel Ponder's marital woes and murder trial, is
resolved by his acquittal in the uproarious trial scene. But the second
story, of Edna Earle's futile attempts to protect Daniel from "the world,"
to keep a decaying hotel (and her way of life) clean and ordered, is left
suspended and unresolved. It portrays one of those battles that is forever
being lost, yet is never forever lost. Edna Earle's voice, in which The
Ponder Heart is narrated like a dramatic monologue, must be heard with
its echoes in the empty parlor of the Beulah Hotel. Her audience, invisible to us but essential in the dramatic monologue, is a stranger who is
there only because his car broke down on the way to some other, more
populous, place. The walls of that parlor are the actual and symbolic
limits of Edna Earle's world. The history of her gradual enclosure is not
resolved by the ending of The Ponder Heart. She goes on talking; her

14. Charles T. Bunting, "'The Interior World': An Interview with Eudora Welty," Southern
Review, VIII (October, 1972), 715.
    15. Ibid., 714.

plight is a human one, not ended until death. Her sense of her individual fate conflicts with her sense of responsibility for the Ponder fate, which she fulfills in taking care of the hotel and Uncle Daniel. Her voice catches this tension at crucial points in the novella. These points are partings of the curtain through which we catch glimpses of a serious struggle between the wish to live with the self and acknowledgment of considerations larger than the self, such as the Ponders, the hotel, the town. *The Ponder Heart*, through its holding of a fine tension in the monologue, makes an important addition to one of Welty's recurrent themes —self versus society.

The lonely struggle of Edna Earle may be merged with those of several women on separate pilgrimages toward love and value—the several "brides" of *The Bride of the Innisfallen*. These seven stories were being written before, during, and after the composition of *The Ponder Heart*, and one book elucidates the other, dissimilar as they in fact are. This collection, much more subtly and covertly than *The Golden Apples*, makes its own integrity in the repetition of image, motif, and nuance. Its boundaries as a single work are drawn ambitiously wide, but there is little left unrealized. Within each story, and from one story to the others, connections are made, the patterns are etched. *The Bride of the Innisfallen* is, I think, the biggest risk and, for that reason, the most strikingly successful example of Welty's technique. But it is not the last word.

In 1969 *The Optimist's Daughter*, Welty's most recently published fiction, first appeared, in a different form, in the *New Yorker*. The first impression is of a confident technique channeling deeply felt and even turbulent emotions into a compact and fully realized work of fiction. Many of Welty's familiar themes, characters, and places are present; but the achievement as a whole seems to me to reach out from the strong base of her previous work. The major objective of the reach is, I think, a sense of resolution such as is felt in Virginia Woolf's *To the Lighthouse*. In reading the work of Virginia Woolf, Welty learned much of her own fiction. The notion of affinity between writers, too deeply rooted and complex for the term *influence*, is no more vividly apparent than in the relationship between these two novels. One can hear, as one hears in *To the Lighthouse*, threats of radical disjunction and despair quelled by patient and loving attention to the people and things in the world.

Because of the similarity of *Losing Battles* to *Delta Wedding* (published almost twenty-five years before), and because of its encompassing theme of history versus myth, it may serve as the resting place for a discussion that aims to gather up the major ideas of this study. All criticism, indeed all reading, takes liberties with a text; I hope that my liberties here are not too flagrant.

The technical decision that makes *Losing Battles* an encompassing work is, as in so many of Welty's works, the discovery of the point of view, here that of an onlooker.[16] In *Delta Wedding* an interplay of viewpoints that, at times and to certain readers, seemed to be confusing, makes for integrity. The earlier novel opens with Laura's viewpoint, and many readers consequently promoted her to a controlling position. I do not think that any single viewpoint in *Delta Wedding* is meant to control, though Ellen's is certainly fuller than any of the others. But she, too, is an onlooker. *Losing Battles* opens with the onlooker's perspective; one of the longest purely descriptive passages in the novel occurs at the beginning and firmly sets the place and the time, the battlefield, beyond the human self. The lines are drawn, then, for the struggle of man to subdue the world to his consciousness and knowledge—the battle that is always new, always old.

The internal connections of *Losing Battles*, its interlocking tissues—images of circles, the family circle, wedding rings, rings of growth in ancient trees, cyclical family stories and roles; and images of the line, roads, no looking back, progress—link the novel with the entire scope of mankind's meditation on the fact of its existence on earth. The circle is the image favored by the clan in their mythic awareness of time and reality; the line is favored by the historical consciousness. *Losing Battles*, through this internal consistency and the quality of its attention to simple, homemade things, discovers battling attitudes toward human history and time. Everybody loses, as Julia Mortimer, the woman at the head of the forces of education and history, learns. But losing with humility, without the hardening of the heart and the loss of its susceptibility, is rewarded with the truth. This is the comic vision in its broadest sympathy.

Eudora Welty's fiction has been received, from the start, by readers who lamented or saluted her mode—southern fiction. Even her most recent novels, though greatly admired, have not completely escaped some condescension as "regional fiction." The fate of her work is

16. Reynolds Price, "The Onlooker Smiling: An Early Reading of *The Optimist's Daughter*," in his *Things Themselves: Essays and Scenes* (New York, 1972), 114–38.

part of a larger prevailing critical attitude. As recently as June 29, 1975, on the first page of the *New York Times Book Review*, a hasty critic granted southern fiction, Welty's included, a brief moment of silent tribute for former influence, but declared that it has since slipped from "the general consciousness."[17]

It is the aim of this study to turn the tables, to show that Welty's fiction truly encompasses "the general consciousness," that it is not primarily regional writing, or even excellent regional writing, but is the vision of a certain artist who must be considered with her peers—Woolf, Bowen, and Forster, among others—who have never been called regional. Welty's fiction is a gift of more than quaint characters and picturesque settings. It is not a tour of the South, although the South is there in its scenes, its various voices, and its various local colors. Welty is always directing the eye to the essence behind the curtain of appearance. The local, the picturesque, even the realistic, are the curtain's fabric. We see individual features instantly; the whole, with its richness and depths, comes into view more slowly. Life is included not only in the subject matter but also in the means of discovering it. This gives Welty's fiction a vitality that is rare and permanent. The fiction starts from the world, returns to it, leaves it richer:

> We come to terms as well as we can with our lifelong exposure to the world, and we use whatever devices we may need to survive. But eventually, of course, our knowledge depends upon the living relationship between what we see going on and ourselves. If exposure is essential, still more so is the reflection. Insight doesn't happen often on the click of the moment, like a lucky snapshot, but comes in its own time and more slowly and from nowhere but within. The sharpest recognition is surely that which is charged with sympathy as well as with shock—it is a form of human vision. And that is of course a gift. We struggle through any pain or darkness in nothing but the hope that we may receive it, and through any term of work in the prayer to keep it.
>
> In my own case, a fuller awareness of what I needed to find out about people and their lives had to be sought for through another way, through writing stories. But away off one day up in Tishomingo County, I knew this, anyway: that my wish, indeed my continuing passion, would be not to point the finger in judgment but to part a curtain, that invisible shadow that falls between people, the veil of indifference to each other's presence, each other's wonder, each other's human plight. (*OTOP*, 8).

17. Richard Gilman, review of Reynolds Price's *The Surface of Earth*, in *New York Times Book Review*, June 29, 1975, pp. 1–2.

# Abbreviations

Abbreviations appear within, followed by page references. The page numbers are from the editions listed below.

BI    *The Bride of the Innisfallen and Other Stories.* New York: Harcourt, Brace, 1955.

BIC   "The Bride of the Innisfallen." Carbon copy of typescript, with author's revisions, in Humanities Research Center, University of Texas at Austin.

CG    *A Curtain of Green.* Complete contents of this collection found in the more readily available *Selected Stories of Eudora Welty.* Introduction by Katherine Anne Porter. New York: Modern Library, 1954.

DC    "The Delta Cousins." Typescript, in State of Mississippi Department of Archives and History, Jackson.

DW    *Delta Wedding.* New York: Harcourt, Brace, 1946.

GA    *The Golden Apples.* New York: Harcourt, Brace, 1949.

LB    *Losing Battles.* New York: Random House, 1970.

OD    *The Optimist's Daughter.* New York: Random House, 1972.

ODNY  "The Optimist's Daughter." *New Yorker,* March 15, 1969.

OTOP  *One Time, One Place.* New York: Random House, 1971.

PH    *The Ponder Heart.* New York: Harcourt, Brace, 1954.

RB   *The Robber Bridegroom.* Garden City, N.Y.: Doubleday, Doran,
     1942.

TL   *To the Lighthouse.* By Virginia Woolf. New York: Harcourt,
     Brace and World, 1955.

WN   *The Wide Net.* Complete contents of this collection found in
     *Selected Stories of Eudora Welty.*

Eudora Welty's Achievement of Order

# I

# Exposure and Reflection:
# A *Curtain of Green*

The publication of A *Curtain of Green* in 1941 was to be a significant event in the issuing of fiction by American publishers. Collections of short stories seldom, according to form and legend, break even; but Doubleday, Doran was bringing out seventeen stories by Eudora Welty. The publishers were not gambling on an unknown, for Welty's stories had made their way from small magazines such as *Manuscript* and *Prairie Schooner* to the national magazines *Atlantic Monthly* and *Harper's Bazaar*. And "A Worn Path" had just won an O. Henry Award.

The reviews that greeted A *Curtain of Green* were on the whole favorable. The major northeastern newspapers were reserved in their appreciation and sparing with the column inches. Other newspaper reviewers, however, took positions along a spectrum of responses. Louise Douglas, writing for the Nashville (Tenn.) *Banner*, was most impressed. "Here a Southerner has used Dixie as a background for her stories yet slyly escaped the bounds of regional limits by her keen understanding of human nature."[1] Several favorable reviews took the same or a similar approach. The regional element was undeniably present, but just as undeniably, it was transcended by a mature and artistic conception of human nature in its universal scope.

On the other end of the spectrum were a few reviews that, for some

1. Louise Douglas, "Genuine Artistry," Nashville (Tenn.) *Banner*, December 10, 1941.

reason, established a critical approach to Welty's short fiction that has thrived for many years. Perhaps Katherine Anne Porter's introduction was a contributing factor. In her appraisal of Welty's stories, Porter emphasizes the "vulgarity" of "Petrified Man" and the case of "dementia praecox" she finds at the center of "Why I Live at the P.O." Those phrases frequently pop up in the reviews. The long-term result has been the identification of Welty, at least in her short fiction, as a purveyor of the Gothic South.[2] Several reviewers saw only, or almost exclusively, the abnormal. "Tale after tale reveals Eudora Welty's preoccupation with mood and atmosphere rather than with incident. Her characters predominantly border on dementia praecox or other forms of insanity; others depend for their emotional effect upon a microscopic revelation of some frustration in the life of a relatively normal human; one or two possess warmth and serenity, only one a trace of humor. For the most part bitterness, pessimism, confusion or sheer horror predominate."[3] The protagonists are seen as "pitiable grotesques" whose lives are plagued by Kafkaesque nightmares and frustrations.[4] The most disappointed reviewers could find nothing of significance in this collection. "Her stories seem mere groupings [sic] into the morbid without the finding of enough to storm our hearts or enlist our interest. The morbid remains morbid, and the reader finds himself skipping pages to find another, better story. He doesn't."[5]

This evaluation of Welty's first work suggests that it merely picks up and dusts off an old tradition in the short story (not just in southern literature)—the gothic or grotesque or morbid—and appears frequently in several critical essays and reviews that have followed the initial comments of reviewers.[6] It is not difficult to see how it might have arisen from naked statements describing selected elements of the stories—dementia praecox, Keela's deformity and his sideshow act of eating live chickens, the image of Clytie's legs protruding from the rain barrel in which she drowns herself. But such statements are not the language of

2. Louise Bogan, "The Gothic South," in *Selected Criticism* (New York, 1955), 207–209.

3. Frances Bunn, "Short Stories," Raleigh (N.C.) *Observer*, April 19, 1942.

4. Frank Brookhouser, "Miss Welty's New Talent in Short Stories," Philadelphia *Inquirer*, December 3, 1941.

5. Sarah Schiff, "Stories Too Green To Burn," Springfield (Mass.) *Republican*, January 11, 1942, Sec. E, p. 7.

6. Marie-Antoinette Manz-Kunz, *Eudora Welty: Aspects of Reality in her Short Fiction* (Bern, Switzerland, 1971), 11. Manz-Kunz gives a condensation of the typical trends in early Welty criticism and reviews.

the stories themselves. Even though some descriptive categories do help in relating the stories in A *Curtain of Green* to each other, these seventeen stories simply refuse to be categorically arranged.[7] Welty herself has been quoted as saying, "The first book covered the longest period of time, so perhaps it is best that way—to say a variety of things in different ways."[8]

Can someone now, more than thirty-five years later, revise the author's own simple description of her stories? I don't think so. What might be done with some profit for both readers and stories, is to show, even among so many stories written over so many years about so many subjects and themes, how there is a resonance in A *Curtain of Green* which suggests an integrating vision and technique that are groping toward discovery. There is the shock of the abnormal, the morbid, the grotesque, and also the reflection after this exposure, in which some heightened sense of reality is attained. The later story collections are certainly not about such a variety of things, nor are they marked by such different styles. They are more poetically and musically composed, more striking in their concerted unities than in the diversity of impressions that the seventeen stories of the first collection leave with the reader. Some of the stories in A *Curtain of Green*, in theme and technique, hint at the direction of the later fiction.

More than thirty years after writing the stories in A *Curtain of Green*, Welty gave the best introduction to their theme and technique in her foreword to *One Time, One Place*. She spoke of the experience of being invisible behind her Kodak, and of how she moved among people in Mississippi places and in conditions of which she was, she admitted, largely ignorant. This learning did not come with the snap of the shutter on the face, the group, or the scene. "It was after I got home, and made my prints in the kitchen and dried them overnight and looked at them in the morning by myself, that I began to see objectively what I had there" (*OTOP*, 7).

This photographic metaphor for the artist's vision—the snapping of

---

7. Katherine Anne Porter, in her introduction to A *Curtain of Green*, reprinted in *Selected Stories of Eudora Welty*, provides some classifications for the stories. See also Eunice Glenn, "Fantasy in the Fiction of Eudora Welty," in Allen Tate (ed.), *Southern Vanguard* (New York, 1947), 78–91.

8. Eudora Welty, quoted in Walter Schmucker, "A Visit With Eudora Welty in Mississippi," Dallas *News*, December 24, 1950.

the shutter, the slow process of development, the examination in objectivity and solitude—may also be the best way of reading these early stories. And insofar as the impulse to make an image, to border and thus to define amorphous experience, is the impulse to discover an order in experience, the same metaphor indicates the theme. As Welty further stated, this order and truth, like a photograph, is not to be rushed. "I learned quickly enough when to click the shutter, but what I was becoming aware of more slowly was a story-writer's truth: the thing to wait on, to reach there in time for, is the moment in which people reveal themselves. . . . Every feeling waits upon its gesture. Then when it does come, how unpredictable it turns out to be, after all" (OTOP, 7–8). The order is beyond the maker, it is in the world, to be reached for. It might not be the order we predicted; our responsibility is not to predict but to discover.

Reading is not to be hurried. In Welty's fiction, style or technique—terms which in their common applications I take to be interchangeable and to describe ways of dealing with one's material—are not means of stating, but of discovering, not means of racing around and ahead of the reader, but of accompanying. In such writing, style is of central importance, for the totality is never, except in the weaker stories, immediately present. Style works like the chemical medium that develops an exposed photographic film to present the totality, "the moment in which people reveal themselves." That moment is never simply achieved.

The presentation of grotesques—half-wits, morons, cripples, defectives, "little human monsters"—is more readily perceived than is the style. In her introduction to A Curtain of Green, Katherine Anne Porter places the stories in a category of which "the spirit is satire and the key is grim comedy." Porter describes the style in these stories as "complete realism" (CG, xxi, xx). But her conclusion seems to me to be based on a reading that stops with the shutter's click. At that moment the reader most clearly sees Uncle Rondo disporting with ketchup in Stella Rondo's flesh-colored kimono, or Mr. Marblehall with his two wives and nearly identical sons by each. But this instant is not the one, I think, in which the stories fully reveal themselves. The thrusting forward of the grotesque is not the gesture that is crucial.

In "Lily Daw and the Three Ladies," the first story of A Curtain of Green, Victory, Mississippi, is the realistic context of the story, a real place with a railroad station and a town band that plays sincerely if not always on key. It is peopled with human beings who drink Orange Ne-Hi, drive Willys-Knight autos, and use Redbird school tablets. The texture is rich and appropriate; the world of Victory seems realistically complete. But, on a second reading, when the carefully selected detail is not so vivid, the story seems to reach beyond itself. Lily Daw is not simply a local grotesque; the three ladies are not simply three ladies to be taken in a spirit of satire. The fiction, by means of its style, begins to reach beyond its roots in the circumstantial; a heightened reality emerges from the exposed film.

Lily's deficiency, considered less clinically, is not a deficiency at all but a surplus. Not encumbered by the civilized conventions of the ladies, Lily behaves according to the urges and impulses of her nature. Her freedom in this behavior frightens the wardens of polite society. The three ladies, not just a trio of prominent women, are as ominous as the Fates of classical mythology. One of them, Mrs. Carson, wearing a tape measure around her shoulders, reminds us that the Fates were seamstresses who spun out and finally snipped the thread of life. The three ladies hover about Lily, itching to snip her life before it blooms too richly; they will commit her to an institution before she can get herself and the town into some kind of Dionysiac "trouble."

A second reading of "Lily Daw and the Three Ladies" discovers the strife between the self, which desires its own freedom and an unobstructed path toward it, and society, which demands conformity and surrender of the self for the common good, the single straight and narrow path. Lily's grotesque quality moves her beyond the realistic context into a realm of allusion and reference, as part of this larger theme. At the end of the story a hat is flung into the telegraph wires. There it stays; there the resolution of the story stays too, for nothing is decided permanently in this fiction and nothing is certain except the urge that lives in Lily and the will of the ladies to channel that urge into the groove of respectability. Eternal conflict is certain; resolution is not a feature of Welty's reality. The nature of her style is, on the contrary, suggestive; it entices the mind to reflect upon the intricate complexities concealed behind the curtain of polite, social self.

The interplay of polite self and private self is a prominent feature of this story. Mrs. Carson, wearing her tape measure like a stole of office, is

the Baptist minister's wife; Mrs. Watts wears widow's black; Aimee Slo-
cum, ironically named, is a spinster with poor skin and a low emotional
threshold. These three cluck their tongues and make other noises remi-
niscent of "the hen house at twilight" (CG, 4, 7). They want to coop
up Lily too, make her conform to the codes of restraint and denial that
they represent, impose upon her an external role that will eliminate the
danger to their facade. To institutionalize Lily, either in Ellisville—literal stone and mortar—or in marriage with a stranger who will take her
away, is their plan.

To this end Lily is betrayed to the xylophone player with a kiss, as her
hope chest vanishes down the railroad tracks on the departing train (CG,
19). The marriage does not bode well. The xylophone player is partially
deaf, shows no inclination to follow Lily to Ellisville (if he should have
to), and inscribes her name, not on an innocent tree or in his heart, but
in a small notebook coldly titled "Permanent Facts & Data."

By means of such suggestion and nuance, "Lily Daw and the Three
Ladies" leaves the hard and fast artistic place of complete realism and
reaches toward a different region of meaning. Life and beauty are betrayed by age and social restraint. Complete freedom, personified in Lily
and in the urges she feels at this crucial stage of her life, is sacrificed to
permanent facts and data for the sake of order. Hope departs; the hens
are left in command.

In other stories of the category "grotesque," this theme emerges more
obviously. Ladies are apparently always the active agents. In "Petrified
Man" the patrons of Leota's beauty parlor display the selfish and vulgar
behavior of women who demand that society (control of which they have
seized) punish all men for repeated transgressions. Mrs. Fletcher's husband must suffer for being responsible for her pregnancy (or for giving her
dandruff), Leota's husband for not working, Mr. Petrie for raping four
women in California. Leota's friends and customers are venal, vain, and
lifeless; they have nothing—looks, taste, youth, or sensibility—to be
proud of. Yet they are never boring. They love to bully men. Images
of pygmy men; of Mr. Petrie; of Leota's husband, whom she calls a
"shrimp"; of Mrs. Fletcher's husband, who has not yet been told that his
wife is pregnant; of Billy Boy, the child whom the ladies smack and
chase, compose a pattern of male denigration that emphasizes the vulgarity and heartlessness of the women. It is no accident that their garden

club is named after the Trojan women. Such pains taken for the sake of a consistent pattern of suggestion in the story are evidence of something more than complete realism; they indicate a striving toward the full moment of discovery, well after the shutter's click. It takes time for the full picture to develop.

"Old Mr. Marblehall" is a similar critique of polite society. The narrator of the story reveals, in addition to the oddity of Mr. Marblehall's bigamy, a contempt for the proper society that knows nothing of his double life, and treats him with a strange mixture of vindictive contempt and hypocritical concern. Mr. Marblehall, who reads *Astonishing Stories* and *Terror Tales* (which feature nude women and dismembered bodies stashed in bureau drawers), and whose bigamy ticks like a time bomb in society's vest pocket, amazes the narrator, who cannot wait for the explosion.

The climax in this story and in "Petrified Man" is the discovery of an action (rape, bigamy) that threatens to undermine the very basis of the stable society of the overwhelming majority. In "Old Mr. Marblehall" the climax is vividly present in the narrator's anticipation of it. That the realistic pattern is not completed—Mr. Marblehall's double life is undiscovered—is not essential for the completion of the artistic whole, the story itself. The wholeness and completion depends upon the integrity of the network of suggestion and nuance. The technique used to achieve such a story discovers an even larger meaning: individual lives, like words, may have their fullest scope beyond the confines of the everyday.

Other stories in the first collection—"Why I Live at the P.O.," "Clytie," "Keela, the Outcast Indian Maiden," and "A Visit of Charity" —repeat this theme and technique. In each story a main character with some defect, physical, psychological, or moral, is universalized, and a point about the nature of individual human existence is made. The grotesque occupies the foreground and lingers in the mind as the general impression from a first reading. But a large body of explication and criticism of these stories testifies to the existence of another aspect of them. "Clytie" resonates with the Greek tragedies of family; "Keela, the Outcast Indian Maiden" with Coleridge's "Rime of the Ancient Mariner"; "A Visit of Charity" with the classical myth of Proserpine. In each case, then, a pattern includes the grotesque; there is a wholeness that develops slowly and in the totality of the story absorbs the reality of the "little human monsters." For a long time Welty has been classified as a southern realist whose accomplishment is the capturing of these freaks. When such "realism" is apparently lacking, she has been chided by northern and southern critics alike.

A majority of the stories in A Curtain of Green, however, are not about certifiable cripples, mental or physical. The technique in most of the stories goes beyond the beginnings listed in the "grotesque" category. Two readers of these stories have given us a truer direction for reading them. Jean Glaser observes: "There is such a tenseness about the stories that it is as if the author is playing on some heretofore undiscovered nerve. However, the stories are far from obvious, and the ache may be difficult to locate."[9] Glaser sensed that there was some larger meaning, not so obvious as the shock of the grotesque. Katherine Anne Porter made a separate category for this type of story. "Let me admit a deeply personal preference for this particular kind of story, where external act and the internal voiceless life of the human imagination almost never meet and mingle on the mysterious threshold between dream and waking, one reality refusing to admit or confirm the existence of the other, yet both conspiring toward the same end (CG, xxi)." Stories in this category ("A Piece of News," "The Hitch-Hikers," "A Memory," "Death of a Traveling Salesman," "A Curtain of Green," "A Worn Path," "Powerhouse") show a heightened level of the suggesting style present in the "grotesque" stories. The technique mingles dream and waking, banishes time and ordinary chronology. It uses for the most part a homemade or natural symbolism and net of suggestion that mark the fiction as evocative, rhythmic, symbolic, concerned with the revelation of life that "never stops moving, never ceases to express for itself something of our common feeling" (OTOP, 8).

The technical achievement is the revealing of life with its never-ceasing movement, that fleeting aspect of life for which the word seems antithetical. A grotesque, a caricature, is essentially static. A mythological allusion moves, but in a predetermined direction. The stories in Porter's "inner-outer" category move like life, pulsating in all directions, discovering the true nature of life's connections which, as Henry James

---

9. Jean Glaser, "Reviews," Ephemera, V (Winter, 1942), 29.

said, stop nowhere. These stories are the most direct entrance into Welty's later fiction.

When the emotion is not scorn, contempt, or shock, when the focus is not the grotesque, attention goes beyond the world of the actual and the case history into the territory of the heart and its timeless existence, or dream. Here the suggestion and connection-making power of the fiction emerge more fully. Often place names are omitted or else chosen to radiate suggestions and symbolic significance. The reader's imagination becomes the place. "A Piece of News" is such a story, in which mysterious and intangible forces throw the characters into an instant of self-revelation, to be engulfed the next instant in the irresistible movement of life.

Ruby Fisher's tremendous vitality and hunger for life are more vivid than the physical setting. Something is set to happen to her heart, and so the place is mysterious and dissolving, like the place of "Death of a Traveling Salesman." Ruby trades her body for a package of coffee, but there is no mention of sexual promiscuity, for the fear of social condemnation occurs only in the ordinary world. Ruby's vitality heals; it does not open such wounds as those made by the ladies who handle Lily or visit Leota's. In the climax of the story, Ruby's reckless and unconscious response to life summons a moment of union for herself and her husband. Their routine is banished; things, in the language of "The Bride of the Innisfallen," "cut more deeply." "Rare and wavering, some possibility stood timidly like a stranger between them and made them hang their heads" (CG, 30). The curtain which separates them, man and woman, worker and dreamer, is parted just for an instant. Then Clyde, the husband, bursts the dream, and life goes on in its ordinary time. But for the instant, a new state of living entered their separate worlds, and the power of its presence abolished their separateness. So powerful is this state that it assumes human attributes and the presence of another character. Something exists beyond the human, and its gift is to unite and to conquer time. It appears later in "No Place For You, My Love."

In "Death of a Traveling Salesman," too, a symbolism of fire, sunlight, fertility, and imminent birth creates a tangible world that, because of its intensity, consumes the dry-as-tinder life of R. J. Bowman. Bowman senses the presence behind the curtain and flees. After fourteen years on the road selling ladies' footwear, Bowman realizes that all of his

vital possibility is gone. Tom Harris, in "The Hitch-Hikers," is a similarly unrooted itinerant whose life has been drained, with his complicity,
of its places, its time, its memories. One of the hitchhikers, Sanford, the
man who plays the guitar, presents Tom with an indictment of his empty
and wasted life, for he talks of a past, of a family, of music. He talks, in
fact, of everything. Sobby, the other hitchhiker, is so angered he kills
Sanford, because "'I was jist tired of him always uppin' an' makin' a noise
about ever'thing'" (CG, 140). Making a noise is one way of making
oneself noticed. Speech implies and requests a connection; Sanford's
music is his personal cry and his invitation to others. Communion, as in
the case of Ruby and Clyde, is rejected. Sobby, especially, cannot endure
such hope as is held out by Sanford's music. Tom Harris is implicated
also. He suggests that Sanford play his guitar for money, and he gets rid
of the symbol, the guitar, by giving it to a black boy in the ending of the
story. Harris is a creature, like R. J. Bowman, who has killed time. "He
himself had no time. He was free; helpless" (p. 141). As his time dies so
does his hope for rejuvenation within the human group. He cannot remember the women who call him; neither Ruth nor Carol receives from
him anything resembling kindness, attention, or passion. He is a derelict
soul adrift in a life without firm shape or substance. Like Clyde and R. J.
Bowman, he cannot abolish separateness with acts of love. The physical
setting of each of these stories pits a warm domestic interior against a
vast, vague, dark, and lonely night, with which the men, hard or exhausted of heart, are associated.

"A Worn Path" shares this inner-outer dynamic movement, for the
fully realized character, Phoenix Jackson, is a match for the mythological
and Christian imagery of which she is the human, life-giving heart. "A
Memory" also radiates an inner life that encounters fully realized characters and situations. The plight of the young, withdrawn, and sensitive
girl of "A Memory" is, in fact, the challenge to reconcile the opposing
demands of inner and outer worlds, for the outer is not obliged to satisfy
the dreams of the heart. Consciously framed approaches to life, such as
the young artist in "A Memory" tries to impose, are not the natural and
personal impulses that will discover the connections. The successful impulses, as Ruby and Sonny's wife show, originate in the heart.

The fiction of this category is, I think, the main channel of Welty's
work. Even though the beleaguered Martha of "Why I Live at the P.O."

and the efficient, neurotic Edna Earle of *The Ponder Heart* are unforgettable, the more intricately fashioned stories, those based on the technique that searches for and waits upon the moment when separateness is abolished and wholeness is so intense it becomes a thing, are truer to Welty's overall achievement. "A Curtain of Green" is the most compact example of this style and meaning.

Mrs. Larkin has seen her husband killed in what the newspapers might have called a freak accident; a tree fell on his car and crushed him. It was a summer day; there had been no warning. Like the girl in "A Memory" Mrs. Larkin faces a numbing, potentially killing fact—love may have no power beyond the lover's heart. "It was accident that was incredible, when her love for her husband was keeping him safe" (CG, 214). Death, far more significant than the nosebleed in "A Memory" but an analogous omen, threatens the very life of love. For if love is powerless to protect, then it is futile and is not part of the actual world. Not of the world, love then is not natural, not real. The emotions of love, therefore, bring pain because they aggravate the wound of separation that divides self from other, self from world. Better to be anesthetized, like Tom Harris. Nevertheless there is the imperative to love—the theme of the fiction—and the imperative to discover wholeness—the technique. So Mrs. Larkin's plight is *the* issue of Welty's fiction.

Mrs. Larkin tries, in retaliation for her husband's death, to bury herself in the nonhuman. She plunges into her garden, plants every variety of flower she can obtain, "rarely" thins, prunes, separates. The ladies of the local garden society disapprove, but their disapproval and they themselves are of no moment to Mrs. Larkin in her attack upon the enigma. The accident had showed her chaos; she rushes toward it. "To a certain extent, she seemed not to seek for order, but to allow an over-flowering, as if she consciously ventured forever a little farther, a little deeper, into her life in the garden" (CG, 211). The curtain of green may conceal nothing, the heart of darkness; but Mrs. Larkin will look upon it, expose its truth, then find the rest she needs.

Not seeking beauty, she encounters its antithesis. She encounters the other, the uncontrollable, in her black helper, Jamey, who kneels among the plants, separated from her not merely by his sex and race but simply and permanently by himself, his other-ness. She approaches his back, a hoe upraised in her hands. Jamey's head is vivid to her in its reality, its "hot woolly hair, its intricate, glistening ears, its small brown branching streams of sweat," and in its inner reality, its inaccessible dream and consciousness (CG, 216). Suddenly Jamey is the enigma. Poised to strike off Jamey's head Mrs. Larkin faces the world the accident had revealed. "So deeply did she know, from the effect of man's danger and death, its cause in oblivion; and so helpless was she, too helpless to defy the workings of accident, of life and death, of unaccountability" (p. 216). R. J. Bowman died fleeing this revelation, the real dream of his own heart's death in life. But Mrs. Larkin is fortunate, for in this moment all is revealed, the wholeness of which death and life are parts. She suddenly sees herself and the enigma together, "what we see going on and ourselves" (OTOP, 8). And she sees, and accepts, the living relationship between the opposites. In this crucial action Mrs. Larkin takes her place at the beginning of a line of Welty's heroes and heroines that includes Clement Musgrove, Virgie Rainey, Ellen Fairchild.

The rain falls, and Mrs. Larkin sees the world around her shine in its totality and in its particularity of separate objects. So does Clement Musgrove when he breaks through his insistence upon explanations. And so does Virgie Rainey in "The Wanderers." It is the reconciliation that does not banish separateness. Fainting, Mrs. Larkin collapses among her flowers. The rain streaks her face. But the panic that Jamey feels is misplaced. Mrs. Larkin is merely sleeping after a long and exhausting battle with grief (CG, 219).

The moment of seeing all things around her in their particularity and in their wholeness is Mrs. Larkin's saving gift. This is the world, accident and love, life and death; and although these are antithetical, their coexistence is not unnatural. Mrs. Larkin had endured her mistake of thinking their coexistence breakable. After her day's work in the garden, enduring life," [s]he would lie in bed, her arms tired at her sides and in motionless peace: against that which was inexhaustible, there was no defense" (CG, 218). Finally her heart is also granted its peace.

The reality of the fiction in A Curtain of Green includes the completely, but merely, real and also searches for the "cause in oblivion." In her first collection of stories Welty focuses sharply and unerringly on the grotesque, the natural habitat of real things and people. Always present and striving in the technique, however, is the will to probe the enigma with language, with fiction, for the wholeness that lies at the root of human life. In some of these stories symbolism and mythological allusion aid, with their literary connections, the entry into the undeveloped shadow around, behind, even within the perceived person and thing. Always there is the effort to coax the vividness and immediacy of the instant's shock into the ultimately timeless state of connection. Mrs. Larkin's great gift is to endure the shock and to enter behind the curtain into the realm of innocent acceptance of life.

That these seventeen stories are varied and different is obvious; choosing the critical structure of categories is a risk. Welty's fiction is not one thing but many things. The effort toward connection through an exploring technique unifies the stories. There is, as Porter says, in every story—and in this collection as an entity—"a sense of power in reserve" (CG, xxiii). That power toward inclusion grows in *The Wide Net*, Welty's second collection of stories, and continues in all her subsequent fiction.

## II

## The Mystery in the Other:
## *The Wide Net*

*The Wide Net*, published in 1943, two years after
*A Curtain of Green*, is different from the first collection. The concern for
connection is not only a theme given flesh and blood in the meetings of
several pairs of human beings, but is also a powerful and subtly unifying
technique that links individual stories and transforms them into something more than a collection. The stories of *The Wide Net* cannot be
segregated into categories, for they do not vary as greatly as those of *A
Curtain of Green*. Fewer in number and composed over a shorter period of
time, they possess the resonance and lyrical wholeness of Welty's later
fiction.

Although *The Wide Net* contains about half as many stories as the
first collection, the new stories are longer, more intricate in plot, more
complex in theme. What Harvey Breit, reviewing *The Golden Apples*,
proposed as Welty's contribution to the short story form—a novelistic
continuity that sidesteps requirements of length and plot—begins with
*The Wide Net*.[1] Here we have eight stories dwelling on a single theme;
related by a common ground (the Natchez Trace); concerned with the
difficulty of love and personal expression; and linked by echoing words
(*silence*, *haze*, *dream*, *still*). In *The Wide Net* Welty's sensitivity to the
language and to the possibilities within style for discovering and making

1. Harvey Breit, "Books of the Times," New York *Times*, August 18, 1949, p. 19.

connections emerges as a unique and forceful use of the short story form. These eight stories are not related simply by being contiguous or by sharing grotesques for characters and the South for setting. Even though the stories are grounded in the history and geography of the Natchez Trace, they take place—as fiction—in a state of heightened imaginative possibilities. The heroes and heroines of these stories find themselves in two worlds simultaneously—the historian's and the dreamer's. By patient attention they discover that the two worlds are indeed one world with extensive winding caves and passages. The discovery does not come through escape into fantasy. Each one of the central characters of these stories moves from the world of history into the region of dream (art, love) and back into the world again.

"First Love," the first story in the collection, centers upon the character of Joel Mayes, an orphaned deaf-mute working as a bootboy in the Natchez country during the time of the magnificent treason of Aaron Burr.[2] The setting blends the charm of a romantic and historically verifiable past with the eerie stillness óf mystery. Young Joel does not have the aid of words or sounds to make his world intelligible. As a human apparently powerless before the brusque world, he is like Mrs. Larkin and all of Welty's potential heroes who face some kind of spiritual waste unless they can discover the life-restoring connection. Joel's world is charged with an immediacy and intensity that render his plight extraordinary, fit for fiction: the winter is the coldest in memory; the drama of Burr's trial sheds oblique light on Joel's silent routine; his own fresh memories of the slaughter of his parents bar his retreat into the past; and the spectacular figure of Burr himself shines in Joel's eyes like an apparition. But Joel's breaking through to this world is in the balance.

The bond between Joel and Burr, which overcomes handicaps to expression and develops into "first love," is the kernel of the story. Burr seems, from Joel's special point of view, to be truly magnificent in stature—dashing, adventurous, as exciting and full of possibility as a dream. Joel watches him so closely—each night as Burr returns from his courtroom sessions, each morning before he leaves again—that he begins to

2. Several fine discussions of *The Wide Net*, such as those of Ruth Vande Kieft and Alfred Appel, Jr., precede this one and differ from it in several ways. See also Daniel Curley, "Eudora Welty and the Quondam Obstruction," *Studies in Short Fiction*, V (Spring, 1968), 209–24; Victor H. Thompson, "The Natchez Trace in Eudora Welty's 'A Still Moment,'" *Southern Literary Journal*, VI (Fall, 1973), 59–69; and Albert J. Devlin, "Eudora Welty's Historicism: Method and Vision," *Mississippi Quarterly*, XXX (Spring, 1977), 213–34.

share in the fluctuations of Burr's spirits. Joel eventually knows Burr's moods and spirits better than he knows his own. Indeed, a connection, a bond of love, is born, even though Burr does not know he is involved (he hardly notices Joel), and even though Joel's youth prevents him from knowing that love is so complex and that such a vast gulf exists between one human and another.

In his altered state Joel undergoes many trials that challenge his new life. He remembers the fear and vulnerability he felt when Indians appeared in the Natchez Trace wilderness and took the lives of his parents and the other settlers. His duties as bootboy are routine. But he also experiences wonderful things in the orbit of Burr, who seems to attract wonderful things as the sun attracts and holds the planets. Each night during the month before Burr's trial, Joel watches silently as Burr and his advisers confer. During the day he watches the militia drill in preparation for the trial and an anticipated insurrection. But the trial itself—outside, in the world of history, not dream—passes unrecorded in the plot. The fiction dwells in the region of Joel's heart and growing love. In a state of love, all is fluid, not fixed and frozen like the historical world of accusations, roles, and convention. The natural habitat, the historically accurate place and time, serves as an emblem of the lifeless world that waits for "first love." It is the coldest winter in Natchez Trace history, and all life is brought to a standstill, forced indoors. The very molecules of all matter slow down; birds freeze and fall from the trees. But accuracy of place and conditions is not its own reason for being in this story. Welty discovers in the facts the parts of a more encompassing whole.

A girl with a violin entertains Burr one evening after the trial, and Joel senses that Burr and the girl know of a territory to the West where they might be free. In his silent drama Joel sees Burr, disguised, gesture to the girl toward the west. She declines; Burr leaves alone. Before he goes, however, he grasps Joel's hand. In that touch, anticipated from the beginning of the story, something is kindled.

The fingers closed and did not yield; the clasp grew so fierce that it hurt his hand, but he saw that the words had stopped.

As if a silent love had shown him whatever new thing he would ever be able to learn, Joel had some wisdom in his fingers now which only this long month could have brought. He knew with what gentleness to hold the *burning* hand. With the gravity of his very soul he received the furious pressure of this man's dream. (*WN*, 28–29. Italics mine.)

In the transaction with the "burning hand" Joel receives a more complex love, a connection and communion in which he transcends the handicaps—his own deafness, the world's cold and lifeless surface—to achieve full growth in love. Joel approaches an awareness so full of possibility that his boy's heart cannot yet fathom it. The heat of Burr's life kindles the slowed molecules of Joel's flesh, and he stirs to life and change, not yet fully aware of the possible outcome for himself and surely not protected against disaster. At the end of the story Joel is following in Burr's path on foot, along the frozen trail out of the Natchez country to the west. The route is called, historically, the Liberty Road. Joel's liberation is real; he does not linger in former roles. The lesson of Burr is that of feisty King MacLain: time re-creates the self—a mystery of both pleasure and pain—and obliges it to enter the world and accept its beauty with its grief. The world that had seemed so oblivious and estranged now lends itself to Joel's growth, as it also lends itself to the fiction. The real name *Liberty Road* plays into the network of suggestion that unifies the story.

This special vision continues in the title story of the collection, "The Wide Net," for which Welty was awarded an O. Henry first prize in 1942. In this story William Wallace Jamieson, a boastful minor-league Paul Bunyan, is jolted to learn, after carousing with the boys all night, that his new wife, Hazel, who has recently learned that she is pregnant, has left a note informing him of her intention to jump into the Pearl River. He is stunned. He fetches his friend, Virgil, and together they call on Doc, owner of the wide net. They will have to borrow the net and drag the river.

This is not quite the way in which Dante set out with his companion Vergil in search of Beatrice. Welty's allusion to the Renaissance Christian epic, though reticent, is not altogether a phantom. Hazel, for example, assumes the character of a madonna, the revered woman, especially at the end of the story when her beatific, serene smile seems to shine down upon her man and thrall (*WN*, 72). William Wallace undergoes his own epic struggles also, though they are less sophisticated than Dante's. He performs feats of physical daring in the Pearl and faces down the local dragon, the King of Snakes. The male's epic, in contrast to Hazel's, is satyric and sweaty. William Wallace hooks a catfish to his belt buckle and struts a phallic dance for his pals. Whereas Hazel is sophisticated and reverent, William Wallace is crude, proud, and

vaunting. That such polarities of epic character can and do live as com-
plements is the ultimate subject of "The Wide Net."

Hazel's body is not found. The men leave the river and return to the
town, Dover, where there are no terrible dragons, only the women at
their Sacred Harp Sing, torn circus posters, and bottle caps pressed into
the asphalt of the streets. Welty eliminated, in one revision, sparkling
shards of broken glass that lent some dazzle to the scene in Dover.[3] The
town might be Purgatorio, a middle, prosaic state between the terrible
and the sublime. William Wallace's cabin, to which he makes his mourn-
ful way, is the sublime, however, for he finds Hazel there. All she wanted
all along was attention.

Hazel has come upon a knowledge that is very deep but not completely conscious to her. Smiling upon her man, content—now—to
have a child grow in her womb, Hazel has discovered time as a steady, in-
exorable flow. The men experience time as a series of bursts of wonder
interspersed with domestic boredom—the fish dance followed by Dover
and the women. The world demands that all of them keep step with its
time. The two sexes try, in the shadows of different epic patrons, to
answer the demand.

This underlying meaning and the tone, irony, are gradually revealed.
Although the epic allusion is subtle, it informs the whole story as the
concern with change appears frequently. "We're walking along in the
changing time [Doc prattles]. Any day now the change will come. It's
going to turn from hot to cold, and we can kill the hog that's ripe" (WN,
48). A more telling and internal change is also imminent. Hazel is
changing from a girl to a woman and to a mother. Virgil takes the pessimistic view of it. "Oh, she's a pretty girl, all right. . . . It's a pity for the
ones like her to grow old, and get like their mothers" (p. 38). The men
of the story do not know that the change with which "The Wide Net"
deals is more serious than physical aging. When William Wallace dives
into the depths of the Pearl River, he faces the specter of change but
does not know it.

So far down and all alone, had he found Hazel? Had he suspected down there,
like some secret, the real, the true trouble that Hazel had fallen into, about
which words in a letter could not speak. . . . how (who knew?) she had been
filled to the brim with that elation that comes of great hopes and changes, some-

---

3. Eudora Welty, The Wide Net (Carbon copy of typescript, in Humanities Research Center,
University of Texas at Austin), p. 20.

times simply of the harvest time, that comes with a little course of its own like a tune to run in the head, and there was nothing but the old trouble that William Wallace was finding out, reaching and turning in the gloom of such depths (pp. 56–57).

The "old trouble" is the problem of mutability. William Wallace, all swagger and self-command, does not fully comprehend that the real trouble is not the King of Snakes. It is time itself, change, decay, eventual death. A hero is needed, but it is not William Wallace. He merely asserts his youthful potency in a ritualistic dance. The women are more likely to be heroes; they preserve the hymns of the Harp Sing from the oblivion of time, and they bear the children that renew the race. Hazel's smile at the close of the story is strong proof: "And after a few minutes she took him by the hand and led him into the house, smiling as if she were smiling down on him" (*WN*, 72). Her stature and serenity transform Hazel into a kind of Beatrice. She, like Joel Mayes and Mrs. Larkin, faces the oblivious phenomenal world and responds affirmatively with love. By moving with time, these heroes can achieve the metamorphosis that turns the random and ambiguous incidents of existence into personal lives and history.

"A Still Moment" also concerns mutability and time. The characters are Lorenzo Dow, an "itinerant man of God," who thirsts for souls so insatiably that he has left a wife behind in New England. Lorenzo sees the Devil's hand in any speck of nature's beauty that might detain him from the next revival in the next clearing in the wilderness. He is driven, never still; he is actually afraid of stillness, as if each moment not spent rabidly in pursuit of heaven is therefore lost in sliding toward hell. Lorenzo is obsessed, not fully human, because love, the major theme of *The Wide Net*, does not quicken the metamorphosis in him. Peggy, his wife in Massachusetts, or God in His distant heaven—neither can provide the immediate experience of love that the burning hand provided for Joel. The world, in which Joel and Hazel find themselves, is for Dow the mirage of Satan. The world must never be entered. "Inhabitants of Time! The wilderness is your souls on Earth. . . . These wild places and these trails of awesome loneliness lie nowhere, nowhere but in your heart" (*WN*, 78). Dow correctly sees men in time, but he places the physical world at odds with the human heart. The world is temptation, not salvation.

James Murrell, the outlaw, springs out of the wilderness and paces Dow stride for stride, so perfectly that the thief seems to be the shadow of the man of God. Murrell, too, is fleeing the stillness. He must have victims just as Dow must have souls. Murrell ponders incessantly the act of murder before he commits it. He is like Dow, who ponders the idea of saving souls. Welty aptly describes Murrell, standing darkly beside Dow, "like a brother seeking light" (*WN*, 82). They are linked by their egotistic insistence upon conquering the world with their dreams. They will not accept the world's time; they prefer their own.

As they stand, breathlessly still, each in his own separate universe, a third man appears. He is Audubon, the naturalist and artist. Audubon is not fleeing, but seeking, the still moment, the ideal of the world's beauty made permanent with his brush and oils. He is like Joel and Hazel, but elevated by an artistic self-awareness. His response to the flow of time, his art, is a form of love.

When a heron appears in the swampy dark, Dow sees, not the heron, but a vision sent by God, part of a sermon trailing from the ether; Murrell sees, not the heron, but his own thumb as he shades his eyes against the setting sun. His thumb bears the brand of his crime, H. T. Then he envisions his plan for a "Mystic Rebellion of Slaves" with himself in the vanguard. Audubon alone sees what is there, the heron. He shoots it.

This is the paradox of art: to make beauty available and free from time, the artist must take it out of its natural habitat and put it within an artistic frame. "All its whiteness could be seen from all sides at once, its pure feathers were as if counted and known and their array one upon the other would never be lost. But it was not from memory that he could paint" (*WN*, 90).

The artist (Audubon and the young girl in "A Memory") creates a stay against mutability by liberating the object from time, by discovering the still moment in which the teeming multiplicity of things and the rushing of time itself are together suspended in the act of beholding what is there. Neither Dow nor Murrell beholds the world; rest and love are, to them, inaccessible. Trapped in time, they can neither liberate nor be liberated. Life remains for them an approaching oblivion and a present waste.

Sabina, the major character of "Asphodel," likewise tries to impose on her world, from the outside, an order and an integrity that do not spring from completely natural roots. Unlike Audubon, Sabina does not see the world from all sides at once. "Asphodel" is a skillfully crafted and ironic version of the classic strife between Dionysian and Apollonian visions of life. Sabina is Apollonian in allegiance. The three spinsters who narrate her story perform the role of the chorus; their words are measured and calm, "like an old song they carried in their memory" (*WN*, 98). At the center of the old story are two houses—the Apollonian house of Sabina, who loves order and restraint in human affairs, and the Dionysian house of Don McInnis, a satyr in appearance and deportment, for whom appetite is both moral and civil tutor. The two houses, ironically, are not separated by a chasm; they are "actually situated almost back to back on the ring of hills, while completely hidden from each other, like the reliefs on opposite sides of a vase" (p. 98). This situation suggests that in reality such opposites are part of the whole, and that someone who could see all sides would realize that. The sly allusion to the Grecian urn (young men in pursuit of maidens loth to be taken) is also part of an ironic pattern. The men, Sabina's father and his ally Don McInnis, overtake and overrule Sabina in her loathing of Don. Sabina, a bride of quietude, is ravished by Don; and the world of competing opposites goes on in spite of her refusal to acknowledge it.

Unlike Hazel, Sabina never acknowledges the change that occurs in her. Driven beyond toleration when Don escorts his mistress into Asphodel before his wife's outraged eyes, she drives the pair from the house and purifies the place by setting fire to it. Don disappears, and Sabina turns upon the town with her fierce desire for order. "At the May Festival when she passed by, all the maypoles became hopelessly tangled, one by one" (*WN*, 105). In the end Sabina's fanatical obsession with order brings her to the post office, which she suspects of fostering a treasonous commerce with the world outside, the world into which the hated McInnis has fled. In an explosion of temper she rips up the mail, then falls to the floor amid the scraps, dead.

As the three spinsters finish the tale of Sabina's rage for order and her defeat, a figure steps calmly from the shadow of one of the ruined columns of Asphodel. No time to mourn Sabina and her dead dream, for this man is the enemy: "He was rude and golden as a lion. He did nothing while the birds sang on. But he was naked" (*WN*, 109). He is at the head of a flock of goats, and they rout the prim chorus.

A similar pattern of opposition organizes "Livvie," although this story does not carry such a heavy freight of irony. Livvie, as her name suggests, represents an urge within the human species to live, to accept change as natural. She marries an older man, Solomon, an independent and fiercely ordered black man whose house and farm bear the print of his own Apollonian temper.

> Going through that room and on to the kitchen, there was a big wood stove and a big round table always with a wet top and with the knives and forks in one jelly glass and the spoons in another, and a cut-glass vinegar bottle between, and going out from those, many shallow dishes of pickled peaches, fig preserves, watermelon pickles and blackberry jam always sitting there. The churn sat in the sun, the doors of the safe were always both shut, and there were four baited mousetraps in the kitchen, one in every corner. (WN, 155)

Solomon's kitchen is a symbol of his temperament, a stay against the encroaching ruin of time. Its deliberate and carefully maintained orderliness and symmetry are Livvie's cage; her escape, like birth, is a matter of nature and of time, which Solomon refuses to acknowledge.

Although Solomon, like Sabina, makes himself "a little still spot in the middle" of the teeming natural world, he cannot prevent the eventual victory of the forces of Dionysus, nor can he keep the world from changing in its natural way (WN, 162). Livvie's natural impulses are first aroused by Miss Baby Marie, an itinerant cosmetics peddler, whose lipstick smells to Livvie like chinaberry flowers. Livvie's waning allegiance to Solomon holds her back from Miss Baby Marie's wares, but her natural instincts pull her away at the same time. Aided by the turn of the year into spring, Livvie finally turns away from Solomon and toward Cash, the black Dionysus of this story. Cash is part of the field, linked with the irresistible germination and growth in the soil; he is the opposite of the geometrical order of Solomon and his rooms. Cash has worked in Solomon's fields, is dressed now in flashy pastels, and sounds the call of Dionysus: "I ready for Easter" (p. 171). The implication is that Solomon is not ready to rise with the reborn world. Livvie follows Cash.

The physical world, which Solomon tries so assiduously to manage, makes a shambles of his life. As Solomon's dream of order succumbs to a natural process, so does he. But he dies without rancor, unlike Sabina. Solomon's final words acknowledge defeat, but they are not a curse: "Young ones can't wait" (WN, 175). He realizes the futility of trying to hold Livvie "from all the young people [who] would clamor for her back" (p. 176). The title under which this story won the O. Henry Award is "Livvie is Back." This title rises from those who have gained in Livvie's return from Solomon, and hints that her captivity, like Persephone's, impoverishes the world.

"Asphodel" and "Livvie" treat the theme of mutability with the distancing elements of myth, either ironically or straightforwardly applied. But "The Winds" and "At the Landing" contain far more intriguing stylistic and thematic treatments that weave the stories of *The Wide Net* into one fabric. For the main characters of these two stories, both young girls, mutability constitutes a challenge to grow that will replace cocoon-like comfort with an ache that shows no signs of being temporary. Like Joel Mayes, the girls face a metamorphosis brought on by love and time. In both stories Welty returns to the style of "First Love" and "A Still Moment": a richly evocative atmosphere of dream, rhythmical cadences, nuances of connections that avoid the overt mythological imagery of "Asphodel" and "Livvie." The intensely lyrical style of these two stories is vitally important to the meaning they explore, for incidents are not as important as the way in which they are perceived, and the resolutions to which both stories confidently move are not within the plot but within the deepened and metamorphosed hearts of the major characters.

In the modern day in which "The Winds" takes place, the old Natchez Trace, locale for the previous stories, is not so much a geographical place as it is a state of imagination and possibility. It has taken on a different name—Lover's Lane. The new name is mentioned frequently in the course of Josie's reverie; it occurs even more frequently in a preliminary draft of the story.[4] Some of these instances have been deleted, but the metamorphosis of the Natchez Trace, the historical habitat of Burr and Audubon, to Lover's Lane, the place in which the fate of the heart is decided, seems quite obvious. In Lover's Lane the girls meet boys, confront love, and begin to deal emotionally with the physical change that Hazel confronted in "The Wide Net." Sexual maturity and sexual experience, the physical and emotional metamorphosis from child to woman, are the large, amorphous areas of experience that "The Winds" and "At the Landing," like Audubon's paintings, strive to make still and set before the reader.

4. *Ibid.*, 4, 7, 11.

Two forces attract Josie, the main character of "The Winds": the equinox and Cornella, her neighbor across the street. The equinox is the season of change, which, in this story, carries special significance. In "The Wide Net" the world enters a season of change and harvest; in "Livvie" the spring means revival and rebirth; in "At the Landing" the spring floods are significant. In "The Winds" the equinox quickly takes up its metaphorical burden. Josie's father explains in simple meteorological terms that the equinox is "a seasonal change . . . like the storm we had in winter" (WN, 119). But it means something more for Josie. The lightning of the storm "seemed slowly to be awakening something that slept longer than Josie had slept, for her trembling body turned under her mother's hand" (p. 119). That something is outside Josie's body, even outside her self. Perhaps a woman knows that experience more vividly than a man ever can; Hazel knows it more vividly and truly than William Wallace. In any case, Josie stays close to her mother, whose eulogy on the equinoctial storm is "Summer is over" (p. 119). And summertime is "the way of the past" (p. 120).

Josie feels change, or metamorphosis, effected by a power beyond and prior to the self. She locates a forerunner in the character of Cornella, who seems to partake of the equinox without intermediaries: "I see Cornella. She's on the outside, mama, outside in the storm, and she's in the equinox" (WN, 118). In the preliminary draft of the story, Josie, in her dream vision, sees Cornella also in Lover's Lane—a vision that intensifies the equinox or condition of change.[5] Even with this small deletion, Cornella's significance seems plain. She is the young girl swept up in the storm of change of which Josie herself feels the intimations. Cornella spends her mornings sunning her yellow hair, making herself as alluring as the princess of the fairy tale. She has passed a marker of change to which Josie feels herself coming; but Josie is pessimistic about catching up with her (p. 125). Their relationship anticipates that of Cassie and Virgie in The Golden Apples. One goes before and blazes a trail into the world in spite of all of its dangers. The other is left in the suspended moment before the movement forward must be undertaken.

Cornella is a symbolic figure, and Josie sees her that way: "Thy name is Corn, and thou art like the ripe corn, beautiful Cornella" (WN, 128). Josie senses both the fertility that Cornella promises and the arid reality

5. Ibid., 4.

of her actual situation—"the nagging odor of cabbage cooking," "the frailest indulgence" by which she is permitted to live with a set of callous relatives, the "voice old and cracked" that summons her to the dreary house (pp. 128, 130).

In the manuscript Josie is summoned from a womblike sleep to a new state made possible because of her relationship with Cornella. "Deep in the little town, close in her father's house, she had not been found or touched. But there was a tapping at the window. A terrible sadness held her."[6] The tapping calls her to a new definition of her relationship with the world, one which, though new, is also, like Joel's, sad. She dreams:

The calming and languid smell of manure came slowly to meet her as she passed through the back gate and went out to the pasture among the mounds of wild roses. "Daisy" she had only to say once, in her quietest voice, for she had felt very near to the cow. There she walked, not even eating—Daisy, the small tender Jersey with her soft violet nose, walking and presenting her warm side. Josie bent to lean her forehead against her. Here the tears from her eyes could go rolling down Daisy's shining coarse hairs, and Daisy did not move or speak but held patient, richly compassionate and still. (*WN*, 131)

Like Virgie Rainey in *The Golden Apples*, who found solace with her head against the side of a cow, and like Lawrence's Ursula Brangwen among the horses, affirming her wish to live, Josie feels a metamorphosis approaching, a change that will require an affirmation from her. This affirmation involves a commitment to her future as a mature woman. There is an intimation of this in her dream. "The future was herself bringing presents, the season of gifts. When would the day come when the wind would fall and they would sit in silence on the fountain rim, their play done, and the boys would crack the nuts under their heels?" (p. 134). Stillness and silence—the moment in which compassion and love, rest and peace are created. It is a moment of tension too, for the boys have yet to advance their requests. Throughout *The Wide Net* such still moments serve as the important crises for characters responding to the summons of love.

After the storm Josie finds a lover's note calling for Cornella to flee in that "direction away" foreshadowed in the trumpeter's note (*WN*, 137). Josie's goddess has obeyed, like Joel Mayes—whose name, like Cornella's, carries the allusion to natural growth—and Josie is left awaiting her

6. *Ibid.*, 17.

own call. Josie has the loving impulse to follow, but a sense of the pain is within her too. She is like so many of Welty's heroines who sense the stillness of love and the pain involved in loving.

Josie "wanted to follow, and by some metamorphosis she would take them in—all—every one" (*WN*, 139). Like the young girl in "A Memory" she must reconcile her desire to know each of her fellow creatures with her human need for an exclusive love. That there is no static resolution, no "happily ever after" of frozen time, is a painful lesson that is hard for both heart and head.

"At the Landing" concludes the collection on this sad, complex chord. Jenny Lockhart chooses entry into life rather than aloof retirement and a changeless future. In fact, given the summons, she cannot refuse without risking the death of her heart. "At the Landing" pulses with nuance and the atmosphere of symbolic connection. On every level, words and style contribute to the entire meaning. This story is very much like "First Love," in major character, theme, and technique. As a closing story, it brings to culmination the unifying themes of *The Wide Net*, for love and communication take on their most mysterious appearances and the style is its most intricate.

In "At the Landing" a male, Billy Floyd, represents the spirit of natural forces. His name, *Floyd*, is a near rhyme for *flood*, of which he seems to be the genius. Jenny's grandfather, on the night of his death, dreams of a flood, and Billy Floyd appears in the dream with the news of high water. Billy Floyd's occupation, fishing; his repeated appearances in town with a large catfish dangling from his hand; his instinctive ability to communicate with the Lockharts' horse—all his attributes indicate a character who is intimate with natural forces. Like Cash or William Wallace, he embodies the vaunting of an aggressively proud male.

After years of sheltered girlhood in the rigid household of her grandfather (an extreme Apollonian, like Solomon), Jenny, with little knowledge of life, meets Billy Floyd and loves him immediately. Her falling in love, however, is not a joyous initiation, for she is beset with an awareness of the imperfections of human love and communication. Sorrow, distance, mystery, and separation seem to her the fate of each heart impelled toward love.

Billy Floyd's first appearance is a "moment of hope" for Jenny, who had "never performed any act, even a small act, for herself" (pp. 184,

183). Billy seems to be her first choice, the first genuine experience of herself at this crucial and equinoctial moment of her life. She soon learns that love, responding to the imperative of a natural force, is not a guarantee of happiness. As she watches a pair of butterflies, her own newly born self-awareness becomes known to her.

At each step they took, two black butterflies over the flowers were whirring just alike, suspended in the air, one circling the other rhythmically, or both moving from side to side in a gentle wave-like way, one above the other. They were blue-black and moving their wings faster than Jenny's eye could follow, always together, like each other's shadows, beautiful each one with the other. Jenny could see to start with that no kiss had ever brought love tenderly enough from mouth to mouth. (p. 187)

And she also learns that the means of communicating her love, any love, are inadequate. Soon she finds herself in what seems to be a necessary and crippling contradiction in human love.

She would find him equally real with herself—and could not touch him then. As she was living and inviolate, so of course was he, and when that gave him delight, how could she bring a question to him? She walked in the woods and around the graves in it, and knew about love, how it would have a different story in the world if it could lose the moral knowledge of a mystery that is in the other heart. Nothing in Floyd frightened her that drew her near, but at once she had the knowledge come to her that a fragile mystery was in everyone and in herself, since there it was in Floyd, and that whatever she did, she would be bound to ride over and hurt, and the secrecy of life was the terror of it. (pp. 188–89)

Stricken with the simultaneous nature of Billy, object to her and subject to himself, Jenny is on the verge of being paralyzed; her loving is in the balance, and so is her life. More clearly than at any other moment in *The Wide Net*, the mystery of love and the imperative to love are presented in the terms of the vital paradox that Robert Penn Warren called "the love and separateness in Miss Welty."[7] To defeat this paradox Jenny must consent to become object; in other words, she must enter the world on the world's terms. She must escape the secrecy of life that is the terror of it. Having committed herself to this action, to love, Jenny discovers that love is real. "A clear love is *in the world*—this came to her insistently as the mussel's bubbles through the water. There it was, existing there

7. Warren, "The Love and Separateness in Miss Welty," 246.

where they came and were beside it now. It is in the bubble in the water in the river, and it has its own changing and its mysteries of days and nights, and it does not care how we come and go" (p. 198). No other character in *The Wide Net* comes into the immediate and powerful presence of this truth about the world—that it is oblivious to everyone and that love is our positive, affirming action in spite of the obliviousness. Jenny reconciles what has always been and will always be in the world— the mercurial but eternal urge represented by Billy Floyd and the flooding river—with what is unique and mortal—her self. In the attempt to reconcile these, there is no winning for the self; there is only victory in conquering the shock and despair that attend the separateness. Both lover and artist recognize the mystery in the other that resists their knowledge. In "At the Landing" Jenny reprises Audubon's dilemma. She faces in love what he faced in art: the gesture that affirms love at the same instant does definite harm to the other simply by making him known.

During the flooding of the river Billy rapes Jenny and feeds her wild meat, which she vomits. After the waters recede, and after the arduous work of cleaning up the mud, Jenny learns that she can no longer live in the town. Her love is known to the "ladies" of the landing; and like the three ladies who take over Lily Daw, they disapprove of her connection with the wild Billy Floyd. Jenny then seeks Billy among the fishermen of the river; and waiting for him to return, she is violated by several idlers. An old woman nods knowingly as the rude laughter of the men covers Jenny's cries; soon the "original smile" appears on Jenny's lips when the men have finished with her. She is aware, as Josie was not, of the price exacted for following her lover's summons. She subjects herself to the world's time, as Audubon had partaken of oblivion and time in killing the heron.

"At the Landing" uncovers the complexity in human consciousness and love, the simultaneity of object and subject, that grows out of the earlier stories in which such depths are felt but not fully known. Josie and Jenny, in their respective stories, approach the brink of this mystery, but Jenny finally plunges into it. The complexity of the theme has its counterpart in the style. Allusion as a means of connection between the human plight of the individual and the larger concepts of time and the physical world progresses from the use of mythology in the earlier stories to a highly complex, intricate, and lyrical technique of nuance and sug-gestion in the later stories. Finally, the patterns of connection become as important as the things connected; for the artist's vital need to discover connection, to coax it out of the apparent world, becomes the issue that breathes life into the fiction. The fatal alternative is to stop, to allow the obliviousness of the physical world to paralyze the heart and force it back upon itself into inaction and the refusal to love. Love, Welty's stories repeat, is the vital, the essential movement of the private self into the world's time.

Yet, after all, let us acknowledge it wiser, if not more sagacious, to follow out one's day-dream to its natural consummation, although, if the vision have been worth the having, it is certain never to be consummated other than by failure. And what of that? Its airiest fragments, impalpable as they may be, will possess a value that lurks not in the most ponderous realities of any practicable scheme. They are not the rubbish of the mind.
Nathaniel Hawthorne,
*The Blithedale Romance*

## III

# *The Robber Bridegroom* and the Pastoral Dream

Miles Coverdale, Don Quixote, Jay Gatsby, Clement Musgrove—a motley fraternity of dreamers with unique approaches to the fulfillment of one dream—all face across the bay of their own puzzling circumstances a disordered world that will not obey their wills or dreams. The dream is fundamentally the same for each—heroic fulfillment, beauty, harmony, efficacious action in the moral or imaginative improvement of life. They believe that the world outside the individual consciousness is amenable to sense, to the dreams harbored in private. Man's desire for a world "commensurate to his capacity for wonder," or for love, or for social good is, each believes, just about to be fulfilled.

The question in their stories is ancient: will the world resist man's attempt to establish his dream of order, harmony, and peace? Can we reopen Eden under new and wiser management?

Very serious human issues are involved. Perhaps there is no connection between the wish and the world; perhaps we are surrounded by envelopes of ignorance that are filled by the airiest fragments of our dreamy misconceptions. It might, after all, be the condition of human existence in the world that events are unleashed and run uncontrollably, that harmony is another shiny piece of junk among the rubbish of the mind. It might be that, the intuitions of *The Wide Net* notwithstanding, subject is subject and object object—forever.

This seems to be a heavy fanfare for *The Robber Bridegroom*, a slim novella that waves no flags and trumpets no messages. But there is significance in Welty's first novella that has nothing to do with length. Most reviewers who read the book when it appeared in 1942, early in World War II, debated but rarely doubted its significance. Strangely, the issues of that debate seem to have been set aside or forgotten in most subsequent commentary on *The Robber Bridegroom*.

Writing in the *New York Times Book Review*, Marianne Hauser praised Welty's charming, clever blending of fairy tale with ironic insight. "It is a modern fairy tale, where irony and humor, outright nonsense, deep wisdom, and surrealistic extravaganza become a poetic unity through the power of a pure, exquisite style."[1] We know this fairy tale very well—it is ours as a nation—and each retelling makes it "modern." *The Robber Bridegroom* is the story of white settlers in the wilderness, pursuing their dream of a new world. Since the first white settlers touched the eastern coast, however, the irony of that pursuit has been learned.

Like *The Blithedale Romance* or *The Great Gatsby*, *The Robber Bridegroom* balances the futility of pursuing the pastoral ideal against the necessity for dreaming it. Miles Coverdale confessed that no dream worth the having would succeed. He knew that even before he got to Blithedale and, once there, found the flaw he had always expected. "It struck me as rather odd, that one of the first questions raised, after our separation from the greedy, struggling, self-seeking world, should relate to the possibility of getting the advantage over the outside barbarians in their own field of labor."[2]

From such ironic detachment as this springs the wisdom of *The Robber Bridegroom*. Human beings must always dream of what they need but will never accomplish. The dream is always more important than "ponderous realities." Irony is the defense of the rational mind. Compassion is the response of the heart; for no matter how unfit man is for living in his dreams, his need for them is vital.

Another first-round reviewer, however, looked askance at *The Robber Bridegroom*. Lionel Trilling insisted that the novella lacked serious content. He saw only the sparkling style, not the complex truth behind it.

---

1. Marianne Hauser, "Miss Welty's Fairy Tale," *New York Times Book Review*, November 1, 1942, p. 6.
2. Nathaniel Hawthorne, *The Blithedale Romance* (New York, 1958), 47.

"But its lucidity, its grace, and its simplicity have a quality that invalidates them all—they are too conscious, especially the simplicity, and nothing can be falser, more purple and 'literary' than conscious simplicity."[3] Alfred Kazin, on the other hand, trusted the seriousness of the novella. He acknowledged its style, humor, and fantasy; and he felt the author moving beyond them. Anticipating a "machine-in-the-garden" theme, Kazin wrote: "If this is an enchanted world, the black forest of childhood, it is also one into which the sadder, newer world is breaking. And the slow, long roll of disenchantment can be heard at the end, where the Indians capture all the characters and decide their fate, as the axe that broke the trees only led the way for the machine that would break the forest."[4]

These excerpts from early reviews suggest that *The Robber Bridegroom* is capable of leaving the reader with variations on two basic impressions: one, the simple amusement of a retold fairy tale, with the easily achieved irony of a cartoon for adults; the other, a serious examination of the theme of disenchantment in the pursuit of a chimeric, pastoral, fundamentally American Eden.

For many years Kazin's tribute and Trilling's objections were overlooked in discussions of *The Robber Bridegroom*. Those who wrote about the novella continued to praise Welty's skill in combining several fantasies, and the ironic humor with which she retold them. If the novella was considered to have serious substance, it was often found beyond the covers of the book, for example, in its thematic connections with the literature of initiation and alienation.[5]

It is my conviction that in *The Robber Bridegroom* Welty, though employing her own style, is consciously engaged in a form familiar in American fiction. Pursuing the dream of a pastoral reality in the new world is, as Leo Marx has written, one of the most stubborn topics in American fiction.[6] It is essential to any interpretation of *The Blithedale Romance* and *The Great Gatsby*. Hawthorne depicted the attempt by his "counterfeit" arcadians; Fitzgerald showed its wreckage at the hands of the very rich.

3. Lionel Trilling, "American Fairy Tale," *Nation*, December 19, 1942, p. 687.

4. Alfred Kazin, "An Enchanted World in America," New York *Herald Tribune Books*, October 25, 1942, p. 19.

5. Gordon E. Slethaug, "Initiation in Eudora Welty's *The Robber Bridegroom*," *Southern Humanities Review*, VII (Winter, 1973), 77–87.

6. Leo Marx, *The Machine in the Garden* (New York, 1964), 355–58.

Welty finds the same story among the half-legendary figures of the Natchez Trace. Each group imported its own evil.

Kazin's review seems to begin in the direction of this theme. He understands how laughter and sadness coexist in *The Robber Bridegroom* without disharmony or "conscious simplicity." Sensing the note of sadness and loss, he detects the effect of the novella's conscious and deliberate style. Following Kazin's lead, I want to consider *The Robber Bridegroom* in the company of other versions of American pastoral laced with irony. But I also want to emphasize that its unity arises primarily from within, in artistic choices often taken for granted; in images, character, and symbolic action.

I realize here that I run the risk of overanalysis, of explaining the jokes. Indeed, in *The Robber Bridegroom* the sustaining power of the humor—of which a few examples follow—cannot be overstated. Rosamond, the damsel of the tale, suffers the humiliation of being robbed of every stitch by a dashing bandit. Is she flustered? Not for a second; she calmly returns home clothed only in her tresses and a straight face. Her stepmother demands to know the whereabouts of the herbs she had sent the feckless girl to gather in her apron. What herbs? What apron? "In God's name," cries Rosamond's father, "the child is naked as a jay bird." (*RB*, 51)

In another instance, the hapless gnome of the story, Goat (an apt name, for he not only has to butt his way into and out of things, he is also the "goat" of Salome's foiled revenge plot against Rosamond), comes upon Rosamond weeping in the tent of her Indian captors:

"Good evening, why are you crying?"

"Oh, I have lost my husband, and he has lost me, and we are both tied up to be killed in the morning," she cried.

"Then cry on," said Goat, "for I never expect to hear a better reason." (*RB*, 150)

Sometimes damsels are more aggravation than they are worth.

And Rosamond, thoroughly pregnant with the hero's twins, has taken to the road to find Jamie, their father. She encounters Mike Fink, who has been exiled from the river for losing face to Jamie Lockhart in a fight. Fink, convinced that he has murdered Jamie, is just as sure that Jamie is a ghost come back to haunt him. Rosamond knows otherwise and tells Fink to notify said ghost, at his next materialization, that he is soon to be a father. "Oh," Fink said. "Ghosts are getting more powerful every day in these parts" (*RB*, 178).

The wry, deadpan tone with which Welty retells the legendary tale of the Natchez frontier propels the novella. In fact, the caricatures may be taken for the whole meaning of *The Robber Bridegroom*. Alfred Uhry, who has written book and lyrics for a musical adaptation of the novella, emphasizes this aspect. He has chosen to omit both the Indians and the serious aspects of Clement's character.[7]

If jokes were all *The Robber Bridegroom* relied upon, then Trilling's objection on the grounds of simplicity could be readily allowed. But the novella is not limited, in its technique, just to the jokes; it reaches for something beyond the momentary relief of laughter. One laughs at Clement Musgrove much differently from the way one laughs at his silly daughter, her slightly ridiculous hero, her lavishly evil stepmother, or any of the menagerie of eccentrics who appear in the brief story. Clement is foolish in the way that Don Quixote is foolish. One laughs at them both with full sympathy; for the cruel, absurd, treacherous world they wrestle with in innocent vanity can never be subdued. Nor can they happily live in the world of "ponderous realities" and "practicable schemes."

Besides Clement, the Indians spark something other than laughter. They are recreated with a depth and quality of sympathy sometimes found in Cooper. Not the whooping stereotypes of greasepaint westerns, they have nobility, mystery, beauty, and pride. They are the spirit of the country. Clement and the Indians furnish a certain gravity in this light-hearted tale.

Welty's choice of a real place for her "fairy tale" infuses it with the undercurrent of irony and deliberate seriousness in which the Indians and Clement move. Of this river country setting Welty has written, "Whatever is significant and whatever is tragic in a place live as long as the place does, though they are unseen, and the new life will be built upon those things—regardless of commerce and the way of rivers and roads and other vagrancies."[8]

7. "The Robber Bridegroom," adapted for the stage by Alfred Uhry and Robert Waldman. Performed by the Acting Company, Saratoga Summer Theatre, August 2, 1975.
8. Eudora Welty, "Some Notes on River Country," *Harper's Bazaar*, (February, 1944), 156.

Rodney, Mississippi, teems with this unseen life. It began its history as a thriving town on the Mississippi River. Delta cotton went to market through its port. Clement Musgrove's crop goes out to the New Orleans market through Rodney; he and his money return through it to begin the story. Sometime after the Civil War, however, the river was to alter its course and leave Rodney a ghost town. In the novella, that doom hovers in Rodney's future, shading the high jinks with a sentence of death. The place in which *The Robber Bridegroom* happens is both real and imaginary, the timeless land of legend and the changing world of real historical and geographical events. Rodney is a ghost, symbolically cut adrift when time and the river went away and left it.

Rodney is not the only ghost whose presence tempers the novella with seriousness. The Indians, who appear at the opening and close of the story and whom all the white pioneers fear as they fear the dark, encircling wilderness itself, are both real and ghostly.

The Indians of *The Robber Bridegroom*, although their tribe is never named, are modeled on the Natchez Indians.[9] The Natchez had been wiped out years before the imagined events of the novella. Yet the facts of their demise ring significantly in the undercurrent of the story. They had been massacred in retaliation for a massacre of their own, and the remnants of the tribe were sold into slavery in Santo Domingo by the French. Besides their name, they left behind the vivid memory of their distinctiveness.

It is not strange to think that a unique nation among Indians lived in this beautiful country. The origin of the Natchez is still in mystery. But their people, five villages in the seventeenth century, were unique in this country and they were envied by the other younger nations—the Choctaws helped the French in their final dissolution. In Mississippi they were remnants surely of medievalism. They were proud and cruel, gentle-mannered and ironic, handsome, extremely tall, intellectual, elegant, pacific, and ruthless. Fire, death, sacrifice formed the spirit of the Natchez' worship. They did not now, however, make war.[10]

The Natchez, in a way the incarnate spirit of the natural place, fell, as the place itself also fell, before the advancing waves of civilization.

9. Eudora Welty, "The Robber Bridegroom," Synopsis and fragments of screenplay (Typescript, Department of Archives and History, Jackson, Mississippi). Hereinafter referred to as Screenplay.

10. Welty, "Some Notes on River Country," 153.

Their residual spirit and the echoes of a thriving Rodney haunt the tale, not with a haunting so "mundane as a ghost," but with questions much more solemn than those of happy endings.[11]

Through Rodney and the Natchez, Welty keeps us aware that no matter what possibilities of wealth and empire the future may seem to offer, human time is finite; and nothing man builds or accumulates is permanent against time. The Indians are in the throes of change and extinction; Rodney is a static omen of the same impending change. The Indians' way of life and its passing dramatize the meaning of change; the presence of Rodney bodes it.

Change is not necessarily progress; here it seems to be loss. The Indians inhabit the enchanted forest of the novella in a mysterious way that contrasts sharply with the noisy intrusion of the pioneers. This distinction creates the theme of oblivion haunting the works of man, for every step the white pioneers confidently take is shadowed by the unseen, doomed Indians, whose harmonious relationship with the forest is coming to an end. The Indians enjoy an organic union with the place, appearing and dissolving in the surrounding forest, to the eyes of the pioneers, as if Indian nature were not restricted merely to the human but partook of the animal and the vegetable as well.[12] White men never spy the Indians first; they see them only after the Indians have chosen to be seen, when escape from a "reckoning" is impossible. Clement Musgrove's memory of his first captivity by the Indians expresses his pioneer astonishment at the Indians' mysterious presence in the surrounding wilderness. "They showed their pleasure and their lack of surprise well enough, when we climbed and crept up to them as they waited on all fours, disguised in their bearskins and looking as fat as they could look, out from the head of the bluff" (*RB*, 21–22).

The cunning art of disguise links the Indians intimately with their natural place. And the lack of it accentuates the pioneers' estrangement from nature. Beyond the closed circle of their immediate, well-lighted camp, the pioneers enter an unknown universe. In their fears, the Indians are always lurking just beyond what can be clearly seen and controlled. The image of the encircling Indians suggests all that the settlers

11. *Ibid.*, 86.
12. Welty, Screenplay: "Their [the Indians'] musing faces simply appear out of the leaves, almost like metamorphosis."

fear—suffering, death, the unknown. The Indians, then, must be eradicated.

*The Robber Bridegroom*, although a "fairy tale," an enchanted story, acknowledges the torture, death, and violence that the Indians inflict on the pioneers, and vice versa. This bloody violence was noted by John Peale Bishop in his review of the novella, but he could not decide what part it was meant to play.[13] The theme of extinction and change did not fully occur to him. Extinction and the fear of it are as much a part of *The Robber Bridegroom* as the cartoons, the borrowings from Grimm, and the frontier folklore. In this theme, violence as an indispensable part of the pioneering enterprise plays an essential part. *The Robber Bridegroom* is properly a "local legend," which "has a personal immediacy, a cruelty, and a directness glossed over in the fairy tale."[14] Beautiful though it was, Rodney was founded on violence. The Indians resisted invasion violently and were crushed. This is the contradiction that maims the pastoral ideal, that cooled Coverdale's enthusiasm for Blithedale, that lay behind Gatsby's "incorruptible dream." The means corrupt the end; he who acquiesces in the end, acquiesces in the means.

Our glimpse of the Indians while they are yet in their full pride, on the peak from which they will be pushed by civilization, comes from Clement's early life history, which he relates to Jamie Lockhart in the Rodney Inn. Clement remembers the Indians as both gay and cruel (*RB*, 21). But, as Jamie comments, "This must have been long ago. . . . For they are not so fine now, and cannot do so much to prisoners as that" (p. 23). The Indians had struck Clement with their imperiousness and fierce pride. They were supreme in their power over their captives. He remembers: "We had to go whirling and dizzied in a dance we had never suspected lay in our limbs. We had to be humiliated and tortured and enjoyed, and finally, with most precise formality, to be decreed upon. All of them put on their blazing feathers and stood looking us down as if we were little mice" (pp. 22–23). Then with scorn the Indians put to death Clement's infant son, and with contempt dismissed him into the wilderness with his daughter Rosamond and future wife Salome.

13. John Peale Bishop, "The Violent Country," *New Republic*, November 16, 1942, pp. 646–47.
14. Francis Lee Utley, introduction to Max Lüthi, *Once Upon a Time: On the Nature of Fairy Tales*, trans. Lee Chadeayne and Paul Gottwald (New York, 1970), 16.

The Indians had full control. Their realm was unfenced, unsurveyed, undivided. The onslaught of pioneers was but a trickle and well within the Indians' power to intercept. In the first "reckoning" episode of the novella, the Indians do decree and pronounce. The time is still their own.

Nevertheless, extinction is their fate. If Jamie Lockhart, the successful bandit and gentleman, has his way, the Indians will be eradicated as if they were ants at his picnic: "The savages are so clever they are liable to last out, no matter how we stamp upon them" (RB, 21). Clement, however, is not so vehement; vengeance does not consume him, even though he, not Jamie, has lost loved ones at the hands of the Indians. Clement contemplates the Indians' fate with a puzzled melancholy. His melancholy springs from that moment of mutual recognition when the Indians turned him out into the wilderness bound to Salome. In that moment a "mark" was fixed on Clement. "There is nothing that you can see," he tells Jamie, "but something came out of their eyes" (p. 23). Clement cannot say what his mark means; but he feels that he shares the Indians' strange and doomed relationship with time: "They are sure of the future growing smaller always" (p. 21).

The future is also dwindling for the two men, the robber and the planter, as they sit and talk in the tavern. The town itself will eventually be removed from the mainstream. Although the Indians and the town of Rodney may be seen as symbols for limited time, extinction, the vanity of human pride and industry, they are never explicitly identified by the author as her symbols. Their meaning would be impaired by direct identification. Welty uses place more subtly, trusting it to generate its own symbolic meaning in its own time: "Place in fiction is the named, identified, concrete, exact and exacting, and therefore credible, gathering-spot of all that has been felt, is about to be experienced, in the novel's progress."[15] The extinction of the Natchez and the eventual death of Rodney are always "about to be experienced"; they haunt the place of this novella. Welty's choice of place is essential to the meaning of The Robber Bridegroom and must be understood to appreciate her technique. It is not the case, as Chester Eisinger has written, that "the accuracy of historical detail constitutes an act of harmless piety."[16]

15. Eudora Welty, "Place in Fiction," South Atlantic Quarterly, LV (January, 1956), 62.
16. Chester Eisinger, Fiction of the Forties (Chicago, 1965), 273.

With the passing of the Indians, an intimate human connection with the natural world passes too. They are so closely united with the world of animals and forest that disguise, as Clement can testify, is as natural to them as their own skin. Beyond the lights and noise of the artificial world of the pioneers, the Indians are always watching, ready to proclaim a "reckoning." When the second and climactic reckoning falls due, the Indians materialize and apprehend the white offenders as if they (the Indians) were the avenging shapes of the forest itself. The bush at Salome's side "comes alive," and she is taken; a "red hand" materializes in an apparently empty forest, and Clement is taken; an Indian suddenly appears before Rosamond "in the mask of a spotty leopard," and she is carried off.

The Indians seize the captives to avenge their people's rape and dese-cration, symbolically committed by Little Harp, the vicious killer of the Natchez Trace, who violated and killed an innocent Indian girl while Jamie's robber cohorts cheered (RB, 132). This violation scene is a de-parture from the fantasy of the fairy tale and a vivid example of the vio-lence that threads through the story as local legend. There is not the least sliver of irony in the scene. On a table littered with the leavings of a meal, Little Harp first cuts off the drugged girl's finger, then throws himself upon her. When he leaves her, she is dead; no magic wand can revive her. A new and brutal power has entered the realm of the pacific Indians. The power is the power of greed; everyone is infected.

Jamie Lockhart's sole interest is the accumulation of capital. "Take first and ask afterward" is our hero's motto (RB, 69). Rosamond, damsel that she appears to be, becomes Jamie's wife and then the mistress of a mansion more lavish than the one her wicked stepmother coveted (p. 183). And Salome herself is the essence of greed: "We must cut down more of the forest, and stretch away the fields until we grow twice as much cotton, twice as much tobacco. For the land is there for the taking, and I say, if it can be taken, take it" (p. 99).[17] It is little wonder that the Indians of history, faced with this plague of human locusts, reacted with violence to defend themselves but were overcome.

The second reckoning of the novella is the Indians' twilight; they

17. Compare the relationship of Clement and Salome with that of Adam and the Eve of Progress in John Crowe Ransom, "Reconstructed but Unregenerate," in Twelve Southerners, *I'll Take My Stand: The South and the Agrarian Tradition* (Baton Rouge, 1977), 10.

appear weary and decimated, faint shadows of their former "blazing" selves. They have been exhausted in the struggle against the intruders; for them "sleep had come to be sweeter than revenge" (RB, 149). When Salome insults the sun, the Indians' divinity, they hesitate to strike her dead. In former times she would have been executed on the spot. "And Clement, from where he was bound, saw the sad faces of the Indians, like the faces of feverish children, and said to himself, 'The savages have only come the sooner to their end; we will come to ours too. Why have I built my house, and added to it? The planter will go after the hunter, and the merchant after the planter, all having their day'" (p. 161).

Clement sees, in the faces of the Indians, the human fate of extinction. They are, to him, just another group of humans overtaken by change, as he himself will be overtaken. He is the planter about to give place to the merchant, Jamie. A stronger, more brutally efficient force is always wresting control of the present. The Indians and Clement become relics of the past.

The town and the Indians are reminders of the universe that resists the fastening of a human dream to a real wilderness. This is Clement's perspective. Through the novella he has resisted and doubted change and "progress," quixotically trying to preserve his illusions in a world of real and treacherous forces. He is an innocent, like Don Quixote. But his dream is not romantic chivalry. He dreams of harmony, of a pastoral gentleness, of the kind of mutually beneficial and cooperative human community that lured Hawthorne's Coverdale and for a brief time held off his skepticism.

Clement Musgrove is a character in a cast of cartoons. He is round and the others are flat. He is the work of a novelist; the others are the work of the skilled caricaturist. The other members of the pioneer cast can be defined as stereotypes—the hero, the damsel, the wicked stepmother— but Clement must be dealt with as a person of considerable dimension. He enters with the naïve innocence of Don Quixote or Candide; and he grows, through the development of his conscience, memory, and foresight, toward an encompassing vision. Like the Indians, he is pushed aside by time and change.

While the pioneers around him are ruthlessly taking everything that is not nailed down, Clement cannot, or will not, push himself over the psychological threshold that bars him from adding to his possessions. His conscience is the barrier. Salome's insistent greed dismays him: "To encompass so much as that is greedy. . . . It would take too much of time and the heart's energy" (*RB*, 99). Ownership, for Clement, is a matter of conscience; it is more emotionally complex than the mere piling up of land or loot. But such is the malleable condition of his conscience, as it grows, that he bends to Salome's desire and adds to his plantation, hoping, with a fair amount of self-delusion, that each new demand will be her last.

The toll of pioneering into the wilderness is collected from Clement's heart. The Indians were cleared away with the trees of the forest; and the guilt of that offense lodges in Clement's heart. The Indians and the forest are the outright victims of pioneering. Clement is a victim in a more complicated way. He carries the burden of guilt; the more he sees, the heavier the burden becomes.

There is no mistaking the quality of naïve vulnerability in Clement when he appears. He steps from the riverboat, during the flush times of Rodney, carrying in plain sight, "a bag of gold and many presents." His riches are protected with nothing more formidable than his own "tight grip," even though the place is swarming with bandits. We also learn that he has sold his tobacco for a "fair price" at a time when fortunes were to be made. But Clement is not a tycoon, not a wheeler-dealer, and not apparently motivated by the desire for great profit. He lives up to his name; he is a fair, clement man, avoiding extremes of profit and poverty.[18] But he lives in a world of wild extremes. And, as if to underline the contrast between his clemency and the wide-open world of the frontier, a fabulous storm whirls into Rodney minutes after Clement debarks.

Another facet of Clement's guilelessness is his gullibility. Rejecting the deceit and deviousness in plain sight (a series of innkeepers whose missing ears signify punishment for past crimes), Clement is duped by dishonesty that he fails to see. At last he meets an innkeeper with both ears intact, but he fails to notice how those ears perk up like a rabbit's at the tempting prospect of such a rich and unsuspecting customer as himself. Clement, to his grief, pronounces this innkeeper an honest man (*RB*, 4).

18. Screenplay: One of Clement's bags of gold slides from the deck of the riverboat. He makes no move to recover it. Jamie, who has had his eye on it, dives into the river and fetches it back.

A shrewder, more worldly person would not automatically accept someone at face value; he would have the imagination of evil to suspect duplicity. But Clement's imagination is, as yet, innocent of such things. He prefers his illusion of worldly wisdom to a real and vigilant cynicism. In choosing Jamie Lockhart to hear his life history, Clement is again guided by face value: "He [Jamie] was remarkably amiable to see. But by his look, nobody could tell what he would do" (RB, 14). Not surprisingly, Jamie entirely misses the import of Clement's story. He listens as a gentleman would, but his bandit's brain all the time calculates how much Clement might be worth.

Clement's story shows that his heart feels the costs of pioneering, in sorrow, loss, general estrangement, and that his mind is beginning to be puzzled about the reasons. There has been a great enduring separation in Clement's life. "The reason I ever came is forgotten now," he says, as the preface to his history. "I know I am not a seeker after anything," he continues, "and ambition in this world never stirred my heart once. Yet it seemed as if I was caught up by what came over the others, and they were the same. There was a great tug at the whole world, to go down over the edge, and one and all we were changed into pioneers, and our hearts and our lonely wills may have had nothing to do with it" (RB, 20–21). After the separation came the homelessness of the displaced person. Clement, without ambition, without the motivation to seek, to pile up, is an alien in the pioneer life.

Clement is only aware of the pain of dislocation, not of its causes. His memory preserves the name of former comfort and peace—Amalie. Her name suggests a natural kinship with Clement, but she is also part of the past that Clement has left behind. The temptation to "go home again" is as strong as the memory itself. Clement confesses to Jamie that he often struggles in a dream with the tensions he keeps down while awake: "In the dream, whenever I lie down, then it is the past. When I climb to my feet, then it is the present. And I keep up a struggle not to fall" (RB, 29).

Clement is moored to the past, like the town of Rodney and the Indians. But, unlike them, he is tied to a long line that plays him into the future. This is an unusual and complicated situation for a character in a fairy tale. Time is not a real consideration for Mike Fink, Jamie Lockhart, or Rosamond. But Clement is part of the author's concern with change. He is the only character in the novel capable of appreciating, perhaps not intellectually, but intuitively, the expanse of time that will eventually erase all human enterprise. Everyone else is wrapped up in the present.

Jamie Lockhart is full of advice for Clement and tells him that when the going gets deep and heavy, he should discard all his useless moral baggage. "Don't fret over the reason," he says, "for it may have been in stars"; and "Guilt is a burdensome thing to carry about in the heart. I would never bother with it" (*RB*, 21, 27). Clement recognizes the advice; he answers Jamie: "Then you are a man of action . . . a man of the times, a pioneer and a free agent. There is no one to come to you saying 'I want' what you do not want" (p. 27).

For Jamie and his fellow pioneers, the chance to grab the wealth of a lifetime in one stroke—the main chance—is too great to be complicated by intangibles like conscience or the reasons for things. This is the irresistible tug that has drawn the pioneers, through acts of greed and violence, toward the goal. Clement knows better than anyone, being married to Salome, how strong is the desire to take, to exploit, to own what no white man has possessed before. Back in civilization, forms, customs, and laws checked unruly impulses like greed and grandiose schemes of possession. But those checks did not follow the pioneers into the wilderness. The lack of them creates a moral wilderness that baffles Clement as much as the literal one. In such a world, he thinks it better to conserve life's energy than to risk it for loot that, besides being ephemeral, collects a tax from the human heart.

For the pioneer, the past has been left behind. But memory of the past is the keystone of Clement's character. His memory of the little group huddled around a campfire just before the Indians effortlessly penetrate the circle and burst the illusion of security, reminds him that nothing he gathers around himself for familiarity and protection is as firm or impenetrable as it seems. In time, Clement learns that even his own family circle (Salome, Rosamond, and Jamie) have left him alone, pursuing, each in his or her own way, dreams of wealth and success.

Jamie Lockhart, even though he locks up the heart of the fair Rosamond, has a locked heart himself. He *seems* to change, to see the futility of his acquisitive ways, but the tone of irony makes it probable that he changes only in appearance. It has been Jamie's delusion that he could be both gentleman and robber. He has applied the berry stain disguise and washed it off so many times that he finally reaches a point at which he is caught, half-gentleman and half-robber (*RB*, 112). Little Harp, whom Welty uses as a dark image of the robber half of Jamie, makes this discovery, forcing Jamie to choose between robber and gentleman.[19] Jamie kills Little Harp. But is the dark side gone forever? Maybe Jamie would like to think so. He goes on to become a wealthy, prominent New Orleans merchant. "[T]he outward transfer from bandit to merchant had been almost too easy to count it a change at all, and he was enjoying all the same success he had ever had. But now, in his heart, Jamie knew that he was a hero and had always been one, only with the power to look both ways and to see a thing from all sides" (pp. 184–85).

Although toads may metamorphose into princes in romance, Jamie's transformation is little more than an outward transfer.[20] Jamie has not been as deeply tested as Clement, whose heart is far more respectable than Jamie's. Jamie has stepped from success to success and never held anything in his heart more complicated or painful "than a dream of true love—something of gossamer and roses" (*RB*, 74). He is the compleat businessman; his satiric foil is Goat, the troll-like bumpkin whose parodies of hard bargaining always result in a self-fleecing.[21]

Jamie is very close in instinct and motto to Salome, herself a sour

19. In Screenplay, Welty deleted the following: "Little Harp for all his repulsiveness is a kind of conscience to Jamie and deserves being let live."

20. This position will cause much debate. Screenplay reads as follows:

Jamie:    Well, sir, I've only uncovered a merchant under the bandit. Who knows what's under that.

Rosamond: His luck holds . . . Maybe you have as many layers as a spring onion, dear.

Clement:  Oh, many more.

Rosamond: (Amused and a little alarmed).

Jamie:    You were the first one, and the most fanatical, to trust me, sir, that night at Rodney Inn. Yet you could see me better than I saw myself, I've found that out. And what are you thinking now?

Clement:  Not that life is at a standstill. Only that it's time for me to go. —My child, when you have a genuine fearless man to contend with, you can take off a hundred coats, a dozen disguises, and his present wealth, too, even his luck—for maybe he stole it—and there he'll still stand, ready for you still. It's Jamie himself to contend with, as always.

Rosamond: I know. But what he contends with, in his heart, Father—for I can tell you—is that robber or husband, he's a hero, and was a hero all the time.

Clement:  Rosamond, you were wiser than we thought all the time, and safer than us all.

Jamie:    I only think the world is wide and new—and that there's plenty of time ahead.

Clement:  (mildly) A hero's words. —And I must go back to my part of the world. My seeds must go down by this Easter moon.

21. Welty, Screenplay synopsis: "[Goat is] convinced he has a good deal of business ability, a common failing among our characters."

distillation of envy, greed, and ambition. Salome is obsessed with taking, owning, and displaying. She urges Clement to absorb more land, place it under cultivation, and make it pay. She envies every ounce of attention Rosamond receives, storing up her revenge for a grand climax. She is described as several animals—a cat, a vulturelike, clawed bird—and she looms like a black shadow on the borders of several scenes. The overstating of her wickedness, however, reaches tall-tale proportions early in the novella; the result is that the reader seldom takes her seriously. Who really fears the evil of the "wicked stepmother"?

But Salome should not be taken too lightly, for her kind of evil is special. It originates in greed and a grudge against the wilderness. The land must be compelled to work for her. She represents the extreme precipitation of the tug that pulled the pioneers into the new lands. In the character of Salome we see the frightening truth of what happens to human beings when the checks of civilization are left behind. Clement sees it also. If the zest to explore the unknown is one of man's noblest activities, then the cold intent to subject the earth to his possession and to make it serve his desires is one of his least noble.

Salome's ultimate dream is "a mansion at least five stories high, with an observatory of the river on top of that, with twenty-two Corinthian columns to hold up the roof" (*RB*, 100).[22] Clement must have been sadly surprised to see Rosamond's happily-ever-after on the shores of Lake Pontchartrain: "a beautiful house of marble and cyprus wood . . . with a hundred slaves" (pp. 183–84). It is more opulent than Salome's dream. The surprise must be all the more aching because Rosamond has always been her father's pet, content to let him think of her as the delicate princess in need of protection and rescue. But she has always been, for the readers, more shrewd than that, and cunning in the way she gets her man. She shows her true colors when she lies to her father about being married to Jamie by a priest. In that moment she uses Clement's innocence as Jamie and Salome had used it.

The last word of the novella, or close to the last, is the last word on Rosamond. Clement is about to return upriver once again with the gold

22. Screenplay makes explicit that Salome's dream corresponds to the actual ruins of the plantation Windsor, which burned in 1890. The proposed fade-out: "Twenty-two Corinthian columns rising in a caney field, which seem to be haunted by something—an owl, a goat, a cat?" Salome has been compared to each of these animals in the novella.

his crop has brought. But Rosamond stays behind, in the city. She is part of the new age that has superseded Clement. The city, the place of doubleness, where vice and beauty live together, is too exotic for Clement. "But the city was splendid, she [Rosamond] said; it was the place to live" (RB, 184).

Clement lives an Emersonian maxim: "Our life is an apprenticeship to the truth that around every circle another can be drawn; that there is no end in nature, but every end is a beginning; that there is always another dawn risen on mid-noon, and under every deep a lower deep opens" ("Circles"). He lives it in his heart, feeling there the unseen, outer circles. He has seen in the faces of the Indians pride and triumph brought down to impotence and weariness as time runs out. And he accepts himself as an end and Jamie as a beginning in the constant revolution of time. But "he was an innocent of the wilderness . . . and this was his good" (RB, 182). It is essential to his innocence that he remain clement, leaving action to the Salomes and Jamies, violent resistance to the Indians. His way is contemplation.

In his moment of private reckoning, Clement sees each individual tree and bird, and also the continuity of all things. Time bothers him most persistently: "What is the place and time?" (RB, 141) The trees grow straight and tall, birds sing from the branches, everything seems to be harmonious and ordered. But there is a menacing presence that threatens the tranquility. "Across this floor, slowly and softly and forever moving into profile, is always a beast, one of a procession, weighted low with his burning coat, looking from the yellow eye set in his head" (p. 141). A beast like that of impending chaos in Yeats' "The Second Coming" haunts Clement's vision. He worries, like Yeats, that the way of the world is down from order, accelerating toward chaos.

Clement's thoughts and emotions in his moment of choice are complex; he is deeply troubled by a sense of the contradictions in things and people. The mutability of all things haunts his consciousness, yet all around him he sees people living in ignorance of it. Clement's personal outlook, in this respect, is a more conscious and reflective version of the outlook of the Indians. His special relationship with them is not an accident. He knows what they only feel—their inescapable doom in the waves of white pioneers. And he knows further that the tug pulling the pioneers will result in nothing more permanent than the life the Indians had. Rodney is the place to verify that.

Two worlds clash in Clement's vision; the old will be destroyed. The beast with the single yellow eye is the harbinger of the new, forever revolving into the present. The beast means to Clement that the end point of progress is not a perfect pastoral Eden on earth. How can that be the culmination, Clement must think, even though the dreams and hopes and images dangling before the pioneers are the most desirable the human imagination can create? How can this pioneering adventure end in idyll when it is based on doubleness, on greed that is called a noble errand, on ambition that shuts out every human consideration except the piling up of fantastic gain?

But the time for cunning has come. . . . And my time is over, for cunning is of a world I will have no part in. Two long ripples are following down the Mississippi behind the approaching somnolent eyes of the alligator. And like the tenderest deer, a band of copying Indians poses along the bluff to draw us near them. Men are following men down the Mississippi, hoarse and arrogant by day, wakeful and dreamless by night at the unknown landings. A trail leads like a tunnel under the roof of this wilderness. Everywhere the traps are set. Why? And what kind of time is this, when all is first given, then stolen away? (*RB*, 142–43)

Just as Coverdale and Carraway attended to the romantic dream of earthly perfection, until the means of getting it proved invalid and false, Clement Musgrove followed the pioneer trail until, in time, he learned the cost to the human heart. To continue to pursue, he would have had to assume a doubleness toward himself and the world, taking what was there while pretending it was free.

*The Robber Bridegroom* accommodates its elements of myth, folk tale, legend, fantasy, blood violence, and historical fact within a theme of the spoiled pastoral—paradise dreamed, desired, lost. Hawthorne made use of such a theme in *The Blithedale Romance*; the ideal society desired by the communitarian reformers was contaminated and finally spoiled by the humans involved. Fitzgerald struck the same note of disenchantment in *The Great Gatsby*; whatever glowing possibilities the new world held out were poisoned the moment man entered to take possession of his dream.

Welty has taken great care in the selection and composition of *The*

*Robber Bridegroom.* Choosing the town of Rodney as the place for the tale and modeling the Indians on the Natchez, are conspicuous choices that deepen the story's theme and meaning. The cycles of the plot and the frequency of individual circle images prove close and delicate attention to construction. There is more here than simple good fun with a few childhood fairy tales.

The integration of society called for in the resolution of a comedy is present only in appearance. Happy-ever-after is not a future in the real world, only in fairy tales. Jamie and Rosamond do live happily and prosperously ever after. But their opulent establishment recalls the grand and futile obsession of Salome.

The time has brought change. The pioneer has given way to the middleman, as the Indians had been forced aside by the pioneers. It is as Clement feared. His dream of a paradise of integrity, where appearance and reality are united, where cunning is nonexistent, has vanished. Welty seems to be saying that the dream of a pastoral paradise on earth is always one step ahead of the dreamers; it is, sadly, only possible in a dream world removed from contact with human flesh and imperfections. But still worth dreaming. Alfred Kazin stated this well in his review. Our myths are always sparking our hopes; reality is always dousing them: "Every myth we tell each other today, or try to restore, is only the symbol for our own longing, and turns upon itself. Not the smallest part of Miss Welty's rather exquisite achievement is the skill with which she reminds us that the enchanted forest is for us to recapture—and is forever dead."[23]

The real hero of *The Robber Bridegroom* is Clement. Like Don Quixote, he wrestles with evil valiantly, and loses. Clement, more authentically than Jamie, has the power to "see a thing from all sides." But seeing the doubleness in all things, he does not attack it; nor does he act as if it were not there. Clement acknowledges the vital necessity of mystery (the limits to human understanding), most of which goes out of the world as time and arrogant human meddling have their way.

Clement, as a hero, retreats. But he has won an integrating vision; he has learned through physical and emotional trial the continuity of time and its concentration in the moment. The technique of *The Robber Bridegroom* works to furnish that moment. The Natchez and the town

---

of Rodney haunt the background as reminders of time past, of human culture and industry done, wiped out, or simply and willy-nilly abandoned. In the foreground the bustle of civilization continues under the spell of progress and profit. But Clement, knowing intuitively the lesson of the past, has seen the future: time is a continuous cycle; the moment of unscaled human vision is the only true stability.

## IV

The artist needs and seeks
distance—his own best
distance—in order to
learn about his subject.
Eudora Welty,
"The House of
Willa Cather."

# Finding a Style:
# "The Delta Cousins"
# into *Delta Wedding*

*Delta Wedding*, Welty's first full-length novel,
was serialized in the *Atlantic Monthly* and published in the spring of 1946.
It was to be, according to several reviewers, a literary event. Many who
had admired Welty's short stories still awaited the traditional acid test of
the American writer of fiction—the successful novel. If the literary jury
was expecting to hand down a clear-cut verdict, however, they were
disappointed.

Among those disappointed by the lack of a traditional plot in *Delta
Wedding*, John Cournos, an informed historian and critic of the American short story, wrote perhaps the most generous negative opinion.
"Rich though Miss Welty is in the creation of background and characters, she does not seem to have any story to tell. Perhaps it is wrong,
nowadays, for a critic to insist that it is the function of a novelist to tell
a story."[1] Other less courteous reviewers faulted *Delta Wedding* for a lack
of social realism and political awareness, a reprehensible omission of
"facts."[2] These reviewers tended to read the novel as an idyll of worn-out
and essentially illusory southern arcadia in which we, as readers and cit-

1. John Cournos, review of Eudora Welty's *Delta Wedding*, New York *Sun*, April 15, 1946,
p. 21.
2. See John Crowe Ransom, "Delta Fiction," *Kenyon Review*, VIII (Summer, 1946), 503–507;
Harnett T. Kane, "Eudora Welty's Authentic and Vital Talent," New York *Herald Tribune Weekly
Book Review*, April 14, 1946, p. 3; Isaac Rosenfeld, "Double Standard," *New Republic*, April 29,
1946, pp. 633–34; and Diana Trilling, "Fiction in Review," *Nation*, May 11, 1946, p. 578.

izens, must no longer indulge our fancy for escape and romance. This was the brave new world, following the Great Depression, the war, and, very recently, the bomb. It was time, these reviewers seemed to say, that we and our writers stop toying with the past and face the hard social, political, and economic world that, in spite of ourselves, we had made.

Criticism of this type was not new, nor has it ever disappeared from reviews of Welty's books. Lionel Trilling had complained in much the same vein about *The Robber Bridegroom*. That southern fiction offers escape from the dull actualities of the real has historically been the opinion of reviewers and critics; sometimes this escape is welcomed, sometimes scorned. Welty's famous short stories, many of the dissenting reviewers wrote, gave us the "new South," a "real South," a South in keeping with their image of it as a backwater with a lush exotic setting and grotesque people with outlandish names and defects. Now that Welty had written a novel, the reasoning went, she should have treated this South in more depth. *The Robber Bridegroom*, with fairy tale characters and ghosts, and now *Delta Wedding*, with its charming rustics and Edenic simplicity and calm, did not seem to the "slice-of-life critics" to be quite proper.

On the other hand, a few critics found *Delta Wedding* powerful because of its innovations in the relationship of style to meaning. Paul Engle praised the novel in language rare among its first reviewers. "[*Delta Wedding*] has, in addition, a slow accumulation of meaning impossible for the short stories [of Welty] to achieve. . . . *Delta Wedding* has a sense of the texture of human experience being entered into deeply and gently and honestly. This is the rare quality above all in fiction. . . . The meaning is one of the great questions of this century, the struggle of the individual to attach himself to a group, to acquire the knowledge of belonging."[3] Engle was right about the technical success of *Delta Wedding*. Without dogmatic preconceptions about plot, storytelling, or the South, he read the novel as it was written, like poetry or lyric fiction with its "slow accumulation of meaning." John Edward Hardy, writing about *Delta Wedding* almost twenty years later, follows Engle's path. "The order of the novel is a poetic order—of recurrent themes, symbols, and motifs of symbolic metaphor. And it must be close-read, as a poem."[4]

3. Paul Engle, "Miss Welty's Full Charm in First Novel," Chicago *Tribune*, April 14, 1946, pp. 3, 12.
4. John Edward Hardy, "*Delta Wedding*: Region and Symbol," in *Man in the Modern Novel*

*Delta Wedding* is an event in another way, for it is a record of a writer's discovery of her distance and in that distance the relationship between herself and experience; in short, it records the discovery of a style. "Things in their natural habitat" do exist in the novel, and several reviewers devoted much ink to the condensation of place, character, and action into a realistic précis. But things transcend their natural habitat and, as Hardy has said, create a fictional world that is much richer because of the poetic style.

The novel is composed of moments when each of the characters through whose eyes the story is told bumps up against the frightening truth that she is not alone but is in a real world with other beings who are equally real. Those who grow from that moment, like Joel Mayes and Jenny Lockhart before them, find love to be a "widened susceptibility." A passage from Elizabeth Bowen's *The Death of the Heart* (1939) is helpful for its illumination of these moments in the theme of love:

There are moments when it becomes frightening to realise that you are not, in fact, alone in the world—or at least alone in the world with one other person. The telephone ringing when you are in a daydream becomes a cruel attacking voice. That general tender kindness towards the world, especially kindness of a young person, comes from a pitying sense of the world's unreality. The happy passive nature, locked up with itself like a mirror in an airy room, reflects what goes on but demands not to be approached. A pact with life, a pact of immunity, appears to exist. But this pact is not respected for ever—a street accident, an overheard quarrel, a certain note in a voice, a face coming too close, a tree being blown down, someone's unjust fate—the peace tears right across. Life militates against the seclusion we seek. In the chaos that suddenly thrusts in, nothing remains unreal, except possibly love. Then, love only remains as a widened susceptibility: it is felt at the price of feeling all human dangers and pains. The lover becomes the sentient figurehead of the human ship, thrust forward by the weight of the race behind him through pitiless elements. Pity the selfishness of lovers: it is brief, a forlorn hope; it is impossible.[5]

There are images in this passage that surprise the reader of Welty: the falling tree (found in "A Curtain of Green"), the lover as sentient figurehead (Easter in "Moon Lake"). Another kind of literary event is

(Seattle, 1964), 183. The themes and forms of memory and nostalgia are discussed by Richard Gray, *The Literature of Memory: Modern Writers of the American South* (Baltimore, 1977), 177–85; and by Mark Robert Hochberg, "Narrative Forms in the Modern Southern Novel" (Ph.D. dissertation, Cornell University, 1970), Chap. 4.

5. Elizabeth Bowen, *The Death of the Heart* (New York, 1939), 220.

presaged in *Delta Wedding*, for Welty's fiction begins to take a place beyond "regional writing," in the company of such novelists as Bowen,
Woolf, Forster and others with whom she shares themes and techniques.[6]

The technique of *Delta Wedding* becomes an essential part of its
meaning. The novel is more lyrical than narrative in its attention to
setting, event, plot, and language. Its thematic territory is not the world
of politics or natural disasters (Welty deliberately chose 1923 for the time
of her story because it was free of such great events); its world is the
human heart and its tangled relationships with others.[7] Such is the territory of Bowen's novel also. The complex nature of theme and technique
in *Delta Wedding* can be more easily understood and appreciated when we
look at its evolution from the unpublished and "unsalable" short story
"The Delta Cousins."[8]

The unpublished story straightforwardly presents the theme of innocence in the character of motherless, sensitive, nine-year-old Laura Kim-
ball, shadowed but never touched by the world of "real" experience that
threatens the peace and wonder of her private world.[9] In the short story,
Laura provides the point of view. The technique, therefore, is not too
complicated. Our vision, like hers, is sensitive but not intellectual; it is
receptive to nuance, to "a certain note in a voice," but is not capable of
Jamesian analysis of it. We see what Laura sees. It is plain to the reader—
perhaps it was as plain to the author—that at several points the burden
of the story is almost too much for a nine-year-old, no matter how sensitive and precocious she might be. Laura detects too much, sometimes too
finely. These moments are most clearly evident when Laura's fascination
with her Delta relations is expressed in long, poetic paragraphs of homage:

All of them in the Delta looked alike—they had a trim fleetness about
them, a neatness that was actually a readiness for gayeties and departures, a
lack of burdens. Without a primary beauty, with only a fairness of color and an
ease in the body, they had a demurring grey-eyed way about them that turned
out to be mocking—for these cousins were in reality the sensations of life and

6. Eudora Welty, *The Eye of the Story: Selected Essays and Reviews* (New York, 1978).
7. Linda Kuehl, "The Art of Fiction XLVII: Eudora Welty," *Paris Review*, LV (Fall, 1972), 84.
8. Schmucker, "A Visit With Eudora Welty In Mississippi."
9. The age of nine has some special significance. It is "so likely to be the most sensitive, most
vulnerable year of childhood." Eudora Welty, "The House of Willa Cather," in Bernice Slote and
Virginia Faulkner (eds.) *The Art of Willa Cather* (Lincoln, Neb., 1974), 9.

they knew it—things waited for them to appear, laughing and amazed, in order to happen. . . . They were forever ready, forever—almost seriously—of the moment; the past (even her arrival) was a private, dull matter, that was understood—wonderful though it had been to Laura at the time. Laura from her earliest memory had heard how they "never seemed to change at all." And yet they changed every moment. Their movements were quick and on the instant, the men's and ladies' both, they were like players who knew a game ever so well. . . . Perhaps they were sluggish and preoccupied too, like other grown people. Maybe their laughter was part of their special intense kind of politeness, like their kissing of everybody in a room, maybe their fleetness and grace were a kind of courtesy to others too, an outward thing, really a protection of themselves. But when they looked at you with their lighted eyes, picked you out in a room for a glance, obviously waiting for you to say something, to ask a question, the smallest thing, of any of them you chose, and so to commit yourself forever—you were aware without question then of their unfailing charm, you had to trust them, for you adored them. (DC, 8–9)

Homage to the clan is an integral part of *Delta Wedding* also, but in the novel we hear it from several different voices. Laura's burden, which is heavy with its fine shades of appearance and motion, is lightened in the novel by being shared with other characters.

Laura's reaction to the Sheltons in "The Delta Cousins" as "players who knew a game ever so well" is also revised. In the novel, suggestions of conscious, or even unwitting, game playing by the clan are removed. The Fairchilds are pure spontaneity and exotic charm. In *Delta Wedding* Laura is reminded of a "great bowerlike cage full of tropical birds her father had shown her in a zoo in a city—the sparkle of motion was like a rainbow, while it was the very thing that broke your heart, for the birds that flew were caged all the time and could not fly out" (*DW*, 15). The shift of the imagery from players in a game to caged and fragile birds is significant, for it alters Laura's reaction to the clan from analysis to wonder. With the image of rare birds come also hints of captivity and extinction of the species, both of which are important elements of the novel's theme.

The sharpening of Laura's character, and the hint of Fairchild delicacy and doom, are not the only beginnings discovered in "The Delta Cousins."[10] The Shelton family of the story has a paragon figure, Raymond, who becomes George Fairchild, the focal point of the women in

10. Schmucker, "A Visit With Eudora Welty in Mississippi."

*Delta Wedding*. In the short story his dimensions are necessarily restricted, but the mythic, religious, and heroic outlines of the stature he is to assume in the novel (and in future fiction by Welty) are clear. In a short paragraph describing Raymond, Welty launches the male character who is to be the original for those whose burden is the blessing of the family, and vice versa. He embodies the family's image of itself in its ideal beauty and excellence, kindness, love, and heroism. Raymond is the forerunner of Uncle Daniel Ponder, of Jack Renfro, of the public figure Judge Clinton McKelva. "And there he was, high above them, above India's father, in his gay protesting way. He talked less than any of them—though he talked a lot. Sometimes they seemed to carry him aloft, like a whole roast pig on a platter, they worshipped him so, and anticipated his wonders so, dared him not to be faultless" (*DC*, 14).

Deleted from the author's revision is the final sentence describing Raymond: "Of course if he was faultless, then they would not have to be, being kin." Welty was already considering the dual role of the clan's hero—savior and scapegoat. Here also is the simple selfishness of the clan; charging one member with the responsibility to be perfect, they pardon themselves. There is insufficient room in the short story for the character of Raymond to manifest even a small fraction of his possibilities as a human figure, much less as a symbolic and mythic figure. Like Laura's imperfect apprehension of the Shelton family, Raymond remains one of the undeveloped resources of the short story.

The nature of the clan, its intricate treaties between self and family, the plight of Raymond (his runaway wife is scarcely mentioned in the short story) are not the only dormant seeds in "The Delta Cousins." The novel concludes on the note of the inevitability of victory for the outside world over the fragile "bower" of clan and plantation. George will make changes and Troy will help him (*DW*, 243). The Fairchilds of the novel are indeed fair children facing away from the necessity of adapting to the outside world. This uneasy detente with disintegration and change is also at the heart of "The Delta Cousins." The story, like the novel, is no *Peter Pan*; there is no victory in not growing up. Evil is present in the story more overtly, yet more hauntingly, than in the novel. The "pact with life" is always being threatened with dissolution.

In "The Delta Cousins" evil confronts Laura first in the person of her nine-year-old cousin, Maurine. Maurine is slow, perhaps retarded, very strong, and unpredictable. She is a "circle-breaker" who turns a circle game into crack-the-whip and flings the other children off the end of the whip with her strength. She would, Laura fears, break her fingers as soon as caress them. The character of Maurine is a static symbol of the unmerciful, unreasonable world; she remains fixed on the fringe of Laura's awareness.

There is also the ghostly figure of the old beeman. Veiled by his beekeeping hat, his voice rasping like the sound of dry leaves, he is a strange and magnetic figure whose presence I miss in the novel. The beeman's importance in the story is essential, for he is the embodiment of evil with its mysterious attraction and easy intrusion into a child's privileged world, and is the symbol of all that the Sheltons, in their splendid innocence, conspire to exclude from the sanctuary of the clan. And, as a symbol for the personal need we "veil" within ourselves, he functions imaginatively rather than intellectually, like a character in a tale by Hawthorne.

Laura and her other nine-year-old Shelton cousin, India, meet the beeman on one of their adventurous walks by the Sunflower River, which runs through the Shelton plantation. Laura is frightened by the meeting; but India, behind a shield of Shelton arrogance, does not shrink from anyone as long as she is on her own ground. The beeman "smiled and looked as if he might stroke their hair" (*DC*, 24). Laura recoils from the veiled face, the veiled evil; but India accepts, for both of the girls, his invitation (or challenge) to ride in his boat to "his house."

There is a dead finch on the porch, which the girls sidestep. But the message is clear. The beeman's house is no joyous human hive, like the loud and teeming house of the Sheltons. Instead, his deserted house carries out the symbolic meaning initiated by his aged, veiled appearance. "They were in a very tall room that was round, dimly light at the top, and going up and around it was a climbing circle or stairway, with nothing to hold it up except its clinging to the wall. It was like being inside an old, round tower that had not fallen" (*DC*, 24).

"Like being inside an old, round tower" is like being in the field of some ancient mystery or phallic power that the two cousins cannot understand. But Laura, with her deep sensitivity, *feels* the threatening force of some power. It is a counterforce to the clan because it creates division. "Laura would not go up the stairs, India would not come down—for a sudden division between them was in the air—full of echoes. At last India came, her face rosy and the ribbon gone off her hair. 'I tied it on the post at the top,' she told Laura. Sure enough, far up in the filtering light was the little white ribbon, like a flag" (*DC*, 25). The imagery of this crucial moment suggests different degrees of sexual knowledge or readiness as causes of division between two characters who had been intimately related within the clan. India sets off toward experience, daring forces that she cannot understand because her lifelong protection as one of the Sheltons has bred in her a kind of hubristic, childish conviction that she cannot be hurt, penetrated, by the world that overwhelms all human beings. Laura, the motherless girl, instinctively fears the unknown; she has lived without such external protection and knows vulnerability.

The beeman takes the girls by their hands and leads them out of his house and back to his boat. His hands are cold, though it is September in the Delta. Both girls shiver. 'Do you want me to help you into the boat?' asked the bee-man, though what he did was to touch his trousers and a little old fish seemed to come out" (*DC*, 26). The beeman's exposure of himself is an effective and telling image for the constant presence of the shadowing world of need and disordered experience. Laura, of course, does not know what she has witnessed; she sees only what her innocence disguises as a fish. The choice of this imagery is significant. In the novel the process is reversed; fish and other underwater creatures represent the existence, beyond the protective walls of the clan, of a kind of worldly experience of chaos that includes sex. Laura, Shelley, and Dabney of *Delta Wedding* find in the Yazoo River, or "River of Death" (which replaces the happy-sounding Sunflower River of the story), these images of the outer world.

"The Delta Cousins" does not sentence the beeman to the depths of sexual depravity. Need, the impulse of his action, is not ignoble. He asks the girls if they wish him to take them home.

"Yes sir," they answered together, and to their surprise they both spoke out of breath, as if they had been running instead of sitting very still in a boat that moved gently over the river. The old man's eyes looked at them gently from down the boat as if he had been running too, at just that distance behind them. He rowed a little faster. But because of the way the boat was made, he could never catch up with them, no matter how fast he rowed. Transfixed and apart they rode, at their distance over the shadowy water. At the right place, willow branches came to meet them overhead and touched their foreheads. The boat touched shore.

They jumped out of the boat, and ran separately forward. In only a moment they were back in the willowy woods. They paused and lifted up their hair, and turned on their heels. They shook themselves. India began to jump up and down and laugh. (*DC*, 26)

In the images of beeman, boat, river, and girls, the major concerns of the story and the seminal meanings of the novel come before the reader. The parallel worlds of aged need and childlike innocence are stopped in their unmixing courses. But the presence of the older, mysterious, apparently sinister world is so near that the girls are breathless under its shadow. Freed when the boat touches Shelton ground, they can run joyously away, shaking off "all human dangers and pains" as a dog shakes off river water. That is their privilege as children.

The burden of "The Delta Cousins," besides resting on the fineness of Laura's consciousness, rests also on this episode. So much more is possible, however, than is actually achieved. There is a complex idea of human nature and need that really requires a wider scope and a slower pace, as Engle observed, than the short story offers. How else to explore such statements as the following:

People were not only what they seemed—if they were all like cousins—they were so much more. More wonderful, more stupid, more beautiful, more secret, more stubborn, more happy, more daring, more anxious—more to be held close-ly, then—if held at all—than had been dreamed of. They were different from one another, different from themselves according to the day. Even the bee-man —perhaps another day he would wear a different mask. It stayed in her head that he had taken some kind of chance when he invited them to go on the river, he had been disappointed—how, she did not know—but they had all failed one another that day, he so easily by having nothing to eat prepared in his house. Another day, he would be successful—like Maurine, she thought abruptly. (*DC*, 31)

Incidental changes from story to novel retain the atmosphere of enclave menaced by the outside. Innisola, the Delta town in which the Sheltons of the short story live and grow their cotton, suggests *island, isolated, in* —a cluster of words having in common the notion of enclave, or separa-tion from a larger world of experience. Shelton becomes Fairchild, the name of the family and town. The name of the Fairchild plantation, Shellmound, continues the hint of self-protection in the *shel* of Shelton.

Changing from Sunflower River to Yazoo, "River of Death," introduces serious symbolic dimensions to the novel, for the river becomes a physical and psychological locale for confrontations with the world of menace and disorder, the former territory of the beeman. Other names and characters are adjusted also to create an atmosphere richer in connotation and nuance than that of the story. But the vital change is the redistribution of the point of view among several distinct characters. This is the technical choice that shifts the novel from narrative to lyric; it presents the characters as stanzas in a poem about love, need, and sympathy. Redistributing the point of view also creates distance, and that is essential in providing the perspective in which the fullness of the novel can be appreciated.

Laura enters the novel first, as she had in the story. But she, like Rosemary of *Tender Is the Night*, should not be established as the principal point of view simply because she is the first to appear. Her significance as character and viewpoint has more to do with the complex nature of her outlook as it takes its place among others. She is an outsider to the Delta, to family life, to the noise and "extravagant talk" of the Fairchilds. Laura's life is lived within herself, secretly and privately, with acutely sensitive sight, feeling, memory, and need. When she is met at the depot by a carload of Fairchild cousins, she is swept into their whirl of talk and bustle and is overwhelmed. When the kin finally melt away, as magically as they had appeared, and leave her at the front door of Shellmound, Laura throws up. She is not used to the tempo of Fairchild living.

The emotional and the physical facts of the clan mesmerize Laura. Two feelings dominate her emotions: her sense that she is vulnerable as long as she remains on the outside, and her passionate attention to the clan in hopes of a sign of her acceptance. Since Laura is the "motherless child" seeking protection, the clan appears to her as blessed, sheltering warmth. Her "stanza" in *Delta Wedding*, then, is devoted to her strong attraction to the comforts of belonging and to her loneliness as an outsider.

Laura records how the Fairchilds, living and dead, form a corporate entity to provide solid protection. She senses the integrity of the generations. "But boys and men, girls and ladies all, the old and the young of the Delta kin—even the dead and the living, for Aunt Shannon— were alike—no gap opened between them" (DW, 14). The clan seems to Laura to act as one. In fact, the singleness of their identity as a clan troubles her. "The Fairchilds' movements were quick and on the instant, and that made you wonder, are they free? Laura was certain that they were *compelled*—their favorite word. Flying against the bad things happening, they kissed you in rushes of tenderness. Maybe their delight was part of their beauty, its flicker as it went by, and their kissing of not only you but everybody in a room was a kind of spectacle, an outward thing" (p. 15).

Where is the individual in this spectacle of clan? That is the kind of question Laura does not consciously ask, but the need for an answer troubles her. They are so public; she is so private. In the midst of the hectic celebration of Fairchilds at home, living in a universe as abundant with "love" as their fields are with cotton, Laura returns again and again to her need for individual recognition, which grows from her strong sense of self. "They had never told Laura they loved her" (DW, 17). Their spoken, public word is the decree Laura, as suppliant at the Fairchild court, begs. But the clan is bound together internally, not by mutual recognition of individuals, but by the communal identity as clan. They are so occupied with themselves that they do not recognize her.

Laura's eager attention to the clan, contending with her acute self-awareness, discloses an aspect of family identity that "The Delta Cousins" does not. The cost of protection and attention as a member of the family is one's individual freedom, or most of it. Wandering into an "empty" room at Shellmound, Laura is startled to hear Aunt Shannon, the oldest living Fairchild, talking to the dead as if they were gathered around her chair like the "mounted blue butterflies on the wall" (DW, 118). Here, Laura is surprised into an understanding of the clan, and its cost:

Aunt Shannon never wept over Laura, as if she could not do it over one mother-less child, or give her any immediate notice. In her the Fairchild oblivion to the member of the family standing alone was most developed; just as in years past its opposite, the Fairchild sense of emergency, a dramatic instinct, was in its ascendancy, and she had torn herself to pieces over Denis's drinking and Denis's getting killed. Insistently a little messenger or reminder of death, Laura self-consciously struck her pose again and again, but she was a child too familiar, too like all her cousins, too much one of them (as they all were to one another a part of their very own continuousness at times) ever to get the attention she begged for. By Aunt Shannon in particular, the members of the family were always looked on with that general tenderness and love out of which the single personality does not come bolting and clamorous, but just as easily emerges gently, like a star when it is time, into the sky and by simply emerging drifts back into the general view and belongs to the multitudinous heavens. All were dear, all were unfathomable, all were constantly speaking, as the stars would ever twinkle, imploringly or not—so far, so far away. (pp. 62–63)

Laura's dilemma is that of the individual, as motherless child, seeking acceptance and protection by the clan, but fearful of the price. To Aunt Shannon there are no individuals, just empty roles to be filled from the succeeding generations; there is no individual notice, only "general tenderness and love." Aunt Shannon's age and memory set individuality into the perspective of a long clan history. The self is like the emerging star; it blazes for an instant, then drops back into the anonymous heavens. The clan exists before and after each soul.

Laura, for better or worse, is not bred for this kind of general existence. She is an only child and used to immediate and exclusive attention to her wishes. She remembers returning home with her parents from an outing in the country just before a storm was about to break. All the windows in the house had to be closed; but Laura's wishes came first. "Before the storm broke, before they were barely settled or had more than their faces washed, Laura cried, 'Mother, make me a doll—I want a doll!' What made this different from any other time? Her father for some reason did not ask 'Why another?' or remind her of how many dolls she had or of when she last said she was tired of dolls and never wanted to play with one again. And this time was the most inconvenient she could have chosen" (*DW*, 231). Laura is used to a kind of exclusive attention that the clan does not offer. The independence fostered in her by this attention never wanes. Even when she is finally enveloped in the warm hug of the Fairchilds as the novel ends, she reserves the right to return to her father whenever she pleases. With her intensely private identity, Laura feels the contradictory forces of self and clan as one thing—need. She needs human comfort; she needs her own freedom.

Need pulled you out of bed in the morning, showed you the day with everything crowded into it, then sang you to sleep at night as your mother did, need sent you dreams. Need did all this—when would it explain? Oh, some day. She waited now, and then each night fell asleep in the vise of India's arms. She imagined that one day—maybe the next, in the Fairchild house—she would know the answer to the heart's pull, just as it would come to her in school why the apple was pulled down on Newton's head, and that it was the way for girls in the world that they should be put off, put off, put off—and told a little later; but told, surely. (p. 76)

Like Portia in Bowen's *The Death of the Heart*, Laura is an extraordinary innocent. The gravity of her need to belong makes her bold to approach the Fairchild clan, to risk rejection. This constant, sharp awareness unavoidably makes her selfish; yet her selfishness does not have the anarchic cast of Maurine's or the pitiful tinge of the beeman's. Laura's kind of innocent selfishness is poignantly clear in her response to her uncle, George Fairchild. As I have said, George is the human focal point of the characters whose points of view define the novel. Each of them feels the necessity of striking a kinship with George, for he embodies, literally, the frank and tactile world beyond the envelope of self. Such personal moments of meeting climax each character's "stanza." Laura's significance, innocence, selfishness, depth, and limitations are summed up in her approach to George with her gift.

After she has tried for a long time to think of the right gift on her own, Laura asks Shelley Fairchild for a suggestion. Shelley, only partially concerned, tells Laura to go to the Fairchild plantation store; anything there she can have for free. The Fairchild store, as Welty describes it through Laura's eyes (in one of the most detailed and sensory passages of the novel, p. 137), becomes the physical manifestation of Fairchild self-sufficiency. Any clan member may have anything he or she needs without paying. But Laura can find nothing there; "Nothing you have is good enough," she says (*DW*, 137). Her gift, her self, must not come from within the clan.

Instead, Laura, according to the "logic of [her] love" for George, makes him the present of his own favorite pipe, which she has hidden for a time in order to whet his need for it. The gift must not be something that might be less than a personal treasure for George. Such is Laura's selfish need for acceptance, that she "uses" George to satisfy it. She has not, as yet, a "widened" kind of love. Because of her innocence, she cannot fully give; and, in turn, life cannot fully give to her.

Besides the pattern of moments of meeting George, there is an accenting pattern in the novel in which the world of street accidents, quarrels, and felled trees intrudes upon the daydreaming self. In *Delta Wedding* these moments occur as each of the characters witnesses disorder, hunger, or loneliness. For Laura, as for her cousins Dabney, India, and Shelley, the moment occurs in the Yazoo, "River of Death." The pivotal moment of the beeman episode, his self-exposure, is deflected by Laura's protective shield of childish innocence. In the novel, her glimpse of the frightening underwater life of the Yazoo is the corresponding moment. Returning from a trip on the river with her cousin Roy, Laura is dumped overboard. "As though Aunt Studney's pack had opened after all, like a whale's mouth, Laura opening her eyes head down saw its insides all around her—dark water and fearful fishes (*DW*, 178)." Laura's immersion is a baptism for which she is not yet ready. She can neither give to the world in perfect love nor receive from it wholly. She is a part of the novel's poem of love, innocence, and need—one vivid human design in the whole mosaic.

Robbie Reid is an outsider too, a Fairchild only by her marriage to George. Unlike Laura she is an adversary, not a suppliant, who thinks of the clan and the one member she loves, George, in purely physical terms. Laura is distinguished by her strong emotion and the thoroughness of her need for recognition; she experiences need in her imagination. But Robbie Reid feels need in flesh and bone:

The pure, animal way of love she longed for, when she watched, listened, came out, stretched, slept content. Where he [George] lay naked and unconscious she knew the heat of his heavy arm, the drag of his night beard over her. She knew what he cried out in his sleep, she was outside herself. . . . She breathed the night in beside him, away from dreams and time and her own thoughts awake—the companion of his weight and warmth. Then she was glad there was nothing at all, no existence in the world, beyond George asleep, this real and forgetful and exacting body. She slept by him as if in the shadow of a mountain of being. Any moon and stars there were could rise and set over his enfolding, unemanating length. The sun could lean over his backside and wake her. (*DW*, 148)

Robbie's insistence upon the flesh and blood of George, his pure animal presence, collides with the desire of the Fairchild clan to have him at their liberty as paragon, hero, and scapegoat. In loving George, Robbie encounters an opposing love, the family's, that transforms the loved one into the most desirable reflection of the lovers themselves. The clan, for example, inducts George into the vacated role of the legendary Denis Fairchild, poet and warrior. Robbie, on the other hand, wants George without masks.

Robbie's love defines her point of view in the novel; it makes her stanza of the novel unique. Her love, like Gloria's for Jack Renfro in *Losing Battles*, seeks the intimate, exclusive relationship between lovers. Her love divides. She clashes with the Fairchilds, whose family love ties individual members to the home ground and the clan gallery of roles. The clan disapproves of members who go "outside"; it loathes those who take its members away. Aunt Tempe's daughter, for example, has fallen from the clan's favor for marrying a northerner; Aunt Primrose, whenever someone mentions Dabney's coming marriage, worries aloud that she will go out of the Delta.

But Robbie defies all bids to proscribe her love for George. She has no family tradition, no store of identity, and no innocence. Life has schooled her to face facts, to insist upon veracity, and to ignore the niceties with which the clan ignores disorder. "'Aunt Mac Fairchild!' said Robbie, lifting her voice again, and turning to the old lady her intense face. 'Mrs. Laws! [using her married name to remind her that she is not exclusively Fairchild] You're all a spoiled, stuck-up family that thinks nobody else is really in the world! But they are! You're just one plantation. With a little crazy girl [Maureen] in the family, and listen at Aunt Shannon [who talks to the dead]. You're not even rich! You're just medium'" (*DW*, 163). It has no effect; they suggest she have a drink of water.

Robbie, with a kind of unblinking stare, faces the outer world that the clan turns from. She has the courage to face the senseless aspect of life that Laura, for one, is not yet equipped to know. She faces it in her love for George. "Robbie desired veracity. . . . It meant coming to touch the real, undeceiving world within the fairy Shellmound world to love George. . . . He was abrupt and understandable to her as the here and now—and now had become a figure strangely dark, alone as the boogieman, back of them all, and seemed waiting with his set mouth open like a drunkard's or as if he were hungry" (*DW*, 149).

In loving George, Robbie faces the mortal world of hunger, need. The vision of the open mouth of human hunger occurs again in Welty's fiction, in *The Optimist's Daughter*, when Laurel Hand must force herself to face her obligation and kinship to those who hunger for love. Robbie makes a creed of it; her insistence narrows her. For she meets George with her own kind of selfishness. She is a militant outsider; compromise with the clan would violate her code of veracity. In her love she denies part of George's identity.

Inside the clan, struggles toward and away from the world are no less intense. Dabney is, in her way, as furious as Robbie, and as self-centered. But, despite her vigorous egotism, she has the virtue of seeing and living life very intensely. Dabney lives as zealously as Laura watches; her self-centeredness is largely unconscious.

Her breaking of the china night light, a Fairchild heirloom that her maiden aunts bestow upon her as their wedding gift, cannot be taken as a totally willed act of rebellion against family constraint. George is on the scene to tell us that the night light is no more than "a little old piece of glass that Dabney would never miss" (*DW*, 53). The heirloom means more to the aunts, for whom, as Ruth Vande Kieft says, it signifies "all that [they] would like to preserve intact, along with their own and their niece's virginity."[11] Experienced sexuality again absorbs the various meanings of the world outside the enclave of Shellmound. Dabney's wedding is a perilous walk near the boundaries for the whole clan. The news of Cousin Mary Denis Summers' new baby, for example, sends ripples of anxiety through the clan. India trumpets the news, then as loudly exclaims that Dabney looks as if she had eaten a batch of green apples. The aunts offer their bed for the bride to rest. But Dabney, stiffened by her egotism, rallies. "'Why, India! I feel perfect!' laughed Dabney, feeling them all looking at her. And all the little parlor things she had a moment ago cherished she suddenly wanted to break. She had once seen Uncle George, without saying a word, clench his fist in the dining room at home—the sweetest man in the Delta. It is because people are mostly layers of violence and tenderness—wrapped like bulbs, she thought soberly; I don't know what makes them onions or hyacinths" (p. 42).

Embracing life beyond the closed circle is Dabney's way of revitalizing the life within. She is passionately devoted to Shellmound, in spite of the family lore that threatens to harden into dogma. Dabney is connect-

11. Vande Kieft, *Eudora Welty*, 106.

ed to the spirit, not tied to the letter. The aunts preserve the lore, the story of her grandfather's duel with the owner of a rival cotton gin. The Fairchild legend is so close to the legend that haunts Faulkner's *Sartoris* and in turn mirrors his own history, that the story of honor, gunplay, and death might almost be the archetypal myth of the Old South. But Dabney rejects the "lesson" of the myth. "Honor, honor, honor, the aunts drummed into their ears. . . . To give up your life because you thought that much of your *cotton*—where was love, even, in that? *Other* people's cotton. Fine glory! Dabney would have none of it" (*DW*, 120).

Her allegiance, on the contrary, is to the spirit of her grandfather's act. "Both gins," in the end, "went on the same" (*DW*, 121). But the duel testified to a passionate attachment to Shellmound and, in that specific attachment, to a larger love for life itself. "She knew, though—even the surrender of life was the privilege of fieriness in the blood" (p. 121). This is the life-giving aspect of Dabney's selfishness; her fieriness will rekindle the life of the clan.

Dabney, like all of the characters of the novel, is drawn irresistibly to George. For her, he is the body of the clan that she passionately wishes may thrive. She remembers a moment of her life before World War I (she must have been nine, the age of Laura, India, and Maureen) when George and Denis came naked from the Yazoo. She was shocked by their nakedness but more concerned with the danger her uncles put themselves in to break up a knife fight between two Negro boys. "But all the Fairchild in her had screamed at his [George's] interfering—at his taking part—*caring* about anything in the world but them" (*DW*, 36). She felt the same intense reaction that Robbie, the outsider, felt at the trestle incident when George put himself in danger to rescue Maureen.

Dabney is intensely pro-clan. And the fieriness she draws from that connection helps her to face the images of disorder that surround her world. She deliberately goes to the Yazoo to stare into its depths.

There were more eyes than hers here—frog eyes—snake eyes? She listened to the silence and then heard it stir, churn, churning in the early morning. She saw how the snakes were turning and moving in the water, passing across each other just below the surface, and now and then a head horridly sticking up. The vines and the cypress roots twisted and grew together on the shore and in the water more thickly than any roots should grow, gray and red, and some roots too moved and floated like hair. On the other side, a turtle on a root opened its mouth and put its tongue out. And the whirlpool itself—could you doubt it? doubt all the stories since childhood of people white and black who had been drowned there, people that were dared to swim in this place, and of boats that would venture to the center of the pool and begin to go around and everybody fall out and go to the bottom, the boat to disappear? A beginning of vertigo seized her, until she felt herself leaning, leaning toward the whirlpool.

But she was never as frightened of it as the boys were. (*DW*, 123)

This confrontation in Dabney's portrayal must not be overlooked. Dabney is the most aggressively affirmative character of the novel. She accepts the world of sex and childbirth; she passionately commits herself to the continuation of Shellmound. Marmion, one of the decaying ancestral houses on the plantation, will be her home. She lines up with what might as well be called the life force; she is about to marry Troy Flavin. An outsider whose red beard and hair bristle with the vitality of a satyr, he appears to the aunts to be half-horse, like a kind of field god. And yet Dabney's "stanza" is narrowed by her self-centeredness. She is so passionately interested in her own life that she is unaware of others. The breaking of the night light has bad connotations, as well as favorable ones, for her character.

Shelley, Dabney's older sister, could never be cast in the role of the ascending queen of the fertility play. Dabney might, if one thought of the wedding ritual as a fertility ritual.[12] Shelley is the opposite of her sister; together they are thesis and antithesis. Dabney feels, Shelley thinks. Dabney rushes passionately into contact; Shelley lingers back, considering, analyzing. She is an intellectual; her stanza has the analytic distance of the intellect. She has her mother, Ellen, worried. "What could be so wrong in everything, [Ellen muses] to her sensitive and delicate mind? There was something not quite *warm* about Shelley" (*DW*, 212).

Lack of warmth keys Shelley's attitude toward the clan. Dabney has the "fieriness in the blood"; Shelley has the coolness of intellectual inspection. In her diary (the very act of writing, when the clan's official medium of communication is oral, sets Shelley apart) she observes, "We never wanted to be smart, one by one, but all together we have a wall, we are self-sufficient against people that come knocking, we are solid to the outside" (*DW*, 84). Her planned European trip will be her escape.

12. Louis D. Rubin, Jr., *The Faraway Country* (Seattle, 1963), Chap. 6.

Shelley prefers privacy to bustle; she quietly considers the images of disorder that Dabney rushes to face.

Theirs was a house where, in some room at least, the human voice was never still. Laughing and crying went rushing through the halls, and assuagement waylaid them both. In contrast, the bayou, in its silence, could seem like a lagoon in a foreign world, and a solitary person could walk beside it with inward, uncomfortable thoughts. The house was charged with life, the fields were charged with life, endlessly exploited, but the bayou was filled with its summer trance or its winter trance of sleep, its uncaught fishes. And the river, that went by the Grove. "Yazoo means River of Death." India was fond of parading the thing they learned in the fourth grade, and of parading morbidity before Shelley anyway, but Shelley looked back at her unmoved at the word. "Snooty, that's what you are," said India.

"River of Death" to Shelley meant not the ultimate flow of doom, but the more personal vision of the moment's chatter ceasing, the feelings of the day disencumbered, floating now into recognition, like a little boat come into sight; and tenderness and love, sadness and pleasure, being let alone to stretch in the shade. She thought this because of the way the Yazoo looked, its daily appearance. River of death of the day the Yazoo was to Shelley, and their bayou went in and out of it like the curved arm of the sleeper, whose elbow was in their garden. (*DW*, 194)

Shelley avoids confrontation. The uninvited confrontations in her experience haunt her with their disturbing omens. Once she had found Robbie crying in the Fairchild store; the moment became symbolic for her. "Shelley stood listening to that conceited fervor, and then Robbie raised her head and looked at her with her tears running down, and then made an even worse face, deliberately—an awful face. Shelley fell back and flew out with the children. An old mother bird dog lay right in the aisle, her worn teats flapping up and down as she panted—that was how public it was" (*DW*, 138).

Again reminders of sex stand in for the "wearing" assault of the world beyond store and plantation. Shelley is sensitive to such reminders. Dabney's wedding seems to take her beyond Shelley's inclination to follow, even in her imagination. And her mother's life of seemingly endless pregnancy seems so heartless that she accuses her father of cruelty (*DW*, 229).

Shelley has an idea of life; she is drawn to George because she believes he is the living confirmation of her idea. His heroic readiness to act in the urgent moment of the trestle incident means for Shelley that she is right to believe that life is made or broken in one instant of choice. She has a premonition that such a challenge waits for her, but not in the cozy circle of the clan.

Shelley's stanza is critical and distanced. She does not engage life directly, but only through the intermediary of her symbol-making intellect. Privacy is her personal habit; a private world of symbols and symbolic combinations is her habit of mind. Because of her devotion to symbols, Shelley's love is narrowed, her susceptibility restricted.

Only Ellen Fairchild is left. She had been Aunt Mim in "The Delta Cousins," slight of build and spiritual stature, and all kindness with no depth or complexity. But Ellen Fairchild is one of Welty's most characteristic heroines, neither adventurous like Dabney, tough like Robbie, nor intellectual and skeptical like Shelley. Ellen is more alive than all of them. Her life is a "widening susceptibility"; she knows Laura, Dabney, Shelley, and Robbie better than they know themselves. And she meets George with no selfish ulterior motivation.

Ellen "was an anomaly too, though no one would point at a lady for the things that made her one—for providing the tremendous meals she had no talent for, being herself indifferent to food, and had to learn with burned hands to give the household orders about—or for living on a plantation when she was in her original heart, she believed, a town-loving, book-loving young lady of Mitchem Corners" (*DW*, 217). In the flash of a family photograph, she is caught in the midst of her eight living children (she is pregnant with her tenth), in the role of mistress of a cotton plantation. She is shown encircled by a clan of people whose ways of boisterous activity and noise are far from her own.

Robbie critically imagines a "pleading mask" over the faces of Fairchild women, as their way of moving the men to follow their wishes. (It is a matriarchy; the survivors are all women. Aunt Tempe is the champion husband-bully.) But Ellen wears no mask. She is herself; she keeps her "original heart." She shuns fancy clothes and pleading ways. "'Your mother *lacks ways*,' Aunt Tempe always said to the girls darkly" (*DW*, 185).

If Ellen lacks the curtsying ways of the belle or the strong-arm brashness of Tempe, she is gifted with serenity and emotional tenderness. Unlike the Fairchilds, she listens with her heart to, as Elizabeth Bowen

wrote of her heroine, Portia, "the knockings and batterings we sometimes hear in each other that [keep] our intercourse from utter banality." [13] Because of her gift the clan, and the novel, gain unity through her
vision:

Not her young life with her serene mother, with Battle, but her middle life—
knowing all Fairchilds better and seeing George single himself from them—had
shown her how deep were the complexities of the everyday, of the family, what
caves were in the mountains, what blocked chambers, and what crystal rivers
that had not yet seen light.

Ellen sighed, giving up trying to make Robbie eat; but she felt that perhaps
that near-calamity on the trestle was nearer than she had realized to the heart of
much that had happened in her family lately—as the sheet lightning of summer
plays in the whole heaven but presently you observe that each time it concen-
trates in one place, throbbing like a nerve in the sky. (DW, 157)

Ellen's vision finds unity in the swarm of the clan. Her imagination
presents the novel with the image of its unity; it is the streak of lightning
that holds time for the picture of its meaning. Ellen's individual story in
the novel is a record of her attention to such moments. With each one
her "susceptible" self grows. In one such moment she meets a strange,
beautiful young girl who is lost in the woods of the plantation. For a moment Ellen imagines that the girl is Dabney; she is happy for the chance
to give her the touch and wishes of farewell that Dabney has been rushing around too hectically to receive. But the stranger is not Dabney; the
moment of meeting is just a flicker. "In the stillness a muscadine fell from
a high place into the leaves under their feet, burying itself, and like the
falling grape the moment of comfort seemed visible to them and dividing them, and to be then, itself, lost. They took a step apart" (DW, 71).
The instant is enough for Ellen to know the girl; she grieves for her as a
mother would when, later, the news arrives that she has been killed by a
train.

Ellen turns to George, as does everyone in the novel, because he
seems, to her, to touch things directly, to move in the realm of certainty.
She realizes that, to the clan, he is "sometimes its hero and sometimes
almost its sacrificial beast" (DW, 63). But she also begins to see him separate from the clan. He seems to live always in the immediacy of a

13. Bowen, The Death of the Heart, 407.

moment like the instant of lightning, or the touch of the strange lost girl. "It seemed to Ellen at moments that George regarded them, and regarded things—just things, in the outside world—with a passion which held him so still that it resembled indifference" (p. 186).

She draws closer to George, as she had unsuccessfully drawn toward the lost girl, and approaches a moment of "wedding." George becomes for Ellen the mystery of the other, "infinitely simple and infinitely complex." Meeting him relieves Ellen of the burden of her self: "There were some people who lived a lifetime without finding the one who relieved the heart's overflow" (*DW*, 222, 223).

This moment is the climax of the novel. Through a patient interplay of viewpoints, the clan and the individual are thoroughly explored. The different aspects of human personality, both self and member of the group, have substantial meaning, enough to give a phrase that defies definition, "infinitely simple and infinitely complex," reality. Ellen's stanza, if it could be separated from the totality of *Delta Wedding*, would be a coda, the resolution of contradictions and incompleteness in a moment of "widened susceptibility."

The technical aspects of *Delta Wedding* are not simple. Readers who approached it with traditional assumptions about narrative in the novel were cut off from the outset from much of its technique and meaning. The real life of the novel is the life of perception as it reaches our awareness through filters of personality and circumstance. The pact of immunity with life, which in a thousand various ways the self tries to preserve and patch up after the tears of experience, is one sided. Life has not signed it.

*Delta Wedding*, like all Welty's fiction, manifests a unique and integrating vision. The complex technique of interweaving several human perspectives on the same issues—clan or self, love and exclusion, innocence and experience—mirrors the meaning itself. The human plight is not static; it constantly rearranges the balance of these issues. Only in moments of susceptibility, when the protections of self are put down, does the order of these contrary perspectives become knowable.

The way in which *Delta Wedding* achieves this merging of self and others mirrors a human relativity. All persons attract and repel each other according to forces of need and defense that are mysterious to them and yet are as natural as gravity. Laura feels the heart's pull constantly in her need; she also feels the effects of her defense. Ellen seems to feel attraction only. Meeting others and the real world in which we exist is a difficult task. There is an uncertainty principle at work: the more concentrated the stare of attention, the more artificial the behavior of that which is studied. The more Shelley searches for meaning, the more puzzled she becomes.

To get at meaning, indirectness is the path. The technique of *Delta Wedding* uses a multiplicity of perspectives that approach the mystery from several angles and tempers. In their simultaneous attempts they approximate the shape of truth. Meaning, as Paul Engle wrote, "accumulates."

The incident of the railroad trestle, in which George Fairchild risks his life to rescue his niece Maureen is a major symbolic event of the novel. Like the "expanding symbol" described by Forster in *Aspects of the Novel*, the trestle incident gradually accumulates meaning as the novel moves through its "stanzas." Each differing human reaction to the event casts a different symbolic light upon it; the varieties of interpretation and reaction represent differing attitudes toward the enigmatic nature of man as both private and corporate being. India, for example, simply reports the event; she is too young to discern symbols or to feel reverberations. But in her simple reporting of Dabney's initial reaction to the news of her cousin's new baby, for example, India's uncolored clarity is telling. India hears Robbie Reid's protest against George's risk, but she does not comment on it. From Robbie herself we hear an interpretation of the event that casts George as the bullied scapegoat whose life is eternally on call by the clan. Ellen sees the event as the keystone in a chaotic summer of marriage and desertion and reunion. For Shelley the trestle is a parable that confirms her assumption that life is a do-or-die proposition. She tries to duplicate George's spontaneous heroism and readiness, but her premeditated attempt is foiled (*DW*, 234). Dabney, watching and remembering, is glad that the clan still acts as one (p. 36).

There are other symbolic actions besides the trestle incident that, because of their common form and their repetition, knit *Delta Wedding* together poetically. There are human encounters—epiphanies—in which the characters meet the puzzle of the other. These are as close to the heart of the novel as the consideration of the clan. Ellen meets the strange girl in the woods; Shelley comes face to face with Robbie Reid in the store; Robbie meets Pinchy, the Negro woman, in a roadside shed as both seek shelter from the heat; Laura meets her uncle in giving him her gift. The shock and immediate fright of bumping another human being, finding mystery where there had been familiarity, is a frequent experience for the characters. It is the equivalent of hearing the telephone ring to interrupt a daydream.

What happens in the next instant? Perhaps no human intercourse is possible; perhaps each encapsulated self is permanently separated from the others with no meaning in meeting and exchange. Except for the miraculous moment when Ellen knows George, there is no communication or knowing. The human family, for stability in a world of disorder and for defense, has assigned each member a role. The result is an imperfect community in which individuals remain safe but unknown to each other within their several shells. The abiding condition outside the circle is loneliness. There is always more emptiness than meeting or wedding. Ventures beyond the shell might sometimes end in danger, ugliness, fear. In private moments the several contemplating eyes in *Delta Wedding* must confront the ugly and the dangerous—the truth of their own mortality. As much as Laura tries to belong, others try to disengage. The issue is not static; Welty's view of the human plight is not that of the dogmatist.

Through the use of recurring, symbolic moments of confrontation with the images of fear, Welty diversifies the meaning of her novel. It is not a social document or even an emotional memoir of the real or imagined pastoral South. The novel faces the insoluble question of belonging in the world as a self and as a member of a larger body. Needs are complex because the human heart is complex. Physical comfort and protection are important, but just as vital is the need for wonder. And so the butterflies, symbols of delicacy and grace, that weave through the world of the novel, are an important motif. They are the presence of a dream world within the waking one. They finally circulate through the windows of the train that brings Laura to Shellmound (*DW*, 3). They flit across George's face and reveal the essence of his interior delicacy to Dabney (pp. 34, 37). They are mounted on boards around Aunt Shannon's head, as the memories of former days and generations at Shellmound are hypnotized and timeless in her stopped world. Ellen, too, sees the butterfly the morning after Dabney's wedding—an omen that the world continues despite what is given up (p. 225). And Marmion, the home Dabney will live in, seems to her to possess the quality of dream, "like a hypnotized swamp butterfly" (p. 120).

Each vital motif, symbol, experience is treated in several different ways. That is the lyrical nature of Delta Wedding. Most readers and reviewers expected a linear plot and were disappointed. They thought the repetition dull, slow, boring; they did not realize that the variation was subtle, that it carried the meaning. Later critics have redressed this imbalance.

"In the end, our technique is sensitivity, and beauty may be our reward," Welty has written in Short Stories. [14] Her technique in Delta Wedding is to present the whole in each of the novel's delicate facets. To this end the lyrical structure of the novel is perfectly suited. The truth is an unfinished and fluid condition of universal human relativity. To place within the story the definite and incontestably "real South" of economics and politics would be to inject an extraneous note. Sympathy, or a widened susceptibility, is the theme of the novel; each of the characters who furnishes a point of view undergoes a series of experiences in which sympathy is to be gained or lost. Only Ellen shows genuine sympathy. She is the heroine, to use the handbook term; her sympathetic vision is the crown of Delta Wedding.

The internal divisions of Delta Wedding signal an approach to the novel that Welty follows up in The Golden Apples. In her next work the viewpoints are more rigidly segregated. The angles of sight upon the same kind of emergency, living in a susceptible and therefore fruitful and loving relationship with the world, are wider. The distances traveled by the wandering self are greater. Stylistically, Welty returns to the mythic and literary allusiveness of her earlier short stories, but the unity and network of connections is more important than individual parts.

14. Eudora Welty, Short Stories (New York, 1949), 52.

V

# The Way Things Emerge in *The Golden Apples*

*The Golden Apples* is more than a short story collection. Reviewers groped for words—"cantos," "movements"—to describe individual stories, for they knew the impression of wholeness was a victory of technique.[1] The unity of *The Golden Apples* is more deeply rooted than the apparent unifying factors of character, place, and theme. It is even more deeply rooted than the mythological allusions, which Welty considers "peripheral."

Unity appears on its most visible level in the fixed cast of characters (listed as dramatis personae between the table of contents and the first story), who are followed through time in the specific world of Morgana, Mississippi. In one story, "Music from Spain," which takes place in San Francisco, Morgana is conspicuous by its absence. On another level unity is created by the network of mythological and literary allusions. The Atalanta and Perseus myths are central. Also supplying images and meanings is the body of Celtic myth introduced by quotations from Yeats. The radiations and interconnections of these networks of imagery and theme create the impression of a firmly wrought whole.[2]

1. Francis Steegmuller, "Small-Town Life," *New York Times Book Review*, August 21, 1949, p. 5.
2. Thomas L. McHaney, "Eudora Welty and the Multitudinous Golden Apples," *Mississippi Quarterly*, XXVI (Fall, 1973), 589–625, traces the networks of imagery and theme. See also Vande Kieft, *Eudora Welty*, Chap. 7; Harry C. Morris, "Eudora Welty's Use of Mythology," *Shenandoah*,

That old black thief who sits on a step below Virgie in the shimmering conclusion of "The Wanderers" is as truly integral to the book's unity as the perception of deep and distant connections between Morgana and the world of Perseus. Not enough attention has been paid to her as the representative of the natural world that nourishes myth. She is to the mythical network of *The Golden Apples* what Phoenix Jackson is to the world of Christian and classical myth in "A Worn Path": a real object that lends its substance to bodiless myth and is in turn made more precious.

In *Delta Wedding* the parts recapitulate and reflect the whole in miniature. This does not occur in a sequential order, but in a simultaneous order that flows from several sources into the moment when the vision of the novel is fully realized. *The Golden Apples* is composed in a similar way and rises to a similar kind of climax in vision. Virgie connects her teeming natural world with the world of mythical and poetic truth. Her world is not hostile to this connection; in fact, it moves toward the poetic. The meeting rich in interconnection is the shimmering moment she and the old black thief share "alone and together." The natural integrity of the world of creatures and phenomena is not the antithesis of the ordered world of the myth but its fellow. Focus shifts from one to the other so easily and so silently that the two "shimmer" in the vision as if with unity.

The motif of meeting has always expressed this vital theme in Welty's fiction, as in Ellen Fairchild's two important meetings, with the strange girl and with George. Perception is the domain of Welty's fiction; images such as curtains, hazes, and glass, which refract the real thing and affect its appearance, are commonly used. To express the human desire to be at home in a world that is rich in allusion and also palpably real is the aim of Welty's technique. That technique begins, in *The Golden Apples*, before the myth, folklore, and literary allusions aid it. As Welty has said, the myth and folklore together were "one of the elements that went into it." The technique was already there, a capacity waiting for its images and gestures to emerge.

Each of the major stories of *The Golden Apples* ("June Recital,"

VI (Spring, 1955), 34–40; Franklin D. Carson, "Recurring Metaphors: An Aspect of Unity in *The Golden Apples*," *Notes on Contemporary Literature*, V (September, 1975), 4–7; Manz-Kunz, *Eudora Welty: Aspects of Reality in her Short Fiction*, 80–93; Allen, "Eudora Welty: The Three Moments," 607–10.

"Moon Lake," "Music from Spain," and "The Wanderers") repeats the essential theme, which widens in meaning by encompassing more experience, more of the world, more of the work itself into a climactic vision. The shorter intermezzo stories, besides possessing their own unique qualities, function as bridges from one major voicing to the next. The meaning of *The Golden Apples* is not, therefore, reducible to a formula, because it is not primarily something known but a way of knowing, of seeing. A sequential order (a traditional plot, for instance) is not the order of *The Golden Apples*. No event or character, once noted, ever stops contributing to the fiction's thrust toward the ultimate connection. A lyrical order that repeats, rephrases, and enriches what has gone before better describes the order of *The Golden Apples*.

A call to growth, a summons to fulfillment moves through the related stories in the person and spirit of King MacLain and the sharers of his vitality. Each of the stories deals with an answer that affirms or fails to affirm King's unavoidable challenge. The summons-answer motif is repeated in a pattern of natural imagery. The changes in the mythological pattern of imagery register the growth of the book's meaning; but this pattern is not the fundamental meaning. The meaning expressed in the most common and homemade things—stance, posture, walls, rooms— emerges less majestically but just as certainly as it does from myth.

The focus of the first story, "Shower of Gold," for example, is not solely the extraordinary allusion to the Zeus-Danaë myth but the emerging or coexistence of that myth with the ordinary details of Snowdie's response to her husband, King. Katie Rainey receives a visit from Snowdie MacLain, who announces that she is pregnant by King. But Snowdie moves in an aura of splendor with her news, none of which is lost on Katie. Katie need not know the story of Zeus and Danaë; in fact, Welty deleted from the story as it appeared in *Atlantic Monthly* a bit of narration in which Katie does show an awareness of such a thing as a Greek god.[3]

The mythic pattern is certainly functioning, but the natural quality of Snowdie's look and presence must also be stressed. "It was like a shower of something had struck her, like she'd been caught out in something bright. It was more than the day. There with her eyes all crinkled up with

3. Eudora Welty, "Shower of Gold," *Atlantic Monthly*, CLXXXI (May, 1948), 42.

always fighting the light, yet she was looking out bold as a lion that day under her brim and gazing into my bucket like a visiting somebody" (GA, 6.) Snowdie, after meeting her husband in the woods, is bold and direct and solidly there, not averted. The technique of *The Golden Apples* places significance in Snowdie's definite stature. Her entry into something larger than herself, King's summons, has stretched her beyond her former limits. The apparently grotesque fact of Snowdie's albinism, her "always fighting the light," joins with the mythical fact of Zeus's (King's) golden brilliance, in a moment that shows Snowdie uncowed by her growth. "The Hudsons [Snowdie's people]," Katie tells us (and the trait will surface meaningfully in Eugene Hudson MacLain in "Music from Spain"), "all hold themselves in" (p. 7). Snowdie answers affirmatively in spite of the barriers of her physical limits and family heritage. She meets King and assumes the challenge of his flesh and blood; she carries his twin sons.

"Shower of Gold," then, is not only crucial to *The Golden Apples* for its introduction of the mythical network. It also announces the emerging of mundane imagery such as Snowdie's albinism and the peculiar nature of her "look" or carriage. Welty's vision of the way things—the things of literary allusion and the things of ordinary life—emerge toward the wholeness of the work has begun even before the networks of myth and image become evident.

Not all meetings are affirmative; not all love is accomplished. The first major statement of the theme in the story "June Recital" deals with the complexities of a failed meeting. "June Recital" is Cassie Morrison's story, her recital. The events that she recites from her deep memory— Miss Eckhart's character, her piano classes with Virgie and Miss Eckhart, the annual June recital, Virgie Rainey's vigorous and challenging character—constitute a story of her conflicting feelings of wanting, yet fearing, to know Virgie and her world. Her relationship with Virgie is complex, for Cassie both envies Virgie and her adventures and strives to realize her own reticent and stationary love.

Cassie's admiration for Virgie is always unstated, confined to her imagination and memory, through which she reveals many more dimensions of awareness than do the characters who venture into the world of action. Virgie, as one of King MacLain's sharers, has a magnetic, mysterious center that tugs Cassie to the limits of her self. Cassie is moved, shaken; but she does not go out. She strives to turn her restraint into love.

Cassie imaginatively links Virgie with an illustration she had seen in an issue of *St. Nicholas Magazine.*

To Cassie she [Virgie] looked like an illustration by Reginald Birch for a serial in Etta Carmichael's *St. Nicholas Magazine* called "The Lucky Stone." Her inky hair fell in the same loose locks—because it was dirty. She often took the very pose of that inventive and persecuted little heroine who coped with people she thought were witches and ogres (alas! they were not)—feet apart, head aslant, eyes glancing up sideways, ears cocked: but you could not tell whether Virgie would boldly interrupt her enemies or run off to her own devices with a forgetful smile on her lips. (GA, 38–39)

Cassie admires Virgie's inventiveness, her endurance of misfortune, her coping, and her familiarity with the rough and "dirty" world. The pose means all of this to Cassie. Virgie is in touch with the real world and can handle enemies. Her forgetful smile is just another of the weapons with which she is armed against this Medusa.

"The Lucky Stone" is not a key to "June Recital," but it is not gratuitously included either. Such is the integrity of *The Golden Apples* that the whole is often reflected in the slightest part. "The Lucky Stone" reflects the central relationship between Virgie and Cassie, uses the imagery of dividing walls, and phrases a theme that unites the stories—the vital summons is not to be denied without drastic human risk. In the intricacy of *The Golden Apples* this theme is not as simple as it seems in "The Lucky Stone," for it revolves around a dilemma. Given that life is full of potential injury to spirit as well as to flesh (Medusas appear in each moment) and that life as growth is pain itself, is happiness and fulfillment a triumph of avoiding pain? or is there a more vital "logic" that meets pain and wrings nourishment and growth from it? Which is the best way to live? Wary, careful to keep distance or walls between the self and danger, so that misfortune is deflected? or is a headlong stride into collision the only way? "The Lucky Stone" returns to Cassie's mind because it echoes the same questions she hears when she watches Virgie.

The girl in the illustration who reminds Cassie so much of Virgie is Maggie Price, an orphan. She lives in the tenement slums with Tilda, "not her real sister," who drinks and keeps late hours during which she indulges in other unnamed vices. Most of the time Maggie is locked within the four walls of a shabby apartment. She has two means of escape. "The settlement," run by Mr. Graham, whom Maggie calls "St. George," had been her escape until Tilda locked the door. The other way is her vigorous and fanciful imagination; her shabby rooms become the chamber of a princess, her spindly geranium an aromatic bouquet, some dry crackers a delicate repast.

Maggie relies heavily on her imaginative power to block out the decaying world of the slum. By telling herself fairy stories, she shields herself against the hardening stare of depravity. The intensity with which Maggie believes those stories is self-hypnotic. "Sometimes," Maggie says, "they [the stories] get so real I half believe 'em myself."[4] This unblinking protection in the face of tenement life, which has taken Tilda to its depths, is the expression that the illustrator tries to portray in the figure of Maggie Price. Cassie identifies it in Virgie.

The plot of "The Lucky Stone" is the testing of Maggie's faith in her illusions. Will she be overcome by disorder, or will her illusions succeed in transforming the world? Another poem by Yeats is echoed here; besides the frequent reminders of "The Song of the Wandering Aengus" there is "The Stolen Child."

> Come away, O human child!
> To the waters and the wild
> With a faery, hand in hand;
> For the world's more full of weeping than you can understand.

Maggie does go away to the "wild," to the country where she finds a stone wall between the farm of her hosts and the rural estate of a wealthy city family. Maggie thinks of this country estate as a castle, in which she imagines a princess. In fact, Allegra, the daughter of the wealthy family, languishes within, the victim of a broken heart and the congenital malaise of the rich. "She [Allegra] was thinking only of herself and of how miserable she was; rebelling because wealth at her command could not buy the heart's desire."[5] Her attendant, Nurse Miggs, sniffs in down-to-earth disapproval; she thinks, to herself, that Allegra is "sulky, selfish."

One day Allegra hears, on the other side of the wall that divides her

4. Abbie Farwell-Brown, "The Lucky Stone," St. Nicholas Magazine, XLI (February, 1914), 318.

5. Ibid., 316.

from the outside world, the rich voice of Maggie discoursing on the existence of fairies. Allegra feels compelled to respond to the voice; she tosses some candy over the wall when Maggie prays for a sign from the fairies. Ensuing installments tell of the adventures in which Allegra encourages Maggie's trust in fairies by appearing in the costumes of several characters from children's stories.

Maggie persists in her belief. She is sure that the princess needs her help in some way. Allegra remains disguised until Maggie, wandering alone in the grounds of the "castle," is brought to the house by the gardener. Allegra and Maggie come face to face. Allegra denies that she is the princess and dismisses the little girl.

Maggie is soon ill with scarlet fever, and Allegra volunteers to nurse her. When Maggie recovers, Allegra stages a lavish fete with guests costumed as fairy creatures. In conclusion, George Graham appears to take Maggie back to her home in the city; he and Allegra exchange looks of love; Maggie is happy that Allegra will now be granted her "heart's desire," love; and Allegra and George announce their intention to enter into settlement work together.

Maggie, impregnable within a cocoon of self-created and self-sustained fantasy, makes life answer to her needs. This is the strength and will depicted in the illustration that Cassie also senses in Virgie. Cassie is, moreover, partially visible in the character traits of Allegra. The wall between her and Virgie is a higher level of involvement in life than Cassie can scale, but it is no less real for its lack of actual stone. The variety, forthrightness, and energy of Virgie's life contrast with Cassie's own apparently arrested growth. In "June Recital" Cassie is poised at a crucial moment of choice. Shall she follow Virgie's lead or stay in her room?

Virgie personifies all that Cassie fears and suspects, but does not know, about the choice facing her. Virgie had not, seemingly, hesitated. "Virgie Rainey had gone straight from taking music to playing piano in the picture show. With her customary swiftness and lightness she had managed to skip an interval, some world-in-between where Cassie and Missie and Parnell were, all dyeing scarves. Virgie had gone direct into the world of power and emotion, which was beginning to seem even bigger than they had all thought" (GA, 52).

The image of the adventurer going before the onlooker occurs in each of the major stories of *The Golden Apples*. The adventurer always goes directly into a realm of heightened possibility and knowledge, while the admirer waits behind, hesitating in the shadow. Virgie goes into the world of "power and emotion"; Cassie feels the summons to leave her protective walls and follow. But the "power" in Virgie, her musical talent for example, seems to Cassie to have been won at too drastic a cost. "She played the *Fantasia on Beethoven's Ruins of Athens* and when she finished and got up and made her bow, the red of the sash was all over the front of her waist, she was wet and stained as if she had been stabbed in the heart, and a delirious and enviable sweat ran down from her forehead and cheeks and she licked it in with her tongue. Cassie, who had slipped around to the front, was spellbound" (GA, 65). For Cassie, Virgie is "magicked," capable of creating a spell, as Maggie Price could spellbind her companions by the purity of her imagination. Virgie's triumph is won at the price of a wound. That spreading red stain from the sash at Virgie's waist could be blood; the wound could be sexual.

Sex is a significant part of the "power and emotion" in which Virgie moves. She uses the deserted MacLain house, next door to Cassie's, for a tryst with a sailor. She and the sailor lie on a bare mattress while Cassie putters in her locked room, her door posted with a skull and bones, tie-dyeing a scarf. Yet something in Cassie registers the power next door. In "Golden Apples," the story as it appeared in *Harper's Bazaar*, this disparity in sexual experience is directly stated. "Sally [Cassie] was wondering this: What did Virgie and the sailor do in the house? What was the point-blank thing?"[6] In a sense Cassie feels shame because of her lack of experience. "Cassie edged back to the window, while her heart sank, praying that she would not catch sight of Virgie Rainey, or, especially, that Virgie Rainey would not catch sight of her" (GA, 32).

Edging back, being closeted, keeping herself averted is Cassie's posture, as Virgie's is one of alert defiance. Evidence of "power and emotion" always has a cowing effect on Cassie. In such moments she meets her limits, her spiritual "walls." Miss Eckhart's playing, for example, forces Cassie back. One morning as a violent storm passed, Miss Eckhart played the piano passionately. "The music was too much for Cassie Morrison. It lay in the very heart of the stormy morning—there was something almost too violent about a storm in the morning. She stood

6. Eudora Welty, "Golden Apples," *Harper's Bazaar* (September, 1947), 318.

back in the room with her whole body averted as if to ward off blows from Miss Eckhart's strong left hand" (GA, 50). Miss Eckhart's whole life, not just her music, is "too much" for Cassie, and for Morgana. Once Miss Eckhart had been jumped by a "nigger in a hedge." Cassie deals with the rape in euphemisms—"attacked," "pulled down," "made well," "terrible thing." This is the violent attack of the outside world that Maggie's imagination keeps at bay. Virgie seems to court it.

But Cassie "remembers." Although the other side of the wall remains a mystery to her, although she hesitates to respond affirmatively to the summons, her heart has not hardened. On the contrary, her heart is acutely sensitive to the danger and the potential loss and to the moments of fulfillment. "She could never go for herself, never creep out on the shimmering bridge of the tree, or reach the dark magnet there that drew you inside, kept drawing you in. She could not see herself do an unknown thing. She was not Loch, she was not Virgie Rainey; she was not her mother. She was Cassie in her room, seeing the knowledge and torment beyond her reach, standing at her window singing—in a voice soft, rather full today, and halfway thinking it was pretty" (GA, 68).

Cassie is not the Gorgon. Her situation has a special bitterness. She sees "knowledge and torment" with a clarity more painful, perhaps, than the actual experience. Some critics have suggested that Cassie's name derives from Cassiopeia and is part of the mythical format of *The Golden Apples*. But her visions of blood and torment, which she can neither communicate or share with another, are the visions of Cassandra, whose brother Hector (Loch) died beyond the walls. (In one version of "The Wanderers," Loch is reported to have been killed in World War II.)[7] It was Cassandra's fate to live with her visions, to have her warnings ignored, to see suffering always avoidable but never avoided.

If Cassie edges away from contact with Virgie or Miss Eckhart, she does face herself.

Cassie saw herself without even facing the mirror, for her small, solemn, unprotected figure was emerging staring-clear inside her mind. There she was now, standing scared at the window, again in her petticoat, a little of each color of the rainbow dropped on her—bodice and flounce—in spite of reasonable care. Her pale hair was covered and burdened with twisty papers, like a hat too big for her. She balanced her head on her frail neck. She was holding a spoon up

---

7. Eudora Welty, "The Hummingbirds," *Harper's Bazaar* (March, 1949), 246.

like a mean switch in her right hand, and her feet were bare. She had seemed to be favored and happy and she stood there pathetic—homeless-looking—horrible. Like a wave, the gathering past came right up to her. Next time it would be too high. (GA, 33)

The posture, frail, unprotected, pathetic, is a reflection of Cassie's spirit as well as her body. She needs walls and protection because she knows too many possible threats. The scarf that she is busily dyeing becomes a symbol for the calm, ordered life she preserves in her room. She is relieved that she did not take it down to the street when she witnessed the brittle encounter of Virgie, Miss Eckhart, and the ladies of Morgana. "There was the scarf. It was an old friend, part enemy. She brought it to her face, touched her lips to it, breathed its smoky dye-smell, and passed it up her cheeks and over her eyes. She pressed it against her forehead. She might have lost it, might have run out with it . . . for she had visions of poor Miss Eckhart wearing it away over her head; of Virgie waving it, brazenly, in the air of the street; of too-knowing Jinny Love Stark asking 'Couldn't you keep it?'" (p. 82) And after the hayride of that evening, Cassie lay in her bed satisfied with the "way she had let nobody touch even her hand" (p. 84).

Although averted from life, Cassie sees the knowledge and the torment. Virgie lives this without thinking it. "In the strange wisdom of youth that is accepting of more than is given, she [Virgie] had accepted *the* Beethoven as with the dragon's blood" (GA, 243). Injury as well as fulfillment abide in each moment. Cassie knows Virgie is her model as Allegra knew that Maggie was hers. But an affirmative response is not simple; nor are the walls between languishing and fulfillment simply overcome. They form a maze that originates within, intimately connected with the sense of self.

Cassie, then, seizes her own truth—a truth of patience, waiting, passivity. Whatever virtues the wanderers claim, Cassie preserves the opposites—for daring, steadiness; for forgetfulness, remembrance; for exploration and discovery, guarding home; for wringing from life, offering it back. Cassie bows to the hummingbird:

The humming-bird! She knew him, one that came back every year. She stood and looked down at him. He was little emerald bobbin, suspended as always before the opening four o'clocks. Metallic and misty together, tangible and intangible, splendid and fairy-like, the haze of his invisible wings mysterious, like the ring around the moon—had anyone ever tried to catch him? Not she. Let him be suspended there for a moment each year for a hundred years,—incredibly thirsty, greedy for every drop in every four o'clock trumpet in the yard, as though he had them numbered—then dart. (GA, 59)

"Moon Lake," the next major story of *The Golden Apples*, is preceded by "Sir Rabbit." "Sir Rabbit" is a reprise of the idyll in "Shower of Gold." Mattie Will Sojourner meets King in the woods as Snowdie had. The outcome is the same—the enrichment of the person, Mattie, who partakes of the knowledge and power of King and the enhancement of the world by his visitation. In "Sir Rabbit" the affirmative note is sounded after the complex chord of "June Recital." In "Moon Lake" the barrier between one's consciousness and another's reality is attempted again. Mattie Will does not think, not before the MacLain twins wrestle her down, or before King adds her to his long list of conquests. Not thinking, just acting upon an uninsured instinct, Mattie Will belongs with the characters who, because of their instinctively affirmative response to the world of danger and pain, seem impregnable, somehow virginal in spite of all they suffer.

Nina Carmichael "thinks" most of her story, while, on the opposite side of the wall, the orphan Easter acts without thinking, lives close to injury, is even once given up for dead. The refrain "Nina thought" echoes throughout the story. It accentuates the abstracting habits of the central character, for whom the summer at Moon Lake is a turning point that ends in a stalemate.

Nina's mind resists make-believe and club activity. She will not join in the chants of the girls as the camp counselors march them to the lake for a cold swim before breakfast. Like Shelley Fairchild, Nina awaits, with an alert intellect, a more dramatic moment. Surrounded by orphans, she feels their challenge to her own "nice" life. "Half the people out here with me are orphans. Orphans. Orphans. She yearned for her heart to twist. But it didn't, not in time" (GA, 104). She tries to force her heart to feel what her head tells her she would like to feel. This split between heart and head, feeling and thinking, is a gap that Nina tries sincerely and consciously to close by getting to know Easter. The motif of yearning to cross barriers, and thereby to unite twins of spirit, reappears in "Moon Lake."

On either side Nina has human alternatives. Jinny Love Stark is a young, spoiled girl whose mind seems closed to all new experience. Her air of self-satisfaction advertises that to be Jinny Love is the crowning glory of human existence. "'Let's let the orphans go in the water first and get the snakes stirred up, Mrs. Gruenwald,' Jinny Love Stark suggested first off, in the cheerful voice she adopted toward grown people. 'Then they'll be chased away by the time *we* go in'" (GA, 101). Jinny is a dissembler, speaking in one voice to adults and in another to her peers. She sees the world divided between *we* and *they*, between what is beneath *us* and above *them*. Jinny is never troubled by an inkling that anyone or anything might add to her life. Her own incompleteness would never occur to her.

On the other side is Easter, first among the orphans. The relationship between Nina and Easter is similar to that between Cassie and Virgie. Easter is Nina's Maggie, a person who moves in a world of power and emotion. Sex is part of Easter's mysterious appeal. "She had started her breasts" (GA, 105). One of the sponsoring deacons, Mr. Nesbitt (perhaps Virgie's erstwhile suitor in "The Wanderers"), notices Easter's budding shape; he "looked . . . hard at her front" (p. 105). Easter bites his hand. She offers the Morgana girls, Nina especially, a vicarious experience of the unsheltered life. "It was wonderful to have with them someone dangerous but not, so far, or provenly, bad" (p. 105).

Nina's attempt to occupy Easter's experience is expressed in two key episodes; in one she is a participant, in the other an observer. The first episode is the thwarted attempt by the three girls, Easter, Jinny, and Nina, to voyage out upon Moon Lake in a leaky rowboat. The beeman episode of "The Delta Cousins" also included boat, voyage, and young girls fashioned into an image of innocence charmed by the immediate force of experience. In "Moon Lake" the voyage is slightly and ironically different. There is no beeman, only the danger of a leaky boat. Moon Lake, like the Sunflower River in "The Delta Cousins," is the dwelling place of imaged evil—snakes, tangled roots, and deep underwater muck. But Nina launches the voyage in spite of these dangers. She is at a peak of hope that Easter's presence will insure their adventure. Characteristically, Nina "thinks" fulfillment:

For a moment, with her powerful hands, Nina held the boat back. Again she thought of a pear—not the everyday gritty kind that hung on the tree in the backyard, but the fine kind sold on trains and at high prices, each pear with a paper cone wrapping it alone—beautiful, symmetrical, clean pears with thin skins, with snow-white flesh so juicy and tender that to eat one baptized the whole face, and so delicate that while you urgently ate the first half, the second half was already beginning to turn brown. To all fruits, and especially to those fine pears, something happened—the process was so swift, you were never in time for them. It's not the flowers that are fleeting, Nina thought, it's the fruits —it's the time when things are ready that they don't stay. (GA, 116)

Images of "the golden apples" of wonder and fulfillment urge Nina to hope for success. Easter, of course, wastes no time thinking. She clambers into the boat without hesitation. Jinny, true to her character, tries to compel Nina and Easter to return to land. "'But I don't choose to sit myself in a leaky boat,' she was calling ahead. 'I choose the land'" (p. 114). She comes aboard when the others ignore her.

The boat scarcely begins to drift when "a soft tug had already stopped their drifting. Nina with a dark frown turned and looked down. 'A chain! An old mean chain!' 'That's how smart you are'" [Jinny] (GA, 116). Nina's hopes for an adventure to share with Easter denied, she retreats deeper into thought. A drifting boat lodges in her mind as a powerful image of freedom from the restrictions of self, which seem to chafe her more irritably than anyone else in "Moon Lake."

Tonight, it was only the niggers fishing. But their boat must be full of silver fish! Nina wondered if it was the slowness and near fixity of boats out on the water that made them so magical. Their little boat in the reeds that day had not been far from this one's wonder, after all. The turning of water and sky, of the moon, or the sun, always proceeded, and there was magical hesitation in their midst, of a boat. And in the boat, it was not so much that they drifted, as that in the presence of a boat the world drifted, forgot. The dreamed-about changed places with the dreamer. (p. 121)

Nina, dreaming about Easter, tries to change places with her. "To have been an orphan," she thinks. She desires release but also wants it safely in her past. Like Cassie, Nina reserves herself, misses the time of action.

Nina's attempt to cross the barrier between her and Easter originates in her intellect. She watches Easter sleeping, and dreams that Night, like a mysterious and caped visitor, enters the tent to take Easter with him. The orphan's hand drops over the edge of her cot and seems to be open to the night, ready to accept its challenge. Nina begs "Instead . . . me instead . . . ," but this crisis, like the abortive voyage, fades away,

Easter retains her privileged relationship with the night, the world of power and emotion. Nina's mind is turned aside. Her own too-conscious thought is not susceptible to mystery. The essence of Easter's King-like charm is its freedom from such reflective thought. Easter, like all of King's progeny, does not stand outside of herself or see herself in two times, being and having been.

Easter's plunge into Moon Lake, the adventure that Nina must only watch, is the orphan's renewed claim to mystery. No one can follow her to the bottom. As Loch Morrison brings her limp body to shore, Nina can only try to think what the orphan has undergone. Thinking, she confronts that internal barrier, a "two-ness," that blocks her from simple wonder. "Nina thought. It's I that's thinking. Easter's not thinking at all. And while not thinking she is not dead, but unconscious, which is even harder to be" (GA, 131). Again, as in the ecstatic moment of Night's entry into their tent, Nina tries to abolish the otherness of Easter by an act of conscious will. "And pressing closer to the table, Nina almost walked into Easter's arm flung out over the edge. The arm was turned at the elbow so that the hand opened upward. It held there the same as it held when the night came in and stood in the tent, when it had come to Easter and not to Nina. It was the one hand, and it seemed the one moment" (p. 132). This close, Nina faints. It is as if, in the drive to identify herself with Easter, her consciousness is overloaded. She revives on the table next to Easter; she can go no closer.

Loch is plunging up and down upon the inert body of Easter in a pantomime of sexual intercourse. Jinny's mother, Mrs. Lizzie Stark (whose dominating female presence shrinks men "to a nuisance—a mosquito, with a mosquito's proboscis" [GA, 131]) is predictably horrified when she walks in upon the scene. "[Loch] crushed in her [Easter's] body and blood came out of her mouth. For them all, it was like being spoken to. 'Nina, you! Come stand right here in my skirt,' Miss Lizzie called. Nina went and stood under the big bosom that started down, at the neck of her dress, like a big cloven white hide" (p. 133).

The shelter of Miss Lizzie's bosom is Nina's ultimate and final refuge. Easter recovers, coughs at the moment when everyone had "betrayed" her to death. "In that passionate instant, when they reached Easter and took her up, many feelings returned to Nina, some joining and some conflicting. At least what had happened to Easter was out in the world, like the table itself. There it remained—mystery, if only for being hard and cruel and, by something Nina felt inside her body, murderous" (GA, 136).

Nina's stalemate is not happy; like Cassie, she is sharply aware of her own incompleteness. The impenetrable wall between her sense of her-self and her sense of fulfillment remains. She has tried to answer the summons addressed to the unified self, body and heart, but too often she finds in herself a second presence, the one that thinks and paralyzes her instinctive self by watching it.

The children of King possess the gift of living in a present moment unencumbered by past or future. They do not stand outside of their time and ponder consequences. Such gorgons might freeze them. Time for them is a moment and each action its own cause and effect. The word that King prophesies to Morgana is that time is not a gauntlet but a splendid moment, a "shower of gold" that transforms those willing to stand in it.

"The Whole World Knows" is an effective bridge from "Moon Lake" to "Music from Spain." The world has changed. "The Whole World Knows" reflects decay in the order of things; futility has surpassed sig-nificance. In a comparison of the two pieces in *The Golden Apples* spoken by characters, the voice of Ran MacLain jars against the voice of Katie Rainey (in "Shower of Gold"). The narrative voice of Katie, as Louise Blackwell demonstrates, conveys the "whole tenor and texture of life in Morgana."[8] Churchgoing, neighborliness, poverty, marriage, family life; the world of Morgana is rich in the filaments that bind the individual to the group, to the place, to friends, even to strangers. (We can think of Katie's story as told to perfect strangers, us.) But Ran's voice is hollow and echoless—the still, maddening chamber of a nightmare. In an eerie, solipsistic vacuum, Ran bludgeons Woody Spights with a croquet mallet. He describes with diseased care the splintering of the tiniest bone. In a similar hallucination he shoots his wife, Jinny, and watches as the bright bullet holes mock him. The world of "Shower of Gold," teeming with all sorts of sound, texture, sight, and smell, has shrunk to the dark, murky prison of Ran's troubled mind.

8. Louise Blackwell, "Eudora Welty: Proverbs and Proverbial Sayings in *The Golden Apples*," *Southern Folklore Quarterly*, XXX (December, 1966), 337.

Things have come to a dead end. In the symbolic action of driving Maideen Sumrall through the night after a date in Vicksburg, the world pulls out its pockets in bankruptcy.

We circled down. The sounds of the river tossing and teasing its great load, its load of trash, I could hear through the dark now. It made the noise of a moving wall, and up it fishes and reptiles and uprooted trees and man's throw-aways played and climbed all alike in a splashing like innocence. A great wave of smell beat at my face. The track had come down here deep as a tunnel. We were on the floor of the world. The trees met and their branches matted overhead, the cedars came together, and through them the stars of Morgana looked sifted and fine as seed, so high, so far. Away off, there was the sound of a shot. (GA, 157)

Is this the same world that received Snowdie's shower of gold, the visitation of wonder that prompted Katie's mingled love and envy? Does Moon Lake exist on the same planet? When there is dearest need of salvation, it seems "so high, so far."

This decay of the world caused by man's pollution of natural and social things is the dark band into which "The Whole World Knows" shifts *The Golden Apples*. Ran, in his narration, confesses it. "I unlatched the little old gate. I caught a whiff of the sour pears on the ground, the smell of August. I'd never told Maideen I was coming to supper, at any time, or would see her mama, of course; but also I kept forgetting about the old ways, the eternal politeness of the people you hope not to know" (GA, 149–50). The pears, the wonderful, transient moments of gracious meeting with the world of possibility—Nina's fleeting moments of "Moon Lake"—lie spoiled. Something natural has been spoiled by human error; the "old ways" that carefully preserved harmony have been forgotten. After the story first appeared in *Harper's Bazaar*, Welty added, "but also I kept forgetting about the old ways, the eternal politeness of the people you hope not to know."[9] Lack of attention to the old ways is symptomatic of a withdrawal from the world, a retreat from the summons. Snowdie complains to her son: "*The Lord never meant us all to separate. To go and be cut off. One from the other, off in some little room*" (p. 152).

"The Whole World Knows," besides darkly echoing "Shower of Gold" in its narrative quality, also reflects another intermezzo, "Sir Rab-

9. Eudora Welty, "The Whole World Knows," *Harper's Bazaar* (March, 1947), 334.

bit." In "Sir Rabbit" the MacLain twins, puberty-stricken, sport freely with Mattie Will Sojourner. But sex has soured in "The Whole World Knows." Ran has parted from Jinny over a "thing of the flesh" (GA, 146) and both parade other partners in an attempt to wound the other. Sex in "Sir Rabbit" is given and taken without grudge. The world—this is King's gift, it seems—is enriched, made golden, by it. But, in the reflecting story, sex means pain and discord. The "thing of the flesh" festers in the flesh, spoiling like the pears. Miss Lizzie Stark tears out at Ran, accusing men of "ailing first," causing all female suffering. Snowdie holds the other position; Jinny's infidelity is a worse sin: *The whole world knows what she did to you. It's different from when it's the man*" (p. 157).

Sex has become a battleground. Maideen, to Ran "a child's copy of Jinny" (GA, 144) is a stand-in for Jinny in his ritual of revenge through sexual domination. He thrusts Maideen into the cross fire between himself and Jinny by taking her to the Stark house. He carries her around like a human shield, knowing that she will suffer from his scorn and neglect as Jinny, a tough ego, will not.

The story builds to a final act of sexual mastery. Ran coerces Maideen into a Vicksburg speakeasy, forces her to drink, takes her for a reckless ride in his car, and winds up in a dark motel room. In the *Harper's Bazaar* version of the story, Ran takes Maideen sexually, then puts a pistol in his mouth and only misses suicide when the hammer clicks without firing. For *The Golden Apples* the climax is subtly adjusted to increase Ran's psychological torture of Maideen. First Ran begins his ritual suicide. Then he takes Maideen, physically and emotionally drained, "so quick." She is just another "throw-away" to Ran.

Next to his father in "Sir Rabbit," Ran is cold, calloused, exploiting. His psychological illness has indeed become a "little room." He is implicated in Maideen's subsequent suicide. Who was hurt when King and Mattie Will met in the woods? Mattie Will did indeed take on King's knowledge with his power, met King's hunger with a fiercer giving.

"The Whole World Knows" is a significant story, both in itself and in its placement in *The Golden Apples*. Within itself it conjures up a polluted, frightening, diseased and spoiling world of jealousy, darkness, suppressed talk, and forgotten harmony. It turns the imagery of golden apples to its shadowed side, turns the technique of first-person narration from an affirmation of community to a denial of it. Between "Moon

Lake" and "Music from Spain" it changes scene, time, and mood. Wonder has gone out of the world; the moment of meeting seems light years distant.

"Music from Spain" embellishes the original theme in a most poetic and complex way. The motifs of walls and time come to deeper meaning. Eugene is the most bitterly confounded of the followers of King. Time dogs Eugene. He is surrounded by clocks and watches in Bertsinger's and is acutely aware of his own age. He is barred from the fullness of his years by a shadow as dense as the one described by T. S. Eliot in "The Hollow Men."

Several of Eliot's poems, in fact, seem like surreptitious recordings of Eugene's private musings and anxieties. They are not inappropriate as a context for "Music from Spain." Eugene is a troubled, sensitive man faced with a hollow future. Love has not renewed him; his speech reflects the confusion in his heart. He scarcely talks to his wife, Emma; the tone and substance of her replies have been fixed since the death of their only child, Fan. Eugene's employer, Mr. Bertsinger, Sr., requires a pleasant *mot* as Eugene enters the jewelry store, a password that Eugene, out of tired habit, patches together as he hits the sidewalk each morning. And the Spaniard he eventually follows neither speaks nor understands English.

"Music from Spain" might be thought of as "The Love Song of Eugene Hudson MacLain," for it resonates with images and tones similar to those of Eliot's poem. There is an essential difference, however; Welty's story presents a world teeming with life, offering salvation that Eugene just barely misses. Prufrock never seems so close to life.

Eugene Hudson MacLain bears his name more naturally than Prufrock, for in it are the names of his father, King MacLain, and his mother, Snowdie Hudson. We know them; we have known them since before Eugene was born. We know Eugene's past, his home ground, his neighbors, and his predicament almost as well as he knows himself. We know the timeless polarity represented in the names Hudson and MacLain, the one reticent, the other bold. Eugene as a character in fiction carries the achieved meaning of *The Golden Apples*. MacLain and Hudson are names for the polarities of human response to love and to the world of action and time.

"The Love Song of J. Alfred Prufrock" opens with the famous image,

Let us go then, you and I,
When the evening is spread out against the sky
Like a patient etherized upon a table.

Soon fog curls and wreaths the two like the medium of unsure perception
or unreal senses. The San Francisco fog announces the beginning of
Eugene's walk and helps to create the impression of his own unsure state
of mind. He steps into the fog uneasy about himself. "One morning at
breakfast Eugene MacLain was opening his paper and without the least
idea of why he did it . . . he leaned across the table and slapped her [his
wife's] face" (GA, 161).

San Francisco's streets seem as twisting and shadowed as Prufrock's;
Eugene's confused thoughts seem just as tormented by tedium and fear.
Tedium, too, is a factor in the hardening and constriction of Eugene's
curious and vital heart. It has been some time since wonder has entered
there. That combustible sense of wonder and freedom that King indomi-
tably possesses in spite of his age has gone out of his son. King seems
younger than Eugene. And the question that Prufrock quietly demurs
from asking, resigning all hope, is the question that King and his sharers
constantly butt against. The question haunts Eugene's intermittent concentration: "Why, in the name of all reason, had he struck Emma? His
act—with that, proving that it had been a part of him—slipped loose
from him, turned around and looked at him in the form of a question"
(GA, 163). The question stares at the heart of his self-image, telling
him that he is losing or has lost the integrity of his flesh and heart. He
has become two—one who acts, one who watches him act. Alienation is
not exactly the word for Eugene's plight. His own blasé assessment ("*The
forties. Psychology*"), because of its throwaway tone, is not only an answer
but, more pointedly, a symptom.

Suddenly a butcher's array of slaughtered beef crosses Eugene's habit-
ual path. The butchers themselves appear in bloody aprons. "The beeves
were moving across, all right, and on the other side a tramp leaned on a
cane to watch, leering like a dandy at each of the carcasses as it went by"
(GA, 165). Eugene is alarmed, and thrilled (for there are still vestiges of
King in him) that "things were a great deal more serious than he had
thought" (p. 165). He is aware that this day is a matter of life and death.

Having decided, or realized, that work (his time clock) was not part
of what he had to face that day, Eugene walks past Bertsinger's and is

immediately surrounded by the curiosities of his world. Recording the placards and ads, Joltz Nature System, Honest John Trusses, No Toothless Days, Strictform No Give Brace, Welty approaches the modern urban world with a detached amusement. Despite the fun and absurdity of the names and slogans, however, there is delight, vitality, a sense of play. There is, in other words, a world to save Eugene.

The vitality everywhere hammers upon Eugene's walls. He does not, yet, try to meet it. "It could all make a man feel shame. The kind of shame one had to jump up in the air, kick his heels, to express—whirl around!" (GA, 166). Ordinary life is more vital than Eugene himself, who has been immobilized by the "marble-like eye" (p. 168) of Emma, the gorgon. Emma, like Medusa, had not always been terrible and ugly. "There had been a time, too, when she was a soft woman" (p. 168), but that time had ended with the death of their daughter.

The transformation puzzles Eugene; the question that follows him is this question of change in life. Is life to have its way with each of us, to decree relinquishment of youth, hope, beauty, to leave only a dry and thin age to be trussed and braced against inevitable ruin? How to escape the leer of that dandy, the marble-like stare or the gorgon, and seize hope and cheer while the flesh is thinning and wasting toward its end? King would not have wasted breath on the question of how to be in and of time and still not paralyzed by its stare. Eugene does not even tentatively begin to ask until, miraculously, the Spanish guitarist appears before him.

The Spaniard is "artist"; for Eugene the artist is the apex of human freedom and power over time. He is Eugene's incarnation of Maggie, Virgie, Easter. The artist makes an experience so real it supplants the mundane. The last time Eugene had been to a concert, his daughter Fan had found the music so real she had reached out to bring it into herself. Emma had pulled down the child's reaching arms. That moment had given Eugene the joy and release of laughter.

In the artist, then, Eugene senses his deliverance from a world hardened by tedium. In Fan's enchantment is Eugene's model of his father's gift. All King's children reach out to seize what they desire, ignore the walls that prevent them from grasping it. But Eugene had come to *prefer* his walls. "And at the same time it would be terrifying if walls, even the walls of Emma's and his room, the walls of whatever room it was that closed a person in, in the evening, would go soft as curtains and begin to tremble" (GA, 179). The yearning for spiritual and physical liberation, for the power to transcend the body's limitations and be present at the limit of vision is, at best, only a promise Eugene hears whispered beyond his walls or in his deep memory.

Eugene tries. His pursuit of the Spanish guitarist is more than a lark. The magnetic field that Cassie had avoided Eugene enters. He is sick and wishes to be healed. And a wish for the return of wonder to his life is a strong but distant motivation. It had moved Cassie and Nina to follow their counterparts of the Spaniard.

Eugene, separated from his place, his soil, is a desperate man. Possibilities for action and delight teem in the world around him, yet he seems to have fatally lost the power to grasp them. Time (he is employed repairing watches) and a sense of his own decay have become his world. Like Prufrock he is no leading actor. Like Prufrock he is a man of suppositions unproven by action:

Why not visit a gambling house? A game of chance would be very interesting. With those red-nailed fingers (Only—and Eugene's hope fell—they were not red now) the Spaniard would be able to place their chips on lucky numbers, and with his sharp and shaming ear listen to the delicate, cheating click of the ball in the wheel. Eugene usually only pressed his lips together—to part them— at the idea of such places, but with the Spaniard along—! For them, as for young, unattached, dashing boys, or renegade old men far gone, the roulette wheel all evening in some smoke-filled but ascetic room . . . how would it be? (GA, 178)

In this daring mood Eugene treats the Spaniard to an enormous lunch. The Spaniard is always chewing or picking little bones from his teeth, while Eugene nibbles at a crust of bread, and thinks. He is trapped in a sink of interrogation. He wonders constantly about the crisis of the moment. For a walk of many blocks, after he and the Spaniard leave the table, Eugene ponders while the artist is received into the life they meet. Eugene seems convinced of his own spiritual and physical mediocrity. When he does notice the world, he sees images of age: "Here came the old woman down the hill—there was always one. In tippets and tapping their canes they slowly came down to meet you" (GA, 185). Or he sees images of decay, "seasoned with light like old invalids the young bungalows looked into the West" (p. 187). Between reminders of age and invalidism, Eugene strives to refresh his life. Thoughts of King return like pillars of fire in the desert. But the path gradually runs out. He and the Spaniard come to the beach, Land's End; no more room for thinking. In "The Whole World Knows" Ran found himself in a similar location, at the end of his road. He backed away.

Eugene almost collapses when the Spaniard grabs him in an embrace that is the moment's crisis, the imminence of grace and wonder that Prufrock unfailingly "scuttles" away from. At that very moment "rain fell on them. In the air a fine, caressing 'precipitation' was shining": a shower of gold (GA, 188). Eugene is taken by surprise; his emotions confuse the Spaniard with his father. "He looked up at his Spaniard and drew a breath also, perhaps not really a sympathetic one, but he seemed to increase in size. Eugene watched his great fatherly barrel of chest move, and had a momentary glimpse of his suspenders, which were pink trimmed in silver with little bearded animal faces on the buckles" (p. 188). For an instant the inert particularity of things is shaken, and King MacLain seems to look out at his son through the buckles of the Spaniard's suspenders.

But Eugene's breath is "perhaps not really a sympathetic one." A cat eyeing its prey diverts Eugene's attention, the cat's eye frozen, "marble-like." The hardening stare vies with the quickening look of the satyr; Eugene is trapped once again in the shadow. He cannot act; he does not decide.

Eugene remains an alien within himself and in the world. The question with which he left his apartment that morning still pursues him in the evening. The Spaniard offers a lily for consideration; but Eugene returns to his slapping of Emma. Still the Spaniard begs attention for the mariposa. "'But in your heart,' Eugene said, and then he was lost. It was a lifelong trouble, he had never been able to express himself at all when it came to the very moment. And now, on a cliff, in a wind, too" (GA, 195).

And so Eugene, finding it impossible to say what must be said, is cut off from the rejuvenating blood and life's breath of his father by the weight of years of stultifying habit and tedium. Events happened quickly; a gap in the wall opened. But action eluded Eugene like his own wind-blown hat and the hat of the Spaniard, which, for a moment of inspiration, he wore. The moment was too much. Eugene recalls a familiar nightmare: "It was as if he were trying to swallow a cherry but found he was only the size of the stem of the cherry" (GA, 197). Eugene himself is not enough.

Again the Spaniard hugs Eugene, swings him into the sea wind, out over the rampart of a seawall. "If he [Eugene] could have spoken!" (GA, 198). But the moment is scotched by the intrusion of "two big common toothy sweethearts." The woman scolds the Spaniard for bullying puny Eugene, and his recreation is effectively stopped. Eugene and the Spaniard return to a cafe. They have coffee, and Eugene says goodbye and hurries away.

For the instant of suspension above the sea, Eugene might have heard the mermaids singing each to each and seen them riding seaward on the waves. But he headed home and "raced up the stairs to the flat" (GA, 201). Was he about to declare, like Lazarus, his return from the dead? If he was, Emma's nagging "You've left your hat somewhere" (p. 201) once again froze his will.

Drowning in the tedium of his life, Eugene reduces his afternoon with the Spaniard to the chitchat of "Saw Long Hair, the guitar player, today" (GA, 201). Then Emma's friend in gossip, Mrs. Herring (certainly no mermaid), chips in that she had seen the freak in question too, at mass, where he had laughed aloud. "'That would be him,' said Emma" (p. 202).

Eugene MacLain, too deep in the shadow, is not revived. The ending of the Levee Press edition of this story is harsher on Eugene, for he is last seen laughing with the women, a partner in their callousness.[10] *The Golden Apples* is kinder to him; Eugene is left silent and watching. In "The Wanderers" his grave in Morgana is visited by a few people who are still puzzled by their wanderer. They remember that he had had an exotic mourner, "a Dago."

The way things emerge in *The Golden Apples* is not by pressure. The context of Eliot's poems provides a sense of the extremity in which Welty creates Eugene. Life tries to break through to him but does not meet his reciprocal effort. Eugene, like Prufrock, has lost something precious and real, his affirmative daring. Averted, busy thinking, or pinched by age, past failure, and sorrow, people do fall short. What emerges from this

10. Eudora Welty, *Music From Spain* (Greenville, Miss., 1948), 62.

parallel is Welty's deep belief in the world as an affirmative and hospitable place; we must only go out to it susceptibly. That the world is really a foggy or underwater world is a vision that *The Golden Apples* does not entertain.

Eugene MacLain, stepping into the shower of gold, which is too much for him, confounded by his own weak hope; chilled by his callous wife, comes back to Morgana, in "The Wanderers," to die. In "The Hummingbirds," the story as it appeared in *Harper's Bazaar* prior to publication in *The Golden Apples*, the last portrait of Eugene shows a fading man.

> Always his light, tubercular body seemed to hesitate on the street, anticipating questions, but when he was back home dying and puttering in his mother's garden, his hands held steady, lifted out a rooted rose cutting from the sand and placed it, every little hair of a root safe, in its pocket of loam. He knew he was dying. Sometimes he looked up the street and said something strangely spiteful or ambiguous, but he bothered no one. "He never bothered a soul," they said at his graveside that day. He would never go to a doctor. He had stayed lonely and quiet, until he wasted away.[11]

Averted, like Cassie and Nina, even spiteful and ambiguous toward the end, Eugene collapsed from within as if the pressure of life's grasp folded him upon himself. He faltered, not because life is sterile or hostile, but because he had become too dependent upon the security of walls. Eugene "never bothered a soul"; that may be his epitaph. In "The Wanderers," those who eternally bother life are granted their "pure wish to live."

"The Wanderers" takes place in a world losing its vitality to machinery and the dollar. Calmly we are informed that Mr. Nesbitt's employees are "the very people that were out depleting the woods" (GA, 205), the woods once full of sweet birds and the golden wonder of "Sir Rabbit." The engines of depletion roar along the same road that Katie Rainey, her sentry chair vacant, once watched. "Only the wrong people went by on it. They were all riding trucks, very fast or heavily loaded, and carrying blades and chains, to chop and haul the big trees to mill. *They were not eaters of muscadines*, and did not stop to pass words on the season and what grew" (pp. 213–14).[12] No one, any more, believes in "golden apples," or enjoys the taste of muscadines.

The people of Morgana have changed, too. Many, like Eugene, have

11. Eudora Welty, "The Hummingbirds," *Harper's Bazaar* (March, 1949), 246–47.
12. Italics are mine.

lived neglected lives. The friends of "Moon Lake" live without the joy of their youth. Nina, who strove for the shocking, affirming experience of Easter's life, is married to the scion of the family depleting the woods. "Nina Carmichael, Mrs. Junior Nesbitt heavy with child, was seated where he [her father-in-law] could see her, head fine and indifferent, one puffed white arm stretched along the sewing machine" (GA, 211). Her life seems vacant and inert; her "puffed white arm" bespeaks a spirit without receptivity or resilience. Her father-in-law spends "a long time contemplating and cheering [her] up" (p. 211). The hidden flaw in her nature, the substitution of "to have been" for "to be," the preference for the finished moment over the moment itself, has ended in indifference. Nina is not moving with the pure wish to live; she is not bothering life.

Jinny, Nina's friend at Moon Lake, now Ran MacLain's reunited wife, enters. "With her hand out, she showed a ring about the room on her way to Virgie. 'I deserved me a diamond,' she went on to say to Cassie Morrison, twisting her hand on its wrist. 'That's what I told Ran.' Softly, abruptly, she turned and kissed Virgie's cheek, whispering, 'I don't have to see her [Katie]—do I, Virgie?'" (GA, 215). Shallow as always, determined to bend everyone to pay homage to her, vain, as untouched by life as the ring on her finger, Jinny is not to be pitied. She is not aware; she never has been. She cannot be said to feel life. "Jinny, who in childhood had seemed more knowing than her years, was in her thirties strangely childlike; was it old perversity or further tactics?" (pp. 224–25). Perversity or tactics—neither is grief, sympathy, human tenderness, the wish to live.

Ran is still Jinny's husband. Although Virgie feels a kind of alliance with him, detects his "passionate" presence during her mother's funeral, there are distressing aspects to his character. He has grown fat. He wears the facile smile of the politician; his hand is quick to find the voter. He enters the Rainey house like a candidate knowing always that the voters like his image—the bad MacLain twin, married to a Stark, ruined a country girl who killed herself over him (GA, 210). Is there an echo of the hollow man about Ran? To some extent his response to life is deadened. In "The Hummingbirds" the mourners arrive at the cemetery, and one of the tots sits astride brother Eugene's gravestone. It does not bother Ran. In "The Wanderers" that episode is exchanged for one in which senile Miss Billy Texas Spights wears her purple election dress to the cemetery. Miss Snowdie, it is commented, would have been shocked.

"Ran's here, but nothing bothers Ran" (p. 231). Maybe imperviousness to "bother" is a mutation of Eugene's "not bothering a soul"; both brothers seem to be, in different ways, beyond the stream of life. Ran has created a life to cover the deep confusion he experienced in "The Whole World Knows."

Cassie's fate is loneliness, like Cassandra's. The sight of her at Katie's funeral, like the sight of Nina, is not happy. "Cassie Morrison, her black-stockinged legs seeming to wade among the impeding legs of the other women, crossed the parlor to where Virgie sat in the chair at the closed sewing machine. Cassie had chosen the one thin, gold-rimmed coffee cup for herself, and balanced it serenely" (GA, 209). Wrapped in black stockings and "gloved" (GA, 214), Cassie is living out her young satisfaction in letting "nobody touch even her hand." She is armored against touch and enriching contact with the world of nature or humans. Her office is to perpetuate the memory of her dead mother in the hyacinths that spell out her mother's name each spring. She tends her invalid father; she carries out the career of Miss Eckhart: Cassie gives piano lessons (p. 239).

But Cassie still lives up to her belief in the greater value of the hummingbird, which she acknowledged in "June Recital." Her parting words to Virgie are heartfelt. "'You'll go away like Loch,' Cassie called from the steps, 'a life of your own, away—I'm so glad for people like you and Loch, I am really'" (GA, 240). In "The Hummingbirds" Cassie (as Sally Howard) did not have these lines. In "The Wanderers" she occupies an isolated and unique position, for she has made an intense life out of passivity, observation, reticence. In a strangely necessary way she may be glad for the wanderers because their daring makes her stability welcome.

King MacLain is also present, feeble, tended by Snowdie from meal to nap, like a child. Yet he is still mysterious to Virgie, whereas Snowdie is not. King is "eating still"; his appetite, like the Spaniard's, is voracious. And his face is the vision that takes up residence in Virgie's heart. "But Mr. King pushed out his stained lip. Then he made a hideous face at Virgie, like a silent yell. It was a yell at everything—including death, not leaving it out—and he did not mind taking his present animosity out on Virgie Rainey; indeed he chose her. Then he cracked the little bone in his teeth. She felt refreshed all of a sudden at that tiny but sharp sound" (GA, 227). King is the archetypal botherer.

Against this tapestry of finished, successful, unsuccessful, dormant lives, assembled from the entire novel, Virgie turns her mourning into her rebirth. Like Laurel of *The Optimist's Daughter*, she finds continuity in the apparent vacancy left by death. Over forty and having had a few temporary love affairs, Virgie is still the Maggie of "The Lucky Stone." As the mourners try to drag her to the coffin, she strikes the pose. "'Come see your mother.' They pulled peremptorily at Virgie's arms, their voices bright. 'Don't touch me.' They pulled harder, still smiling but in silence, and Virgie pulled back. Her hair fell in her eyes. She shook it back. 'Don't touch me'" (GA, 212). Virgie's hair is the flag of her indomitable self-possession and vitality. Indeed, every cell of Virgie's flesh is alive to the world. Wading into the Big Black River she feels each grain of sand and each blade of flowing grass. The immersion is a rebirth. Unlike Cassie, Virgie eagerly touches the world with her naked skin. Like King, she always wants more. After her rejuvenating swim, "[she] would have given much for a cigarette, always wishing for a little more of what had just been" (p. 220).

Her kinship with King need not be literal. She has his spirit. Long ago she had "calloused over, gone opaque." "She had known it to happen to others; not only when her mother changed on the bed [dying] while she was fanning her. Virgie had felt a moment in her life after which nobody could see through her, into her—felt it young. But Mr. King Mac-Lain, an old man, had butted like a goat against the wall he wouldn't agree to himself or recognize. What fortress indeed would ever come down, except before hard little horns, a rush and a stampede of the pure wish to live?" (GA, 233). King is the father of Virgie's rebirth, giving life to the sleeping self secreted behind layers of callous "fortress."

The ending of *The Golden Apples*, then, is reserved for Virgie. She alone is left to win, through her transcendence of walls, rooms, barriers, even her own flesh, the full moment of time. This is the quest of all of King's kin ("The Wanderers" was provisionally titled, in manuscript, "The Kin."). This has always been King's gift, a blank check on possibility.

She [Virgie] knew that now, at the river, where she had been before on moonlit nights in autumn, drunken and sleepless, mist lay on the water and filled the trees, and from the eyes to the moon would be a cone, a long silent horn, of white light. It was a connection visible as the hair is in the air, between the self and the moon, to make the self feel the child, a daughter far, far back. Then the water, warmer than the night air or the self that might be suddenly cold, like any other arms, took the body under too, running without visibility into the mouth. As she would drift in the river, too alert, too insolent in her heart in those days, the mist might thin momentarily and brilliant jewel eyes would look out from the water-line and the bank. Sometimes in the weeds a lightning bug would lighten, on and off, on and off, for as long in the night as she was there to see. (GA, 236)

Virgie's life has reached an apotheosis; the word is too wan next to the richness of this passage. Here, as elsewhere in *The Golden Apples* the prose is fashioned into a rhythmic, vivid beauty to mark the moment of peace and fulfilled consciousness to which the motifs run. *The Golden Apples* is more than separate but related stories; it is a distinct work of art.

The mythological network that, critics have shown, so tightly unifies the work is dependent on this natural wholeness. Each moment, however humble, is alive with this kind of exaltation, especially for Virgie in her apotheosis.

Cutting off the Medusa's head was the heroic act, perhaps, that made visible a horror in life, that was at once the horror in love, Virgie thought—the separateness. She might have seen heroism prophetically [like Cassie-Cassandra?] when she was young and afraid of Miss Eckhart. She might be able to see it now prophetically, but she was never a prophet. Because Virgie saw things in their time, like hearing them—and perhaps because she must believe in the Medusa equally with Perseus—she saw the stroke of the sword in three moments, not one. In the three was the damnation—no, only the secret, unhurting because not caring in itself—beyond the beauty and the sword's stroke and the terror lay their existence in time—far out and endless, a constellation which the heart could read over many a night. (GA, 243)

The apparent threefold nature of time is just that—apparent. The moment itself is an integrity. The self—this is King's message and gift—that seizes time in the moment thus seizes its own essential unity. Prophecy is indeed human too, but it introduces a separateness that eventually widens into indifference, spitefulness, ambiguity. Individuals are self-conscious beings and things in the physical world. It follows that they are both the critics of mythology and the rapt hearts that read the constellations "over many a night."

Virgie lives out the successful unifying of the self. From the impulsive child to the reflective woman of "The Wanderers," she perseveres in her demands upon life. She always goes forward into life, keeping up with time itself, remaining therefore ever young, maintaining her right to the name Virgie—ever new, whole.

Welty brings us to this point through Virgie's musings, triggered by the October shower. And we see the old black woman in a bright light. Although she is an old beggar and not a student of classical mythology, she too hears the "running of the horse and bear, the stroke of the leopard, the dragon's crusty slither, and the glimmer and trumpet of the swan" (GA, 244). Which is to say that the natural world gives myth its wonder and vitality, that myth is not man's escape from the world but his way into it.

Put one of his [Faulkner's] stories into a single factual statement and it's pure outrage—so would life be —too terrifying, too probable and too symbolic too, too funny to bear. There has to be the story, to bear it—wherein that statement, conjured up and implied and demonstrated, not said or the sky would fall on our heads, is yet the living source of his comedy—and a good part of that comedy's adjoining terror, of course.
Eudora Welty,
"In Yoknapatawpha"

VI

# Comedy's Adjoining Terror: *The Ponder Heart*

Certain readers of *The Ponder Heart* have made the connection between Welty's review of Faulkner's *Intruder in the Dust* and her own comedy in *The Ponder Heart*. Her understanding of Faulkner's comedy-terror relationship has been interpreted as a kind of self-recognition. The comic theme is so important to an understanding of Welty's fiction that it would be well to probe *The Ponder Heart* beneath the humor for the terrible story that Edna Earle refuses to tell lest the sky fall on her head. There is the danger here, as there was in the discussion of *The Robber Bridegroom*, that taking the serious tone will scant the humor of *The Ponder Heart*. Perhaps it is necessary to say that Welty's comedy is not the burlesque of rural types and manners that the Broadway adapters made of the novella.[1]

*The Ponder Heart* is told by Miss Edna Earle Ponder in the quiet parlor of the Beulah Hotel in Clay, Mississippi. The walls, the room itself, the stillness inside and outside, the fidgeting captive stranger who must listen, are the elements of the "too probable" story beneath the bright, farcical surface of Uncle Daniel's troubles with marriage and murder. More than plot and subplot, there are two stories here. Uncle Daniel's Ponder heart freely prompts him to any act of generosity and love. Like

1. Joseph Fields and Jerome Chodorov, *The Ponder Heart: Adapted from the Story by Eudora Welty* (New York, 1956).

a mythic figure, he is not constrained by mortal or social contingencies. Edna Earle's Ponder heart, however, is wrung with a thousand concerns for the orderly way of life she sees dropping into oblivion before her attentive eyes. She tries to preserve the order while Uncle Daniel behaves in such a way as to jeopardize it. Edna Earle's travails in the struggle for order are necessary to the comedy; they present its "adjoining terror."

Edna Earle's story possesses the formal qualities of the dramatic monologue.[2] She tells the entire story; one auditor, restless, silent, is present to us only through a few reactions reported by Edna Earle. The actual dramatic issues of her story she treats indirectly. Her monologue, taking place after these facts, is her continuing attempt to gain control over what has long since left the sphere of her control, if, indeed, the large facts of her existence were ever susceptible to her will. We are asked to have sympathy for Edna Earle in her fight. The sympathy that we do feel for her is similar to that we feel for Clement Musgrove who also strove with changing "times." But does Edna Earle break through to peace at the end, as Clement does?

Edna Earle's plight is not unfamiliar in Welty's fiction. There are several stories about troubled souls caught on a pressure point between their private desire for fulfillment and personal freedom, and their felt obligation to heed society's nurture and authority by filling the role prescribed for them. These characters are, more often than not, women; going against the dictates of society means opposing stalwart "ladies" whose office it is to work from within to insure stability of home and community. Life runs headlong into a way of living.

"The living source" of the comedy in *The Ponder Heart* is this vital balance between laughter and outrage, between stability and the terror of chaos, between that part of Edna Earle's awareness that seeks to keep Daniel under wraps and the unvoiced part of her that desires her own free expression of love. These opposing selves create the conflict for a drama in which the standard denouement is not a neat resolution. Life colliding with external restrictions upon its expression, whether in two persons or within the complex nature of one, releases the vital energies that Robert Penn Warren found in Welty's fiction.

2. The description of the dramatic monologue is condensed from Robert W. Langbaum, *The Poetry of Experience: The Dramatic Monologue in Modern Literary Tradition* (New York, 1957), Chap. 2.

It is not that there is a standard resolution for the contrasts which is repeated from story to story; rather, the contrasts, being basic, are not susceptible to a single standard resolution, and there is an implicit irony in Miss Welty's work. But if we once realize this, we can recognize that the contrasts are understood not in mechanical but in vital terms: the contrasts provide the terms of human effort, for the dream must be carried to, submitted to, the world, innocence to experience, love to knowledge, knowledge to fact, individuality to communion. What resolution is possible is, if I read the stories with understanding, in terms of the vital effort.[3]

Warren is reviewing *The Wide Net* in this essay; but the extension of his perception of "the vital effort" to the struggles of individuals in *The Ponder Heart* is not reckless.

Edna Earle and Uncle Daniel are Apollonian and Dionysiac ways of living locked in a loving struggle for supremacy. Edna's ideal is orderliness, knowledge, experience. "It's always taken a lot out of me, being smart. I say to people who only pass through here, 'Now just a minute. Not so fast. Could *you* hope to account for twelve bedrooms, two bathrooms, two staircases, five porches, dining room, pantry and kitchen, every day of your life, and still be out here looking pretty when they come in?'" (*PH*, 10). Uncle Daniel's urge, on the other hand, is to follow the spontaneous promptings of his heart, which invariably lead him to do the kinds of things—ogle chorus girls, admire Intrepid Elsie Fleming, marry Bonnie Dee, and tell the truth about her death—that rattle the secure world busily maintained by Edna Earle. The humor of the story endures, not solely because of the popular success of its characters and situations, but also because of its basis in universal human experience.

In a radical sense, the drama of *The Ponder Heart* is both moving and still. No ground is won or lost, except to the ultimate victor, Time. On the surface, of course, the melodrama of the murder and trial is brilliantly and ironically entertaining. But the verdict of the very partial jurors, far from deciding the question of Bonnie Dee's death, blithely ignores it. The resolution built into the melodramatic form of the trial sequence has no bearing on the resolution, or absence of one, in the adjoining story. For in that story of Edna Earle's heart there is far more serious thematic significance than the ending of the trial can ever satisfactorily resolve.

Edna Earle's constant effort to order the life around her runs into a challenge from a Dionysiac character. And, since she is still talking at the
end, we must assume that she has not conceded defeat.

Ruth Vande Kieft calls attention to Uncle Daniel's kin—King Mac-
Lain of *The Golden Apples* and Don McInnis of "Asphodel." They can
be easily recognized by a certain wonderful appearance. Uncle Daniel
has white hair, forget-me-not blue eyes; "he dresses fit to kill, you know,
in a snow white suit" (*PH*, 11). Like the other two, Uncle Daniel sports
a hat as wide and legendary as a banner. King MacLain and Don Mc-
Innis appear in their respective stories in their later years; their youths
are remembered from that perspective. Uncle Daniel is in his fifties, "and
still the sweetest, most unspoiled thing in the world. He has the nicest,
politest manners—he's good as gold" (p. 11).

These external similarities spring from the sharing of a common spark
of vitality that is characteristic of the Dionysiac type. Their nature includes a spirit of spontaneity that throws them into conflict with the
forces of conservatism and responsibility in society, usually the ladies.
They practice a great, unmotivated generosity that is also a splendid
self-centeredness. They share a claim to innocence in this respect; they
have never grown up to social maturity or respectful acceptance of the
prescription of behavior handed down to them. This is why Welty wrote
of Uncle Daniel: "He should be an integrity of innocence, for example
he should be as innocent about money as about sex—and breaking his
father's will would never occur to him, or the use of those legal terms,
etc. . . . . He can't be offering reasons of logic or argument or wit."[4]

Uncle Daniel's character, then, is basically nondramatic. He does
not develop; he *is*. Adapting him to the necessities of a Broadway show
revealed this basic truth. The adapters' attempts to insert greed and
jealousy, or other ordinary motivations, although successful on the stage,
are finally inappropriate to the character. Uncle Daniel is a mythic figure
to the extent that he is beyond motive; he embodies the Dionysiac response to life, which does not recognize social convention or even the
context of history and time. He is outside the psychological, too, not as
a case of arrested development, but as a splendid innocent preserved by
the community of Clay, which he in turn nourishes with the spectacle

4. Eudora Welty to Joseph Fields and Jerome Chodorov, March 28, 1955, in Department of
Archives and History, Jackson, Mississippi.

of his charmed, golden freedom. "Work? . . . What would I want to work for? I'm rich as Croesus" (PH, 132).

Unlike King MacLain and Don McInnis, however, Uncle Daniel does not enjoy unrestricted freedom to roam. He is guarded by the society that he delights, although his agitations threaten to raze the foundations and formulas upon which Clay operates. Don McInnis and King, by their satyric ways, created havoc when they chose to, but lived beyond the pale also by choice. Uncle Daniel is kept within the world by love.

His generosity is the least serious of his agitations. In a closed society like Clay, agreements among the members can be reached by which the potential chaos of Uncle Daniel's giving can be defused. You just give it all back after he leaves the scene. But, when Uncle Daniel's agitation turns in the direction of the opposite sex, the sharpest clashes and the closest calls occur. He almost gives the girl at the bank an all-expense-paid trip to Lookout Mountain, and almost goes with her. Edna Earle intercepts him in time. "He's good as gold," she repeats, "but you have to know the way to treat him; he's a man, the same as they all are" (PH, 16).

When the carnival hits Clay, the tempo of Daniel's agitation picks up. He is right up on stage with the chorus girls, handing each one a banana ice cream cone. And he pays too much attention to Intrepid Elsie Fleming, according to Edna Earle.

Intrepid Elsie Fleming rode a motorcycle around the Wall of Death —which let her do, if she wants to ride a motorcycle that bad. It was the time she wasn't riding I objected to—when she was out front on the platform warming up her motor. That was nearly the whole time. You could hear her day and night in the remotest parts of this hotel and with the sheet over your head, clear over the sound of the Merry-Go-Round and all. She dressed up in pants.
Uncle Daniel said he had to admire that. (PH, 22)

The siren song of Elsie's motor disturbs Edna Earle; the pants are a flagrant announcement of her attitude toward the role of women in the domestic order.

The women Edna Earle fears, the same women Uncle Daniel admires, are not accomplished in the domestic arts of cleaning, sewing, cooking, and looking pretty in the acceptable way. They are dangerous because they are potential underminers of the stable household structure. What kind of housekeeper and mother would Intrepid Elsie make? But

Uncle Daniel, a natural man, is naturally attracted to these women. Attractiveness is their essence. He cannot stay married to Miss Teacake Magee, the devout Baptist lady approved by both his father and by Edna Earle. Miss Teacake, a widow, a regular member of the choir, is the exemplar of social regularity. She is the top candidate when Sam Ponder decides "to be strict for the first time" with Daniel by "forking up" a wife for him. A good wife is the woman who will draw the man into the fabric of quiet society. Marriage, according to Grandpa Ponder, is to be a permanent enclosure, an asylum to be utilized when the institutions of brick and mortar are too inept for containing the "problem."

Bonnie Dee Peacock is another problem, for she runs counter to all that Edna Earle, as the voice and walking embodiment of Clay, stands for. Bonnie Dee is a serious threat to the tranquility of the Ponder world; her kittenish, doll-like appearance is no evidence to the contrary. The possibilities that she may be after Uncle Daniel's money and that the fear of being cut off plays a large part in Edna Earle's jealousy are only negligible ingredients in the plot. (The adapters, needing more conventional dramatic motivation, expanded the hint into a certainty and had the same results they had with the character of Uncle Daniel.) The real danger is that Bonnie Dee, as a Peacock, as a nondomestic, apparently erotic sister to the Elsie Flemings of the world, might successfully corrupt the Ponder order.

Bonnie Dee is one of several women in Welty's fiction who represent this selfish, potentially disruptive, erotic element. Fay Chisom of *The Optimist's Daughter* is the most recent appearance of the type. Laurel McKelva arrives at an understanding of Fay, finds the way in which Fay fits into her (Laurel's) world. But Edna Earle never has such luck with Bonnie Dee; she just can't see her in the world.

Bonnie Dee's taste in fashions, or lack of taste, is additional evidence of her sisterly traits with other disrupting women in Welty's fiction. De Yancy Clanahan remembers Bonnie Dee "all in pink" (*PH*, 39). And Edna Earle sees the image of a kewpie doll, "a little thing with yellow, fluffy hair" (p. 29). She had come from the country and could do little more than make change at the ten-cent store. Her household usefulness is nil. Her pastime is to order off for all the latest appliances, and so replace the personal kitchen of Grandma Ponder with the impersonal trademarks of G. E. or Frigidaire.

Most dangerous and threatening of all, Bonnie Dee has youth. "Except Bonnie Dee, poor little old thing, didn't know how to smile. *Yawned* all the time, like cats do. So delicate and dainty, she didn't even have any heels to speak of—she didn't stick out anywhere, and I don't know why you couldn't see through her. Seventeen years old and seemed like she just stayed seventeen" (*PH*, 42). If she had grown older, if she had had to scratch to keep herself from sliding back into the country, she might have become Fay Chisom. The resemblance is striking. Both women are small, slight, and kittenish or cat-like. Both have a penchant for pastels—Bonnie Dee for pink and Fay for "peach satin." Both stock a house, already furnished with the personal objects of a more domestic woman, with the chrome and electric marvels of a mechanized age. And both share a kind of agelessness, an appearance of lasting youth that somehow signifies the extent of their spiritual growth. Bonnie Dee will always be seventeen; Fay, though she is in her forties, still seems to be a girl. The elder Mount Salus ladies, as they gossip in Becky's garden, reveal their worst fear of Fay: because of her "youth" she will outlast them all.[5]

Bonnie Dee is a member of a peculiar sisterhood in Welty's fiction. She represents the nondomestic female whose presence poses a constant threat in the ordered, steady, closed-curtain society of the ladies. Edna Earle and Laurel face similar challenges from the nondomestic intruder, who threatens the family name and the principle of restraint and order itself. Bonnie Dee, with her doll-like looks, her flashy lack of taste, and her easy disregard for such institutions as marriage (she prefers a "trial" before committing herself to Uncle Daniel in wedlock), makes a direct attack on Edna Earle's domain.

Uncle Daniel's marriage to Bonnie Dee, while it is the source of a lot of laughter, is also the point of great personal tangle at the heart of this novella. It places before Edna Earle a crucial challenge to her heart and understanding. It is not as if she were not aware of the challenge, for she always reveals more than she means to:

And she [Bonnie Dee] didn't know what to do with herself all day. But how would she tell him a thing like that? He was older than she was, and he was good as gold, and he was prominent. And he wasn't even there all the time—*Uncle Daniel* couldn't stay home. He wanted her there, all right, waiting when he got back, but he made Narciss bring him in town first, every night, so

5. Eudora Welty, *The Optimist's Daughter* (New York, 1972), 115.

he could have a little better audience. He wanted to tell about how happy he was. (*PH*, 48)

Edna's sympathy for Bonnie Dee's lonely situation succumbs to her desire for Uncle Daniel's happiness. Her formulaic phrase, "he was good as gold," shuts out objective viewing of the plight of Bonnie Dee. She is trapped in a doll's house; Edna Earle could say it if she would allow herself.

After Bonnie Dee escapes and is coaxed back, she turns Uncle Daniel out of his own house. Still Edna Earle's understanding of the complexity of the situation omits the darker side. "And to tell the truth he was happy. This time he knew where she was. Bonnie Dee was out yonder in the big old lonesome house, right in the spot where he most wanted her and where he left her, and where he could think of her being" (*PH*, 66).

Uncle Daniel had a wife and couldn't keep her; the blame is not entirely the wife's. Uncle Daniel's essential being is not domestic, or even governable. Like Don McInnis, who affronts his wife, Sabina, by taking his mistress in the front door of Asphodel, and like King MacLain, who is seen everywhere but at home, and whose offspring are said to make up a sizable bloc in the county orphanage, Uncle Daniel is a wanderer, through attachments if not across geography. He breathes the spirit that is so necessary to housed and communal man—the spirit of untaxed freedom to pursue whatever seduces his eye. And the community, through the chairwomanship of Edna Earle, grants Daniel his upheavals of the order—giveaways, a divorce, even some possible responsibility in the death of Bonnie Dee—because the vicarious experience of his unbounded love is a current of fresh air in a closed room. One thing that Edna Earle does not recognize is that Bonnie Dee is the fit mate for Uncle Daniel. At the end, and beyond the end, she is still talking, still trying to ignore that difficult fact.

The attitudes toward Uncle Daniel, Don McInnis, and King MacLain are similar in the reservation of censure. Each man is implicated directly or indirectly in a potential rebellion against the status quo and in the personal sorrow of others, who are almost exclusively female. Yet each one is accommodated, loved, "enjoyed" for the vital possession of life each offers to the world. Phoebe's reaction to the appearance of the naked old goat, Don McInnis; Virgie Rainey's encounter with King at her mother's funeral; and Edna Earle's exchange of "looks" with Uncle

Daniel near the end of the trial are indications of the available vitality of these men. For Phoebe and for Virgie, something is transferred from the old men to their lives. Even Laurel gains something through Fay. But Edna Earle remains unchanged.

Although her character seems closely related to the narrator of "Why I Live at the P. O.," Edna Earle is a woman of Sabina's creed. Consecration to order and to self-denial, which became the consuming fanaticism of Sabina's wronged life, are the basis for Edna Earle's self-esteem. Uncle Daniel spends and gives away, lives in a kind of splendid moment of enjoyment and wonder; Edna Earle cleans and maintains the Beulah Hotel, preserving the environment in which Daniel lives. While he is full of zest for the next face, she harks back to the time when the town had not yet "gone down so." For her each moment is not a miracle, but the slipping of time into the past, with the nagging persistence of a dripping faucet.

Edna Earle is absorbed in the way the past takes over the present. Time, of course, is her adversary; it undoes all that she arranges and preserves. Her absorption in time passing is one of the most serious notes of her narration in *The Ponder Heart*. Her introductory words to her captive listener (whose car is, unluckily for him, in the repair shop of a Bodkin, kinsman to the blind coroner) repeatedly snag on the related topics of decline and the irretrievability of the past: "But oh, when the place used to be busy! . . . This is like the grave compared. . . . And with the town gone down so—with nearly all of us gone (Papa for one left home at an early age, nobody ever makes the mistake of asking about *him*, and Mama never did hold up—she just had me and quit; she was the last of the Bells)—and with the wrong element going spang through the middle of it at ninety miles an hour on that new highway, he'd a heap rather *not* have a hotel than have it" (*PH*, 10, 13).

The word and idea *last* toll through Edna Earle's narration with a persistence that counterpoints the humor. In the light and dark moments alike, *last* appears to remind us that one aspect of *The Ponder Heart*, the fate of the milieu that encloses it (and the fate of the person who embodies that milieu), is not bright with the future.[6] The episode of Uncle

6. Welty to Fields and Chodorov, March 28, 1955: "I think the texture of the play is a little thin. In the book it was designedly thick, and Edna Earle—who supplied the narrative, background, all living detail, and point of view—was the walking embodiment of this texture."

Daniel's escape from the state asylum is a humorous victory for goodness over rationality and expedience. But Edna Earle dates that episode according to "the last year we had a passenger train at all" (*PH*, 16). Even in the funniest moments, then, *last* echoes in her voice. As these echoes accumulate, we gradually see a woman motivated by forces more complex and shadowy than the broadly comic motives of the officious spinster stereotype.

Abrasive encounters with the Peacocks accelerate her obsession with the past and with time passing for herself and for what she knows as her world. At Bonnie Dee's funeral, Edna Earle dons the robes of her social prominence. Clay is above Polk in the chain of being; Edna Earle, as a Ponder and a pillar of Clay society, is miles above the Peacocks, who are "the kind of people keep the mirror outside on the front porch, and go out and pick railroad lilies to bring inside the house, and wave at trains till the day they die" (*PH*, 29). But the symbols of Edna Earle's impermanence and the unknown causes of her constant worry are plainly to be seen. In the most direct and least humorous address to the audience in her story, Edna Earle finds herself in the presence of her own and Clay's future.

Once outside, up on the hill, I noticed from the corner of my eye a good many Peacocks buried in the graveyard, well to the top of the hill, where you could look out and see the Clay Courthouse dome like a star in the distance. Right *old* graves, with 'Peacocks' on them out bold. It may be that Peacocks at one time used to amount to something (there *are* worthwhile Peacocks, Miss Lutie Powell has vouched for it to Eva Sistrunk), but you'll have a hard time making me believe they're around us. I believe these have always been just about what they are now. Of course, Polk did use to be on the road. But the road left and it didn't get up and follow, and neither did the Peacocks. Up until Bonnie Dee. (pp. 78–79)

This hilltop vision is important for a sympathetic understanding of Edna Earle. The causes of her frenetic neatness, her desperate attempts to ignore adversity and to keep the closed world of her own existence as perfectly preserved as possible, are real human worries. The social and personal situation is constantly in flux around Edna Earle. Clay's courthouse dome shines like a star today; but the dilapidated cabin of the Peacocks looms as a dark omen of the future. The road had left Polk behind it; it could also leave Clay. In fact, it has; the time in which Edna

Earle narrates the story is the heyday of the superhighway, when the community's resources may be turned into a lighted arch over that highway, calculated to lure people back to Clay.

The Peacocks themselves are the prolific hordes of coming change, just as Edna Earle is the bathed, neat, and proper survivor of the old regime. Her tone is rattled by worry that she might not be able to weather the siege. She peers over the parapets of her social elevation, her income, her Ponderhood, and can easily see the numbers of the Peacocks. "*They're* not dying out" (*PH*, 87). Mother Peacock, obese, shod in sneakers, shamelessly displaying fingers swollen like sausages, is the prolific breeder that Edna Earle is not. In this comparison Edna Earle has the cosmetic favor, but Mrs. Peacock, even with her clownish ignorance, has the future.

Instead of adding to the Ponders, Edna Earle has had to guard their dwindling numbers. She has been compelled to sacrifice much of her individuality and her womanhood.

Poor Grandpa! Suppose I'd even attempted, over the years, to step off—I dread to think of the lengths Grandpa would have gone to to stop it. Of course, I'm intended to look after Uncle Daniel and everybody knows it, but in plenty of marriages there's three—three all your life. Because nearly everybody's got somebody. I used to think if I ever did step off with, say Mr. Springer, Uncle Daniel wouldn't mind; he always could make Mr. Springer laugh. And I could name the oldest child after Grandpa and win him over quick before he knew it. Grandpa adored compliments, though he tried to hide it. Ponder Springer—that sounds perfectly plausible to me, or did at one time. (*PH*, 26–27)

Poor Grandpa? He can take care of himself. Poor Edna Earle, for she must have somebody and must also believe that Grandpa would go to "lengths" to keep her around. Even the slim pickings of Mr. Springer have been denied her. The knowledge of her loneliness and incompleteness nags her. There is the memory of her own parents. Her father left; her mother, "the *last* of the Bells" (my italics), died young. The specter of spinsterhood hangs before Edna Earle. Miss Cora Ewbanks, the previous manageress of the Beulah Hotel, died an old maid. The possibility of a similar end haunts Edna Earle. "He [Tip Clanahan] gives me a little pinch. The day I don't rate a pinch from a Clanahan, I'll know I'm past redemption—an old maid" (*PH*, 84).

This worry of spinsterhood, last-ness, the disappearance of the Ponders, peeps through Edna Earle's narration several times. It builds within her until she can no longer suppress it. "Now I'll tell you something: anything Uncle Daniel has left after some future day is supposed to be mine. I'm the inheritor. I'm the last one, isn't that a scream? The last Ponder" (*PH*, 146). We should wonder about her scream, whether it is to be laughter, protest, or a reaction to the "adjoining terror" of her plight. She is both funny and pathetic, in the way that Nabokov's Kinbote, in his paranoia, is funny and pathetic. Edna Earle can see her destroyers, as Kinbote envisions his Gradus. They are various forms of life itself, Peacocks, speeding motorists, chorus girls, lady motorcyclists, "the wrong element." They bring the message that life is change, to which one must, because one eventually will, bow. Uncle Daniel's surrender of things and cash is his lavish way of being humble before life.

In Edna Earle's campaign of resistance, her private life is stifled. She knows that time will carry others forward along with herself. But she tries to cover her anxiety with a willed version of the events, particularly the events of Bonnie Dee's death. This resistance to chaos is funny until we see her place her hope for the future in the death of Bonnie Dee. The look that communicates that hope stuns Uncle Daniel. It is a false hope, not only because it embraces death, but simply because it is misplaced; there is Johnnie Ree, Bonnie Dee's sister, to pop into her place.

The plight of Edna Earle is a comic version of the struggle between the sexes and between the champions of life and of order. The vital effort to resolve this conflict goes on, for this is a struggle that will continue as long as two people breathe on the earth. This comedy may seem, as it did to its adapters, to be on the surface only, a first cousin to Erskine Caldwell's comedy. The complexities of its narrator and of the true subject put it in another class. The conflict that carries *The Ponder Heart* forward is inherent in human consciousness.

Similar conflicts occur in several stories of Welty's. Edna Earle's plight and the "adjoining" story in *The Ponder Heart* become clearer in the context of the related stories of *The Bride of the Innisfallen*. In that collection, which followed *The Ponder Heart*, several women face a crucial challenge, for they are surprised by collisions with life from which they must draw that life into themselves, not keep it at arm's length. Edna Earle is their sister, but she is not as successful as they are in seeing life in a larger, more comic order that includes contradiction.

Only by the form, the
    pattern,
Can words or music reach
The stillness, as a Chinese
    jar still
Moves perpetually in its
    stillness.
T. S. Eliot,
"Burnt Norton"

VII

# Rhythm in Stillness:
# The Bride of the Innisfallen

*The Bride of the Innisfallen*, following the great success of *The Ponder Heart*, presented its first reviewers with fiction very different from the traditional narrative storytelling the majority of them had always expected from southern writers, Welty included. John K. Hutchens preferred *The Ponder Heart*, "swift, straight-forward, witty," to *The Bride of the Innisfallen*. He found the new stories diffuse, imprecise, and "chilling," even though some of them were, in his estimation, as good as any short fiction by Bowen or Woolf.[1] Sterling North, though less restrained, was more colorful. He called the stories "literary gumbo" and felt the experience of reading them like an exile "way down upon miasma river."[2] The reaction of William Peden, in his hesitance to praise what he feels is a significant accomplishment, is close to the mean of the reviews.

But the story seems top-heavy, overburdened by a mass of detail and obscure or undecipherable symbol. Unnecessarily indirect and self-consciously elliptical, "The Bride of the Innisfallen" [story] seems not so much a story as a highly *private* game. Only the initiated are invited to participate. The uninitiated can jolly well go about their own prosaic business. This excruciatingly perceptive

1. John K. Hutchens, "Miss Welty's Somewhat Puzzling Art," New York *Herald Tribune*, April 10, 1955, p. 2.
2. Sterling North, review of Eudora Welty's *The Bride of the Innisfallen*, New York *World-Telegram*, April 7, 1955, p. 22.

story seems to be almost a parody of Miss Welty's effectively individualistic method; even after several readings I could neither accept it on a realistic level nor understand it on any other level.[3]

Peden goes on in his review to lament a lack of clarity and a "mass of detail" in most of the stories in the collection. He has a feeling that something is going on, but it remains "undecipherable" to him.

*The Bride of the Innisfallen* is not a cipher to which a lucky reader may have the key. It is a book of fiction, and nothing more unusual than critical approaches through the pattern and rhythm in fiction, discussed by critics E. K. Brown and E. M. Forster, but not the usual approaches of most readers, offer an introduction to the meaning and the form of the stories in this collection.

Rhythm, a pattern moving through time, expresses truth that the declarative statement, direct and forceful, cannot. Denying change, rhythm subordinates the material in the pattern—thread, sound, words —and exalts the form itself, something by comparison insubstantial (perhaps not "realistic") but nevertheless free from the corruption that plagues all material substance. That incorruptibility in the form answers an abiding question in human beings; much if not all of art is aimed at it.

With an ear for rhythm, then, the first readers might have reached a different assessment of *The Bride of the Innisfallen*. Reading the dedication page, they certainly would have picked up an important indication of the theme these stories address. *The Bride of the Innisfallen* is dedicated to Elizabeth Bowen. Her fiction frequently asserts the independent and real existence of "the heart," the kernel of each human's identity. The heart is susceptible to dream, memory, sensation, and a host of other forces, but it remains in mystery because it is neither material nor analyzable. The heart lives its own life, in its own time. Whereas the flesh can anticipate only death and corruption, the heart looks forward to that stillness and perfection of Eliot's Chinese jar, something commensurate to its own nature.

The seven stories of *The Bride of the Innisfallen*, individually published between 1949 and 1954, assert that there is truth in the life of the heart, and that this truth is daily obscured by a prosaic attitude to life. The obscuring attitudes may be dispersed by attention to the rhythm possible

3. William Peden, "The Incomparable Welty," *Saturday Review*, April 9, 1955, p. 18.

in fiction. In the stories of this collection something new in the potential of fiction is realized. In the collection itself Welty discovers a form more complex than the simple assembling of stories and sheds light in areas of human experience and consciousness not generally illuminated in most novels.

"No Place For You, My Love," the first story in the collection, is the story that Welty herself uses as an example in her essay "How I Write." The particular motifs of which the patterns of the fiction are composed are introduced and tested in the first story. The theme of the life of the heart is one element. Welty, according to an early biographical sketch, had met Bowen in 1949, and had even worked on the title story of the collection while in Ireland at Bowen's Court.[4] The theme as Welty approaches it closely resembles that which Bowen treats in such novels as her *The Death of the Heart*.[5] Place, a long-standing concern of Welty's fiction, also operates in these stories, but more metaphysically than before. The motif of the journey or pilgrimage, with the latter's connotations, is important. The effects of large bodies of water, as barriers and obstacles to humans, are used in each of the stories. The divisions between the sexes are used as central dramatic conflicts in which the heart is caught. The frequently repeated pattern of these and other motifs results in a collection of stories with a rare and effective unity. It is odd that *The Bride of the Innisfallen* has not touched off the debate about its genre that followed *The Golden Apples*.[6]

In "No Place For You, My Love" an unnamed woman from Toledo, out of place in the steamy world of New Orleans, is likewise out of place in the world because she possesses a loving and sympathetic heart. The geographical division of North and South, part of the important consciousness of place in this story, is the surface manifestation of a deeper division that is not so static as regional boundary. The sympathetic heart of the woman is embroiled in a territorial dispute, a border war, with the heart of the man from Syracuse, who needs but also opposes her healing

4. Katherine Powell Hinds, "The Life and Works of Eudora Welty" (M.A. thesis, Duke University, 1954), 20–22.

5. Vande Kieft, *Eudora Welty*, 181–83; Wild, "Studies in the Shorter Fiction of Elizabeth Bowen and Eudora Welty"; and especially Elizabeth Bowen, review of Eudora Welty's *The Golden Apples*, in *Seven Winters and Afterthoughts* (New York, 1962), 215–18.

6. Franklin D. Carson, "Eudora Welty's *The Golden Apples* and the Problem of the Collection-Novel" (Ph.D. dissertation, University of Chicago, 1971); Bunting, "'The Interior World'"; Rubin, *The Faraway Country*, pp. 131–54; John K. Hutchens, "Books and Things," New York *Herald Tribune*, August 18, 1949, p. 13; Steegmuller, "Small-Town Life," 5.

presence. Just as Alpheus pursues the nymph Arethusa in Ovid's tale, the man from Syracuse pursues the woman from Toledo. There is a rhythm in repeated approaches and retreats, in passages over water, in the all-important calls of the heart going unheeded. The first story strives through a deliberate style to invite the reader into its pattern and rhythm, to begin the pilgrimage to the stillness.

The heart of the Toledo woman is radiant with its gift. "It must stick out all over me, she thought, so people think they can love me or hate me just by looking at me. How did it leave us—the old, safe, slow way people used to know of learning how one another feels, and the privilege that went with it of shying away if it seemed best? People in love like me, I suppose, give away the short cuts to everybody's secrets" (*BI*, 3–4). The Toledo woman feels not only exposed but pressed forward and rushed, like Arethusa. Her memory of a gentler rhythm in human relations, of learning and shying away, is just that: a memory.

The man from Syracuse, also out of place in New Orleans, responds to the woman. Is it out of his desire to possess; a vestigial memory of love, which the woman awakens in him; or a perverse impulse to refuse that which approaches his own secret and hard heart? The relationship unfolds in mystery. Together, the man and woman are nevertheless separate; a radical difference or antipathy keeps them apart. Eliot's lines from "Burnt Norton" make some sense of the rhythm of their estrangement.

> Desire itself is movement
> Not in itself desirable;
> Love is itself unmoving,
> Only the cause and end of movement

The man is desire, pursuing; the woman is love.

Their drive down into the bayou is real but is also a symbolic pilgrimage—always near the water and, once crossing the river, coming to "the end of the road," "the jumping off place" (*BI*, 15, 16). The margin of the road is alive with the images of a haunted outer dark threatening to the heart. "Back there in the margins were worse—crawling hides you could not penetrate with bullets or quite believe, grins that had come down from the primeval mud" (p. 8). That darkness seems to infiltrate the heart of the man. When the woman asks a sympathetic question, "What's your wife like?," he repels her approach with a hard, screening hand (p. 14).

The barrier the man throws up is both physical and spiritual. Both the people on this pilgrimage are keeping their distance; the woman is no exception—"Her distance was set," "her measuring coolness" (*BI*, 11). Individual hearts remain separate behind impenetrable barriers unless the call to place them in the balance is heeded. "Deliver us all from the naked in heart," the woman ironically prays as she watches a thick-hided alligator on the deck of a river ferry. She is herself the naked heart that is causing unrest.

The man, however, handles her as if she were an object. Their dance at Baba's Place, the shrimp and beer shack at the end of the road, is measured "gratefully, formally" (*BI*, 21) against the wilder shrimp dance advertised for later that evening. And they dance under the eyes of a few idle shrimpers, the human symbols of that outer dark they both fly past too swiftly to see. At dusk they leave Baba's, "still separate hearts," "immune from the world," "in need of touch or all is lost" (p. 22). They have pretended an intimacy but never released themselves to it. Baba's was for them a place of danger and possibility, the brink or jumping off place for a more meaningful pilgrimage. But they fend off both love and ruin.

The man speeds back to New Orleans. Safely in the city again, he drops the woman at her hotel. "Something that must have been with them all along suddenly, then, was not. In a moment, tall as panic, it rose, cried like a human, and dropped back" (*BI*, 26). In its place, in the place of the cry for loving connection, separation and silence enter again. The man remembers the years of his youth in New York City when such possibilities amounted to "the lilt and expectation of love" (p. 27).

The two hearts on this aborted pilgrimage retreat before their passage even begins. Both man and woman shield their hearts from the possibility. From the city and their public selves they make a journey into the primeval region of the bayou. They might have jumped free of their individual lives, found the pleasure or the disillusionment of casual sex, or found some deeper relationship. In retreat they race back along the narrow roads to the lights of the city. The connecting impulse is ignored; it drops back into oblivion. The elements of place and of the heart's beckoning play significant roles in the story. Place is not primarily geographical; it is the region of human hearts projected into a landscape that moves from order into darkness and back into order. The movement in which the call is denied is the revealing climax of the story.

Lesser elements of the style help to voice the issues at stake. Things, scenes, sounds rush past the two central characters before they have the chance to make sense of them. Transitions are often omitted to lend the place and condition an air of disconnectedness. "She watched the road. Crayfish constantly crossed in front of the wheels, looking grim and bonneted, in a great hurry. 'How the Old Woman Got Home,' she murmured to herself. He pointed, as it flew by, at a saucepan full of cut zinnias which stood waiting on the open lid of a mailbox at the roadside, with a little note tied onto the handle" (*BI*, 7). Each person stays in his or her own zone while the world flashes by or is crushed beneath their vehicle. In the woman's murmur is the hint of a wish to be elsewhere. They might as well be in separate worlds; they are still in Toledo and Syracuse, unknown to each other. Silence is their comfort, for nothing said is nothing risked. The woman's question about the man's marriage is the story's center; its moment of risk. In that moment she pokes her head above the fortress of distance and aplomb ("Just how far below questions and answers, concealment and revelation, they were running now —that was still a new question, with a power of its own, waiting. How dear—how costly—could this ride be?" [p. 13]); she learns that she may be as summarily crushed as one of those hurrying crayfish.

The ride is indeed very costly, for nothing ventured is nothing created or changed. Their pilgrimage is abortive and ends where it had begun, with each one separate and "safe." The man guards himself, the woman draws back. They have effectively frustrated the rhythm of the heart toward loving; they have, as Welty herself has written of this story, "court[ed] imperviousness in the face of exposure."[7]

Rhythm, moreover, is the keynote of this story's theme and technique. The man and woman are two characters from whom a third, their relationship, is almost born. The third character, Welty has written, is the point of view outside of them. It is the midpoint of a rhythmic swing. "It was what grew up between them meeting as strangers, went on the trip with them, nodded back and forth from one to the other—listening, watching, persuading or denying them, enlarging or diminishing them,

---

7. Eudora Welty, "How I Write," *Virginia Quarterly Review*, XXXI (Spring, 1955), 249.

forgetful sometimes of who they were or what they were doing here, helping or betraying them along." There is always this rhythm between victory and failure, a fruitful pilgrimage or a spoiled one, "happy or sinister, ordinary or extraordinary" fates.[8] Precisely this vision of human reality always in the balance calls up the rhythmic style.

Through style in the first story an initiation process begins. The prose uses few and oblique transitions. At several moments the woman and man think of love, but they do not find it or any contact that promises love. They remain separate souls, with no place for love. The incidents of the first story establish important motifs—place, journey or pilgrimage, relationships of the heart threatened by routine or hardness, the marking and withholding of commitment and love. Each of the stories in *The Bride of the Innisfallen* elaborates upon these motifs; they reappear rhythmically as part of the pattern of the collection as a whole.

The dangers facing heart and flesh in "The Burning," for which Welty won a second place O. Henry Award in 1951, are more overtly violent. But the style and its objectives are similar. The accelerated violence is most evident in the act of sexual violation. Whereas the bruise on the Toledo woman is handled mysteriously, the rapes of Miss Myra and Delilah are presented more directly. In the version of this story that appeared in *Harper's Bazaar* (March, 1951), Miss Myra is pursued around the parlor by a Yankee soldier sent to announce the impending destruction of the plantation by Sherman. She is, in the *Bazaar* version, merely thrown to the floor. In the later version, however, the rape is made more obvious by the addition of a short phrase: the intruder also "dropped on top of her" (*BI*, 30). The rape of Delilah, called Florabel in the *Bazaar* version, is similarly elaborated in the collected version.

The point of the change, I think, is not to court sensationalism, even though "The Burning" has plenty of that—madness, fire, murder, suicide, miscegenation, and the oppressive pall of Sherman's burning. The point is that the author fits these familiar elements of southern gothic fiction in the pattern of *The Bride of the Innisfallen*. In spite of the undeniable fact that "The Burning" is a Civil War tale full of all sorts of traditional concerns of southern writing, it assumes a different meaning in the collection. A world "inflicted" upon the woman's heart (*BI*, 38),

8. *Ibid.*, 247.

and the reaction of that heart in its suffering, is the bit of the pattern that "The Burning" fulfills. Women are the sufferers; men are the inflicters. The rhythm of "No Place For You, My Love" continues.

Miss Myra is comforted by a cushion of madness and by her sister, Miss Theo, whose tough hand strokes her hair after she is raped by the soldier. Theo croons, "Don't mind this old world"; she is dedicated to keeping her sister "asleep in the heart" (*BI*, 31). To that end, by her own demented logic, Miss Theo coaxes her younger sister into a noose. Then she hangs herself. "Inflicting" is what women are for, says Theo, before she puts a stop forever to the inflicting.

Delilah survives them. Her race has been enslaved, her body used by her master and violated by the soldiers, her child taken from her. Her heart, her flesh, her sanctity, her offspring are all vulnerable to the world. The mirror, the medium of her vision, reveals all.

> The mirror's cloudly bottom sent up minnows of light to the brim where now a face pure as a water-lily shadow was floating. Almost too small and deep down to see, they were quivering, leaping to life, fighting, aping old things De- lilah had seen done in this world already, sometimes what men had done to Miss Theo and Miss Myra and the peacocks and to slaves, and sometimes what a slave had done and what anybody could now do to anybody. Under the flicker of the sun's licks, then under its whole blow and blare, like an unheard scream, like an act of mercy gone, as the wall-less light and July blaze struck through from the opened sky, the mirror felled her flat. (*BI*, 44)

This moment announces a purpose more complex than a retelling of Civil War thrills and gothic chills. In this instant Delilah's vision becomes the central vision of the story and of the collection, for she has a glimpse of the deep over which the pilgrimage is made. The violence of Sherman and the Civil War becomes symbolic of a world of misery from which all checks of conscience, "mercy," and humanity have fled. The world does not acknowledge the heart, Delilah sees. Sherman did not discriminate among his targets, nor does the world into which Delilah survives discriminate, with mercy for those who have suffered. In the first two stories of the collection, place and time, the coordinates of an actual world, merge into a symbolic universe in which the ordeal of the human heart is enacted.

"Circe" echoes, in main character, imagery, and theme, "The Burning" and "No Place For You, My Love." Circe's life is one of routine and

preservation, of the domestic arts. Men no more respect her life and la-
bors than Sherman and his men respected Myra, Theo, Delilah, or any
of the plantations they burned. Circe, as Welty portrays her, is a woman
first and a figure from mythology second. Her "wiles" are sewing, a broth,
a highly polished floor. But she feels her spell counteracted by one that
Odysseus has cast upon her. She falls in love with him, conceives his
child, but must still remain in silence and frustration as he and his men
sail off whenever they please. Circe knows that she must stay to preserve
the harbor for other wayfarers. In Circe's passionate surrender, this story
repeats the motif of pilgrimage halted, the heart denied by the breadth of
the sea that stretches between the self and the object that is its dream of
fulfillment. Deep within Circe there is a rage of the heart because the
connection she desires dies in the obliviousness of Odysseus. Her heart
has been violated just as surely as her house and her sex have been used
by the inflicters of "Circe," Odysseus and his cronies.

"Ladies in Spring" deals with similar circumstances and subject material
through a point of view that Schorer describes as not just "delimitation,"
but "definition." The point of view is that of Dewey Coker, a schoolboy
with an experience of life's complexities that is too lean to deduce plots
from the strange and disconnected incidents that happen before his wide
eyes. The story begins simply. Dewey's father, shouldering two fishing
poles, passes his son's schoolroom and Dewey, foregoing a reading of *Ex-
calibur*, tags along. "Might as well keep still about it at home," (*BI*, 85)
Dewey's father says. Thus two sources of authority and order, home and
school, both tended by women, are evaded. The established pattern
emerges once again.

Evasion of women and authority is a form of the infliction that is the
pattern of the collection. Dewey's father, for instance, would rather not
catch up with rainmaker-postmistress Hattie Purcell, who walks ahead
of them on the road. After they reach a secluded fishing spot, another
woman flits into Dewey's vision like an apparition. She calls "Blackie"
plaintively, but Dewey's father, "black-headed" (*BI*, 84), will not
answer. Then she disappears. "Dewey could easily think she had gone off
to die. Or if she hadn't, she would have had to die there. It was such a
complaint she sent over, it was so sorrowful. And about what but death
would ladies, anywhere, ever speak with such soft voices—then turn and

run? Before she'd gone, the lady's face had been white and still as magic behind the trembling willow boughs that were the only bright-touched thing" (pp. 87–88).

The lady calls a second time. Blackie refuses to acknowledge the call, but the stress of refusal tells upon him; "he looked down at his son like a stranger cast away on this bridge from the long ago, before it got cut off from land" (*BI*, 88). The third time the lady appears, she is silent: "She didn't even have one word to say, this time" (p. 89). Dewey's father rises and knows that "the one *that* lady waited for was never coming over the bridge to her side, any more than she would come to his" (pp. 89–90). Including both Dewey and his father, the point of view communicates a sense of what might happen and of what will not happen, what is known and what is secret at the same time. In the words of Schorer, such a point of view enriches and renews our interest in the world of action by showing us its many facets and mysteries.[9]

The permanent division between the father and the lady does not impress Dewey consciously. He is not ready to receive her heart's complaint. "Fifteen years later," however, "it occurred to him it had very likely been Opal in the woods" (*BI*, 99). Opal, Hattie's niece, was indeed the lady in the willows. She is a restless heart, like Circe: "Someday old Opal was going to take that car and ride away" (p. 96). But not with Dewey's father, for a force stronger than the restless heart of Opal is the ordinary world of social circumstance and convention. Thus the rhythm continues in the call of the heart and the denial in silence. The sense of distance, imaged in bridges, and of the desire to cross is vivid.

When Dewey and his father return home, with the lone six-inch fish Dewey had caught, they, like William Wallace and his pals, reenter a world administered by ladies. Dewey's mother and sisters are doing all the chores. Only the women of Royals, apparently, are capable of getting things done; Hattie Purcell makes rain and puts up the mail. Dewey offers his fish to his mother. But his gesture moves out of a pure world and into the adult world of pain and concealment. The gift becomes an incitement to his mother, and she blurts out her anger and frustration, as Circe might have, had she not been so self-controlled. "'Get away from me,' she shrieked. 'You and your pa! Both of you get the sight of you

9. Schorer, "Technique as Discovery," 201.

clear away!' She struck with her little green switch, fanning drops of milk and light. 'Get in the house. Oh! If I haven't had enough out of you'" (BI, 100).

Dewey is not bruised. Later, alone, his pure vision is still intact. He hears the note of the story and of *The Bride of the Innisfallen* as a skillfully made whole: "The lonesomest sound in creation, an unknown bird singing through the very moment when he was the one that listened to it" (BI, 100). The note is not only the sort that can be heard with the physical ear; it is also the cry of the pilgrim's heart. It is heard throughout the collection and serves to weave it together.

Welty's intricate technique in "Ladies in Spring"—telling the story of longing and loneliness through the point of view of a character too innocent to admit anything but the story itself—succeeds in illuminating new areas of meaning. The motifs of pilgrimage, passages toward fulfillment of dream, lonely souls in need of response, calls sent out in hopes of connecting with other lonely hearts tie this story with the collection as a whole.

This technique also reveals the coexistence of two worlds—an external world of time, in which the heart is bound and pinched and all but ignored because of the primacy of public, social life (Dewey's mother is caught in this world), and an internal world in which the heart plays with dreams of "crossing," "bridging," and "riding away." Opal's call, and its reappearance in the singing of the unknown bird that Dewey hears, comes from hearts in the private world, suffering loneliness and dreams that are grander than the world usually satisfies. Between the actual and the wished for is a rhythm, constant and like the pulse. The time of this world is not measured by clocks.

In "Kin" two young women, Kate and Dicey, meet the heart in its pilgrimage and discover the different time in which these hearts move. To frustrate the critic's neat but sterile scheme, one of the pilgrimaging hearts in "Kin" is that of a man, Uncle Felix. The vital fact is not the sex of the pilgrim but the quality of the heart's life. The pattern, as it moves through "Kin," not only brings forth Uncle Felix as a pilgrim, it also discovers for Dicey her great-grandmother as a model for the pilgrimage that confronts every susceptible heart on the brink of life and love.

Like "No Place For You, My Love," "Kin" emphasizes place. Although Mingo, a town in rural Mississippi, functions as setting, that is not its only importance in the story. In a passage Welty canceled from the opening paragraph (the bracketed section is the crucial deletion), Dicey, the narrator, expresses a metaphysical sense of place. She describes it as being "like *something* instead of *someone*. [I must have forgotten how places are the heart and soul of what goes on and what you talk about here—not ideas, like at home. Back here, what makes a story a story was where it happened— some place they could take you to show you. Part of it would always still be standing. Of course they thought I knew Mingo, and I finally remembered, but] I'd been making a start" (*BI*, 112).[10] Perhaps this is too early in the story and too direct in manner to outline one of the key issues—place is not merely the inert ground on which humans act and things happen but is the lively medium that makes things possible and confers identity. A place is never lost in time: "Part of it would always still be standing." Away from her northern home, back in Mississippi, Dicey is plunged into a surviving tenacious past that, to her surprise and delight, includes herself. People, things, and places are still present, still persist in the memory, and assure her of a self she seems always to have been and always just about to become.

The pilgrimage she had counted on was to visit her Aunt Ethel, whose frail health might not sustain her until a later time. Contrast impresses Dicey: "The cut grass in the yards smelled different from Northern grass" (*BI*, 114); her girlhood home is now occupied by a different family, and its aspect has changed (p. 115). As her heart mulls these changes, she confronts another. Her engagement "up North" has pulled her allegiances not only away from the geographical place but also away from the psychological place her heart had known when she was a child, a single girl, and a young woman. As fiancée, Dicey finds her heart on a much different pilgrimage. At first she does not feel the movement. Welty dramatizes Dicey's internal conflict obliquely.

"She [Sister Anne] used to get *dizzy* very easily." Aunt Ethel spoke out in a firm voice, as if she were just waking up from a nap. "Maybe she did well—maybe a girl does well sometimes *not* to marry, if she's not cut out for it."

"Aunt Ethel!" I exclaimed. Kate, sliding gently off the arm of my chair, was

10. Eudora Welty, "The Bride of the Innisfallen" (Carbon copy of typescript, in Humanities Research Center, University of Texas at Austin), p. 1.

silent. But as if I had said something more, she turned around, her bare foot singing on the matting, her arm turned above her head, in a saluting, mocking way. (p. 120)

Four women are shown in response to marriage, the pilgrimage traditionally prescribed for the woman. Each one illustrates, in her tone of voice or in a slight gesture, her response.

At Mingo, Dicey begins to act out a more complex response when she sees that "the corner clock was wrong" (*BI*, 128). Soon she confesses that her estrangement is more acute than she had felt "in a way, still, just at first" (p. 114) back at Aunt Ethel's: "I feel like a being from another world" (p. 132). Sister Anne, kin by some network of marriage and blood, bustles about, vainly attentive to the itinerant photographer who is using her front room for his local studio. She has banished Uncle Felix, infirm and dying, to a cramped utility room. Her self-centered callousness troubles both Dicey and Kate.

But a visit with Uncle Felix, not outrage at Sister Anne, is the aim of the journey to Mingo. Felix's grip, hard and bony, on Dicey's arm starts her on a pilgrimage. The word *remember* chimes through the following pages of the story. Dicey's heart and memory summon the images, smells, sounds of the family gathered for Sunday dinner at Mingo (*BI*, 141). What Welty had stricken from the first paragraph begins to work itself out dramatically in Dicey's heart and memory rather than in her mind. Stirred by Felix's commanding grasp, Dicey tours a past largely beyond her living memory. Her sense of time begins to alter, fulfilling the promise of the image of the clock displaying what she knew to be the wrong time.

Dicey finds herself, in this new time, before the portrait of her great-grandmother, "the one picture on the walls of Mingo, where pictures ordinarily would be considered frivolous" (*BI*, 147). The subject of the portrait carries more meaning than Dicey could have foreseen. Time past and time future converge on the present.

The yellow skirt spread fanlike, straw hat held ribbon-in-hand, orange beads big as peach pits (to conceal the joining at the neck)—none of that, any more than the forest scene so unlike the Mississippi wilderness (that enormity she had been carried to as a bride, when the logs of this house were cut, her bounded world by drop by drop of sweat exposed, where she'd died in the end of yellow fever) or the melancholy clouds obscuring the sky behind the passive figure with the small, crossed feet—none of it, world or body, was really hers. *She* had eaten bear meat, seen Indians, and had married into the wilderness at Mingo, to what unknown feelings. Slaves had died in her arms. She had grown a rose for Aunt Ethel to send back by me. And still those eyes, opaque, all pupil, belonged to Evelina—I knew, because they saw out, as mine did; weren't warned, as mine weren't, and never shut before the end, as mine would not. I, her divided sister, knew who had felt the wilderness of the world behind the ladies' view. We were homesick for somewhere that was the same place. (pp. 147–48)

The portrait symbolically frames this story's themes and motifs—ladies, pilgrimages, wilderness, loneliness, homesickness for a place for the heart. Dicey receives the message for an eloquent if still moment that prophesies her own pilgrimage into marriage, "unknown feelings," the wilderness of the world of which she won't be warned, to which she won't shut her eyes. She finds both courage in the face of the wilderness and the will to follow the "ladies' view" into the world, across the jump-ing-off place. There are no promises of mercy, not even remote sympathy should she end like Evelina, bereft of body and setting, and left only the eyes—her soul.

The grace accepted in this successful pilgrimage has immediate re-sults. Dicey verbally smites Sister Anne (*BI*, 150). And going back to Felix, she interprets the message he scrawls: "River—Daisy—Midnight —Please." The message confounds Kate, who tries to match each word with the facts of Felix's life. He had no wife named Daisy, for instance. But Dicey is touched by the "Please." The note of supplication at the end hurts her (p. 152). Felix's heart seeks a meeting with a lady by the water. Dicey understands the implications, hears the solitary note, like Dewey. Felix is a fellow pilgrim, even though he is a man, still nurturing in his parched age a moment of communion and touch, a voluntary surrender of his immunity from the world. As Dicey leaves Mingo, she sees the lin-gering group of neighbors on Sister Anne's porch as "passengers on a ship already embarked to sea" (p. 154). Driving away, she thinks of her lover and hopes that he is now thinking of her. She leaves Mingo hoping for connection, straining her ears for the note of the solitary bird she needs to hear.

"Going to Naples" concerns actual pilgrims aboard ship and bound across the Atlantic for homecomings, reunions, and holy visitations; to take the vows of the priesthood or of marriage; and to die. But none of the numerous characters pursues such a heartfelt pilgrimage as Gabriella Serto, a girl-woman whose ample flesh "came through [a hole in her stocking] like a pear" (*BI*, 156). Overweight, out of the running for any beauty crown, Gabriella nevertheless feels her need to give, to be accepted, to make enriching connections beyond herself. It is ironic, but fitting, that the ship carrying them all should have been christened *Pomona*, after the goddess whose special attention is fruits and orchards (here is the link between the goddess and Gabriella, whose flesh suggests a pear), and who was so beautiful she had a hundred suitors and ignored them all. Gabriella has no surplus of beaux.

Images unify this story, which otherwise might be justly indicted for wandering, discursiveness, and a blurring of focus—the kind of private indulgence of which Mr. Peden and other reviewers complained. The birds that follow the *Pomona*, screaming in its wake, initiate part of the network of nuance and symbol. Gabriella, too, screams and screeches as life registers upon her in extremes of pleasure and pain. She is paid as little attention as the gulls, which in Italian are called *gabbiani*. The singular form is *gabi*, which may also mean gull, or fool. Gabriella's name echoes this hint of her plight, for she is certainly, in the end, a kind of saintly fool. Pointing out nuance at work, however, is delicate business; it is touching the chime.

Members of the crew, all male, frequently take shots at the *gabbiani*. In one instance they come on deck with their rifles as Aldo Scampo, Gabriella's boyfriend, sleeps by her side. Her Vertumnus, in his sleep, protests the killing (*BI*, 174). Awake, however, he joins the other men in their sport.

Marriage also plays a part in the pattern of the imagery. A bride waits for Poldy, one of the passengers, somewhere in Italy, and he carries the bridesmaids' dresses in his baggage. His constant references to *his* bride and to *his* marriage keep the idea of male possession before the reader and before Gabriella. She feels a kinship with the unknown bride, as Dicey had felt herself a "divided sister" with her great-grandmother.

Poldy's and Aldo's laughs met like clapped hands over Gabriella's head and she could hardly take another step down for anger at that girl, and outrage for her, as if she were her dearest friend, her little sister. Even now, the girl probably languished in tears because the little country train she was coming on, from her unknown town, was late. Perhaps, even more foolishly, she had come early, and was languishing just beyond that gate, not knowing if she were allowed inside the wall or not—how would she know? No matter—they would meet. The *Pomona* had landed, and that was enough. Poor girl, whose name Poldy had not even bothered to tell them, her future was about to begin. (*BI*, 198)

Gabriella's heart, on its pilgrimage, strikes a kinship with the heart of an unknown girl. In the story of the crossing Gabriella's heart is sounded and the echo returns from depths unfilled by love. She is a woman like Circe or Opal; men—Odysseus, Blackie, Aldo—merely walk away. Motifs of touch and of eating weave this element into the pattern. Early in the story, early in the relationship of Gabriella and Aldo, she "set her teeth into his sleeve. But when she pierced that sleeve she found his arm—rigid and wary, with a muscle that throbbed like a heart. She would have bitten a piece out of him then and there for the scare his arm gave her, but he moved like a spring and struck at her with his playful weapon, the toothpick between his teeth" (*BI*, 165). This woman's need is playfully repelled and denied, as the man from Syracuse had kept the woman's hand distant in spite of her offer of sympathy. The need for human food in love, the substance of the other transformed by the chemistry of love into the regenerated self, is evident in Gabriella's need. She is always hungry, like the gulls that follow the ship.

Taking is not the only direction of the process. Aldo gives to Gabriella.

Aldo buried his face in Gabriella's blouse, and she looked out over his head and presently smiled—not into any face in particular. Her smile was as rare as her silence, and as vulnerable—it was meant for everybody. A gap where a tooth was gone showed childishly.

And it lifted the soul—for a thing like crossing the ocean could depress it— to sit in the sun and contemplate among companions the weakness and the mystery of the flesh. Looking, dreaming down at Gabriella, they felt something of an old, pure loneliness come back to them—like a bird sent out over the waters long ago, when they were young, perhaps from their same company. Only the long of memory, the brave and experienced of heart, could hear such a stirring, an awakening—first to have listened to that screaming, and in a flash to remember what it was. (*BI*, 166)

In a flash also the artistic integrity of the story appears; in the bird alone over the vacant waters echoes the sound and the image of the unknown bird heard by Dewey Coker in "Ladies in Spring"; in the language of "heart" echoes the concerns of love and communion that link all of the stories of *The Bride of the Innisfallen.* In such moments the power of the rhythmic technique to pull narrative time to a point, to summon the various nuances and images of the stories to one effect, not only brings this individual story to a climax but also brings the entire collection to a still focus.

Beneath the roughness of their comradeship, Aldo and Gabriella live the same fate as Odysseus and Circe. For an ephemeral moment they achieve a kind of union that is nearly sacramental. But it is only temporary. In parting, Gabriella touches the case of Aldo's cello; it is "the golden moment of touch, just given, just taken, in saying goodby" (*BI*, 207). Then, in the same instant of the touch, there is only Aldo's back—Odysseus' back—as he goes his separate way. Every moment has this rhythmical aspect of touching and parting, of present and future. It is the moment that Virgie contemplates in "The Wanderers."

"Going to Naples" shows the heart again denied its refuge in the other, but stronger for the denial. Gabriella's heart, concealed in flesh that does not conform to a fashionable standard of beauty, is rich. It summons from those who watch her embracing Aldo and dancing alone (*BI*, 186) the awareness of a truth in the human plight of the necessary pilgrimage and its inevitable denial, the voyaging of the heart without the protection of a harbor. Gabriella's victory is not her jolly exterior, but the depth of her heart, its stamina in the voyage. Like Bowen's Portia, she is cherished and ignored; her heart inspires and disturbs. Unlike Pomona, Gabriella is mortal, and so she does not have Olympian insurance against unrequited love. With no chance of deprivation, however, there can be no heart. Pomona's tears do not enrich the earth.

The title story, "The Bride of the Innisfallen," is the linchpin of the collection. It is the third story in the arrangement of the contents of the volume, but it is the most complex of the seven and, in its way, is the summation of the collection as an entity. The journey or pilgrimage of the American girl achieves its goal, the renewal and rededication of her heart to the world. Through a painstaking technique that frequently reticulates a network of imagery, the story accents the character and plight of the woman who flees her husband and her role as wife, and

rhythmically builds toward a moment of thematic and technical fulfillment. Passengers cross a mysterious, dark body of water, and arrive on
the other side to the greetings of dawn and bells. The chief pilgrim is
not denied, not held off. Courageously her heart turns to embrace the
world in its complex and inevitable rhythm of love and loss; each moment can be its own fullness and the beginning of the next moment's incompleteness and want. In love and faith the woman consents to be the
world's partner, its bride, in this paired existence.

Welty builds the story upon nuance and suggestion, images, bits of
conversation. From the outset a personal and cultural challenge confronts the American wife "leaving London without her husband's knowledge" (*BI*, 48). Her fellow passengers constitute a set of cautions and reminders of the gravity and cost of her move. The woman in the broadly
striped raincoat bids goodby to a man in Paddington station. A young
wife is sent off with loud good wishes from a party on the platform, and
"she smiled calmly back at them; even in this she was showing pregnancy, as she showed it under her calm blue coat" (p. 50). "A pair of lovers
slid in last of all" (p. 50). The American wife, then, is surrounded by
mates alone or in pairs, emphasizing the bond she has just unilaterally
begun to dissolve by leaving.

Also, signs of matrimony and the woman's biological and emotional
role in marriage challenge her. A red-haired infant, a "boy with queenly
jowls" (*BI*, 53), causes a flutter of adoration among the women of the
compartment. The young, pregnant woman speaks for the majority: "But
this is *our* train . . . Women alone, sometimes exceptions, but often on
the long journey alone or with children. . . . But oh, I tell you I would
rather do without air to breathe than see that poor baby pass again and
put out his little arms to me" (p. 54). Her sentiments receive the ap-
proval of the other passengers, for they confirm what the society expects
from the woman.

There is no deviation from this norm. The man from Connemara
tells a story about ghosts, Lord and Lady Beagle, "Married still!" (*BI*,
64); his own birds live only in procreative pairs; and a matched pair of
greyhounds click down the corridor outside the compartment. Through
nuance and suggestion, repetition of the married pair motif, the train
becomes a microcosm, and its route becomes the soul's pilgrimage along
the edge of the abyss, the vacant water. "The train stopped again, start-

ed; stopped, started. Here on the outer edge of Wales it advanced and hesitated as rhythmically and as intermittently as a needle in a hem. The wheels had taken on that defenseless sound peculiar to running near the open sea. Oil lamps burned in their little boxes at the halts; there was a pull at the heart from the feeling of the trees all being bent the same way" (p. 73). The rhythm in the stopping and starting reinforces the rhythm of the story, for the "bride" is caught in a crucial and ambivalent progress towards a moment of decision.

In this universe of married pairs, the American wife, on her own, finds the course of her pilgrimage to be rough. The world is calculated to force her back into the role she has left. A Welshman, a fellow passenger, reads aloud her passport information: "It was not that he read it officially—worse: as if it were a poem in the paper, only with the last verse missing" (BI, 75). And the man from Connemara, another male passenger, becomes the voice of another warning: "Once the man from Connemara sat up out of his sleep and stared at the American girl pinned to her chair across the room, as if he saw somebody desperate who had left her husband once, endangered herself among strangers, been turned back, and was here for the second go-round, asking for a place to stay in Cork" (p. 77).

In neither instance, however, is the American girl's identity caught and "pinned" upon her. She keeps it a secret, and as a secret it remains vital. "If she could never tell her husband her secret, perhaps she would never tell it at all" (BI, 81). That secret that the American girl protects so closely is important in the story. In the typescript another reference to it is canceled: "In Wales I knew I still had my secret, like the money to spend when the journey was over. The Welshman was getting close, but he stopped in time."[11] Her secret is a self that the information on her passport cannot define. Only the incomplete and growing world of her relationships with others and with the world itself can define her. Her leaving London was the first move to open that world, and her secret keeps it expanding.

She persists beyond simple escape. She pilgrimages toward renewal of her heart. When the *Innisfallen* glides into the harbor of Cork, a new day dawns. "After the length of the ship had passed a ringing steeple, and the

11. *Ibid.*, 47.

hands had glinted gold at them from the clockface, an older, harsher, more distant bell rang from an inland time: *now*" (*BI*, 78). A new time calls for a renewal of one's vows with the world. The revisions of the last few pages of "The Bride of the Innisfallen" indicate that the author was deeply engaged with material and style, trying to discover in nuance and suggestion the essence of the vows and a climax for the story in keeping with the technique. The revisions appear in pen, in gray, and in red pencil, suggesting that three sessions may have been needed before the ending was satisfactory. Welty's usual practice involves little revision other than accidentals; no other story in the typescript shows this amount of work.

References to the distant husband and the marriage left behind in London are deleted. With "the pencil . . . it was a London pencil" goes memories of the unpleasant and suffocating London flat—"the cretonne, the linoleum, the fog (as if the disgusting powdery patches of where all her handkerchiefs had dried on the mirror were everything), the very beds. . . ." Deleting the pencil, "its whole length and substance," the beds, "the mutual hungers of London," "Cock Robin with a shaft through his breast" (BIC, 47–48) removes all evidence of an arid or de-structive conjugal life, a harm to be fled *from*. Perhaps the pencil and the beds were discarded because they too overtly symbolize that relationship and do not suggest the possible future. But the typescript bears witness to the abiding concern of *The Bride of the Innisfallen*—the fate of the women in the world, risking their hearts and flesh on the love of men.

The impact of place as foreign is lessened in the revision and thus the American girl's profile as an alienated soul is lowered. Welty deleted the following: "It appeared that you could not leave people [your own], you could only go looking into new countries, go as you were looking into countries that were already, long ago, here" (BIC, 48); and "this stranger from another country, from two other countries . . ." (p. 49). The American girl's alienation is played down; the facts of her nationali-ty, like the information on her passport, are not the essential facts of her identity. The revision eliminates the factual in favor of the suggested.

The secret life, which she brings cupped like a weak flame, is the most important feature of the ending. The confirmation of that self is the reward of her pilgrimage. Something about her marriage had constricted her, a poverty of possibility. "You expect too much," the husband's only words in the typescript (BIC, 49) are altered to "You hope for too much" (*BI*, 82). Hope is a virtue, with a wider range of suggestive power for pilgrims.

Alone in Cork, the woman plunges unafraid and with growing joy into the possibilities of the world. In contrast with the moribund and stale flat in London is the city of Cork, the description of which (*BI*, 82) is essentially unchanged from typescript to published version. The American woman's response to Cork is, however, much more complex than the description of it. Here Welty encountered, if the revision is a true record, her greatest difficulty. The pilgrim is bound to express the joy that she feels, but life has taught her to be circumspect. "You must never betray pure joy—the kind you were born and began with—either by hiding it or parading it in front of people's eyes; they didn't want to be shown it. And still you must tell it" (p. 81). The Toledo woman faced the same difficulty but found no solution. In the typescript the woman debates various ways of expressing her joy: "If she could tell it now, ask it now, quickly, even to the man pausing at her shoulder politely to see what she might be defacing the wall with: Is there no way to express joy except by making love, by eating and drinking, laughing, crying, singing, dancing, asking the time of a stranger—is there no way? For here I've come. Do you tell by seeing?" (BIC, 48). The rising description on page 82 of the story follows, as if in answer: yes, joy may be told by seeing. The eye moves upward toward the point of transcendent joy.

"Do you tell by seeing?" Art expresses joy in the world perceived, and in the act of perception. Out of the trouble of these final pages the resolution comes, a moment of vision. Point of view discovers this climax and the fruition of the pattern of nuance and imagery. Though a good deal of description of Cork and its streets is canceled in the typescript, the sight of the anonymous woman at the window is kept. In that moment of perception, the prosaic world, whose emblem is the cigarette butt, reveals its other nature, becomes transformed into "the tableau that could tell her everything" (BIC, 49). In the moment of the heart's victory, a simple moment of seeing in joy, a new vitality surges through the heart of the "bride" of the story and into the prose; the "golden moment" of touch and parting becomes the renewal of vows, a dedication. It is not told by straightforward telling, but by seeing. The American woman turns to a strange pub, revels in the "lovely" faces within, and thereby participates in the vital rhythm simply by going on into the world and into the life she has. The life she had drops behind when her letter home drops unfinished to the pavement.

The revisions of the "Bride of the Innisfallen" reveal the central goal of the theme and technique of these stories: inside the business and circumstance of the world is a serenity and a stillness toward which the heart naturally moves. This movement is rhythmic, for the heart itself is rhythm. The stillness is moving; as Eliot also says in "Burnt Norton," ". . . at the still point, there the dance is." Each of the women of *The Bride of the Innisfallen* strives toward the stillness, serenity, and joy of vision that redeems the heart from its hopeless isolation in the corruptible world. Each of the pilgrim hearts in the collection approaches this goal, and some attain it. But it is never so vividly won as it is in the title story.

Without attention for the rhythmic technique, this and other stories in *The Bride of the Innisfallen* could well seem "obscure and undecipherable" even to the reader of goodwill. A careful measure of analysis makes the stories much more accessible. In the widest sense, theme and technique reveal a world for the heart within the straightforward and circumstantial world of time and action. The heart lives in its own time and has its own gestures that are rhythmic and just as validly considered signs of life as the pulses that register on hospital machines. There are matters of life and death in every moment. The possibilities for joy, and for hopelessness, are constantly before us.

From its first story, *The Bride of the Innisfallen* should be read with the discipline Welty herself employs. Her earlier collections of short stories exhibit the early stages of this technique—meaning by slow accumulation of suggestion and nuance, with single stories casting light and meaning on one another, the whole collection knit into something more than so many pages of an arbitrary number of stories. Welty has contributed to the short story and to the collection the lesson of rhythm and pattern as ways to art. In *The Bride of the Innisfallen* she followed her talent into unexpected regions. As Louis Rubin said, "She is steadily extending her range." [12]

12. Louis Rubin, "Two Ladies of the South," *Sewanee Review*, LXIII (Autumn, 1955), 671.

## VIII

# Myth and History:
# The Foes of *Losing Battles*

After *The Ponder Heart* and *The Bride of the In-nisfallen* there was a long silence broken by "Where Is The Voice Coming From?" (1963), "The Demonstrators" (1966), and "The Optimist's Daughter" (1969), all of which appeared in the *New Yorker*. There were also several book reviews from Welty, as well as readings and lectures in colleges and universities around the country—in all, enough work to cast doubt on the validity of the phrase "long silence." To the novel-reading public, however, and to the reviewers who were accustomed to new work from Welty, the fifteen years from 1955 to 1970 were a long wait.

When *Losing Battles* was published in the spring of 1970, with a near-ly unanimous welcome from reviewers, Welty was acknowledged as an American artist of the first rank, no longer the regional phenomenon toiling for a place in the Southern Renascence with the likes of Faulkner, Porter, O'Connor, and Tennessee Williams. James Boatwright called *Losing Battles* "a major work of the imagination and a gift to cause gen-eral rejoicing."[1] Joyce Carol Oates praised its perfection, symmetry, and theme of domestic love as gifts of artistic wisdom and beauty, coming too late, perhaps, for a "troubled contemporary America."[2] Reynolds Price

1. James Boatwright, review of Eudora Welty's *Losing Battles*, in *New York Times Book Re-view*, April 12, 1970, p. 1.
2. Joyce Carol Oates, "Eudora's Web," *Atlantic Monthly*, CCXXV (April, 1970), 120.

called the novel "an almost frightening gift . . . of such plenitude and serene mastery as to reveal with panicking suddenness how thin a diet we have survived on."[3] Again and again *Losing Battles* was hailed (for once the hackneyed blurb genuinely applies) as a masterpiece worthy of comparison with *War and Peace*, *The Tempest*, and the novels of Jane Austen.

There were, of course, dissenting voices. Christopher Lehmann-Haupt called the novel an American masterpiece that no one would read; he thought its comedy veered too close to banality and sentimentality.[4] Alan Pryce-Jones found *Losing Battles* ultimately "tiring," even though he granted it the title of "a kind of southern *Tristram Shandy*."[5]

The reviews testify to several things. Welty's reputation in American literature, far from waning during the years of her "silence," actually grew. *Losing Battles* was submitted along with Saul Bellow's *Mr. Sammler's Planet* and Joyce Carol Oates' *The Wheel of Love* to a Pulitzer Fiction Jury that could not decide upon a "single, unanimous, persuasive choice."[6] "The [Pulitzer] Board seriously discussed recognizing Eudora Welty for her lifelong achievements as a leading American writer" but in the end could not decide.[7] Even without the prize, *Losing Battles* occasioned a serious reevaluation of Welty's stature and accomplishments.

John W. Aldridge wrote that the power of "the ladies' fashion magazines" in the 1950s, with their "delight in grotesquerie . . . [and] those wisteria-scented effusions of Madison Avenue Gothicism" had forced Welty's fiction into a kind of parody of southern fiction. The result, says Aldridge, was a narrowing of her range, an "exquisite" fiction rather than a "robust" handling of her materials. *Losing Battles*, Aldridge rejoiced, was a departure from those doldrums of tepid imitation of Faulkner and the other big names. In the new novel Aldridge read a "civilized and profound criticism of life" from an ironic point of view located close to that of Julia Mortimer.[8] Sometimes close to sentimentalizing the Renfro-Beecham reunion, Aldridge says, the author always holds her distance,

3. Reynolds Price, "Frightening Gift," Washington *Post*, April 17, 1970, Sec. C, p. 1.

4. Christopher Lehmann-Haupt, "Books of the Times," New York *Times*, April 10, 1970, p. 37.

5. Alan Pryce-Jones, "Almost a Winner," *Newsday*, June 2, 1970.

6. John Hohenberg, *The Pulitzer Prizes* (New York, 1974), 321.

7. *Ibid.*

8. John W. Aldridge, "Eudora Welty: The Metamorphosis of a Southern Lady Writer," *Saturday Review*, April 11, 1970, pp. 21, 22, 36.

indicating how a pastoral tradition might put the nimbus of nostalgia around the crude hill people, yet never herself doing so.

John Aldridge's essay is long and thorough. By placing Welty in a special relationship with southern literature and the demigods of its renaissance, he does her the great and enduring service of placing her work in a larger context, of estimating a magnitude for her achievement that has seldom been so publicly stated.

Jonathan Yardley also goes back to the 1950s to begin his essay on *Losing Battles*. *The Ponder Heart*, he says, may have been too successful ("too charming?"), because its popularity led to a "severe case of misinterpretation." *Losing Battles*, he writes, will not be so easily enjoyed and absorbed as an entertainment. Even though Welty celebrates the family in this novel, she also shows its "cruelties and narrowmindedness." In balancing the harsh and the funny, Yardley says, Welty makes a statement about the human struggle and the need for survival, for "coming through" it, that may well be "a more meaningful affirmation than anything Faulkner gave us."[9] Moreover, *Losing Battles* may not be just a nostalgic farewell to a lost South, but also a good-bye to a lost southern literature. In short, Jonathan Yardley reads *Losing Battles* as a significant novel, perhaps the last good southern novel. His *ave atque vale*, though generous to Welty and *Losing Battles*, betrays his allegiance to an old stereotype of southern fiction.

Welty's themes and technical approach to difficult subject material in *Losing Battles* deserve more than a reverent elegy. Yardley suggests that *Losing Battles* is the culmination of a hypothetical Mississippi trilogy begun with *Delta Wedding* and continued with *The Ponder Heart*.[10] This view does provide an interesting perspective on the novel, but it does not adequately allow for the flowering of point of view and style within *Losing Battles* itself.

*Losing Battles* elevates Welty's "homemade" symbolist technique, her unique evocation of place, and her vision of human life as a constant rhythm of "lonesomeness and hilarity," community and divisions. After the sharp focus on the embattled and "losing" individual in *The Ponder Heart*, after the limited and individual point of view of Laurel Hand, her attention returns to the clan. If *terrifying* is the word for the submerged

9. Jonathan Yardley, "The Last Good One?" *New Republic*, May 9, 1970, pp. 33–36.
10. *Ibid.*, 35.

half of *The Ponder Heart*—indicating rather than exploring the depths of one of Welty's recurrent themes and characters—*Losing Battles* is celebratory, beautifully interwoven with nuance and the colors and sounds of a world. Its lonesomeness is real but not terrifying.

*Delta Wedding* is this novel's closest relation in Welty's fiction. The earlier novel shows a wealthy Delta family in good economic times. *Losing Battles* is about the poor farmers of the Mississippi hill country during the depression of the 1930s. In *Delta Wedding* the complex interplay of divided viewpoints often led readers into confusion about whom to place where within the transparent frame of the novel. But *Losing Battles* circumvents that confusion; its frame is cosmic, but *there*.

Because the novel pits the uneducated reunion against the forces of learning led by Julia Mortimer, the schoolteacher, readers have been drawn to partisan interpretations of *Losing Battles*.[11] As always, fixed interpretation is hasty and a mistake. It is essential to read *Losing Battles* with an ear for the comic and ironic tone. We must keep in mind what M. E. Bradford says in his review of the novel: "The human lot beneath the noise of politics or intellectual, religious, and economic change, remains constant."[12]

Readers who take this view have a more balanced perspective on the combatants in the novel than readers who believe the novel to be a case made on behalf of Julia Mortimer's passionate dedication to education as the remedy for all the hardship and ignorance that plague innocence and the small yeoman farmer in the modern world. The partisans of Julia Mortimer's beliefs have a blind spot concerning the comedy of her own isolate determination (for example, continuing classes in the middle of a tornado). Those claiming the more balanced view find virtue and liability on both sides of the losing battles, but they still locate the novel's greatest achievement in the sharp and serene remembrance and evocation of things past: the Mississippi hill country around Banner, *circa* 1930.

In a sense, however, Welty has made a remarkable novel as a whole. By skillful maneuvering of incident, imagery, and dialogue, she displays,

11. Although Mr. Aldridge's review takes this "partisan" viewpoint on the battles, a better example is Carolyn R. Ruffin, "Sensitivity Runs a Poor Second," *Christian Science Monitor*, June 11, 1970, p. 13.

12. M. E. Bradford, "Looking Down From a High Place: The Serenity of Miss Welty's *Losing Battles*," *Recherches Anglaises et Américaines*, IV (1971), 96.

in the time- and place-bound particulars of Banner, Mississippi, the time-less combatants of a larger battle, one that can genuinely be termed cosmic. In *Losing Battles* myth and history battle for the allegiance of men's minds and lives, the timeless fights the temporal, the circle struggles against the line. Welty views her people and their condition with the depth and breadth of the philosopher who sees the universal in each moment.

To summarize: just as on the wider scale myth or the mythical view of existence involves, by myth's very nature, an avoidance of contact between man and history, a prevention of man's confrontation with novelty, irreversibility, change, so on the personal level man is freed from his personal history and its conse-quences by evolving a technique of evasion, establishing, thus, in his ritual, a reunion between him and the order of cosmos, a harmony between him and nature. Implied, on both levels, is a "terror of history"—the phrase is taken from Eliade—which is not something merely archaic.[13]

Welty knows (if we accept the novel as testimony) that the battle for human consciousness is not definitively lost or won at any single time or place. She knows that the battles continue, that the casualties mount, that the fierce loyalties do not fade away completely because it is "the desperation of staying alive against all odds that keeps both sides en-couraged" (*LB*, 298). From her elevated point of view, Welty sees that these battles are always losing but never finally lost.[14] Above myth and history is the novelist's point of vantage on the battles. She can listen to and watch both sides, feel with each, and know that the all-encompassing world is friend and foe alike. This is a complicated perspective, three spheres overlapping and conflicting. The wonder of Welty's achievement in *Losing Battles* is that, in her multifront battle, her casualties are almost nil.

The world of the natural creation, the battlefield, the place of the novelist, has important meaning for the wholeness of the novel.[15] M. E. Bradford mentions the conscious "lushness" of the opening segments of *Losing Battles* and takes the view that these passages constitute the com-pact bud of the novel from which the more elaborate blossom of "tale

---

13. A. C. Charity, *Events and Their Afterlife* (Cambridge, England, 1966), 16–17.
14. Bradford, "Looking Down From A High Place," 929
15. In the context of his stylistic approach to *Losing Battles*, John F. Fleischauer says some-thing similar. See his "The Focus of Mystery: Eudora Welty's Prose Style," *Southern Literary Jour-nal*, V (Spring, 1973), 64–79.

telling" unfolds. Considering the novel in terms of a myth-history battle, these early pages take on another meaning.

The overarching world of natural creation contains the human worlds
and battles, provides symbolic meanings, and works, through Welty's use
of descriptive similes, to restrain the human world of speech and action
from bulging out of perspective. These similes are the heart of Welty's
descriptive technique in this novel. The opening paragraphs of the novel
abound in similes: a change of air as if a wooden door had been opened,
a house like an old man's silver watch, a point of the ridge like the
tongue of a calf, a shaft of heat solid as a hickory stick. Similes in such
numbers might obstruct the flow of the prose, if they yoked together
things too disparate to be associated easily. But the ease and naturalness
of these homemade similes stems from their yoking of neighbors in the
natural world. The world of air and houses and calves' tongues remains
intact, part of, but distinguishable from, the human worlds of myth and
history. Welty keeps the natural world present in the novel through her
use of such similes; we are always aware of the field of battle, and the
fact that no one possesses it.

The natural world also supplies the novel with its symbolic meanings.
The bois d'arc tree called "Billy Vaughn's Switch" presides over the reunion like a symbol of the family. "The tree looked a veteran of all the
old blows, a survivor. Old wounds on the main trunk had healed leaving
scars as big as tubs or wagon wheels, and where the big lower branches
had thrust out, layer under layer of living bark had split on the main
trunk in a bloom of splinters, of a red nearly animal-like" (*LB*, 181). Besides carrying the marks of the past generations, the tree springs from a
miraculous event, the overnight blossoming of an ancestor's staff. The
family of mythic consciousness remembers its origins not in fact but in
legend. The tree also suggests an aspect of the reunion's master symbol,
the circle, for its rings of growth record the lives and events of the
family and hold all generations in permanent and equal relation.

Fundamental to the mythical consciousness, according to A. C.
Charity, is the repetition of archetypes, the eternal recurrence of the
ritual.[16] It is fitting that the reunion should think of itself as a circle,
should celebrate Granny Vaughn's birthday as a ritual reaffirming its
solidarity. Welty invests the reunion with the circle motif. The story of

16. Charity, *Events and Their Afterlife*, 16.

Jack Renfro's run-in with the law and subsequent imprisonment begins with a gold wedding ring, follows a circular path into the whole past of the family, and returns to the ring itself. Aunt Cleo, the catechumen, asks, "'Are we back around to that?' 'It's the same gold ring, and all the one sad story,'" Miss Beulah said. (LB, 219)

The continued survival of the reunion demands, in its recurring archetypal celebration, that the family be reaffirmed by the annual birthday party and by repetitions more deeply psychological. On the slim evidence of postcards and entries in the family Bible, the reunion happily concludes that Gloria, Jack's wife, is really a Beecham and part of the family by blood as well as marriage. Jack becomes a reincarnation of Sam Dale Beecham, his uncle who died young, about the age of Jack himself. Both young men are the apple of the family's eye. Both are taken from the circle by a foreign thing called the government. And both courted red-haired girls with mysterious pasts. The reunion insists that Jack recapitulate the abbreviated life of Sam Dale; the motivation is the deep-seated psychological need of the mythical consciousness to keep novelty and individuality at an absolute minimum while it affirms the archetypal cycles.

Welty thoroughly invests the reunion with the circle motif, allying the family with the daily cycle of sunrise, sunset. With the rise of the sun in the first section of the novel, the life of the family begins. With the darkness the reunion comes to a halt, and there is nothing to do but "stand it." "'I've got it to stand and I've got to stand it. And you've got to stand it,' said Miss Beulah's voice. 'After they've all gone home, Ralph, and the children's in bed, that's what left. Standing it'" (LB, 360). The day, sunlight, the visible presence of family, the time of growing is the proper place of the reunion.

In addition to symbolic meaning and the use of the circle motif, Welty portrays the reunion in ways that leave no doubt about its mythical consciousness. The reunion celebration itself is the reenactment of the cosmogony in which its consciousness is grounded. It occurs at a crucial time, for, in addition to the fact that Granny is "the last Vaughn in the world" (LB, 426), the land is "going back" on the people.

Like the origin of "Billy Vaughn's Switch," the early days of the family's existence with the land are enhanced by legend. "Cleo, the old place here was plum stocked with squirrel when we was boys. It was overrun with quail. . . . It was filled—it was filled!—with every kind of good thing, this old dwelling, when me and the rest of us Beecham boys grew up here under Granny and Grandpa Vaughn's strict raising. It's got everlasting springs, a well with water as sweet as you could find in this world, and a pond and a creek both. But you're seeing it today in dry summer" (*LB*, 193). In shorter words, Banner was an Eden, a place of harmonious living with nature that is now fading. "It's the fault of the land going back on us, treating us the wrong way. There's been too much of the substance washed away to grow enough to eat any more" (p. 194). The result is the breakup of the circle; the younger men have to move away, even give up farming, maybe run for office like Homer Champion. Eden has been invaded by snakes and candidates; the reunion copes with one of each.

The natural world in this instance shows itself to be oblivious to human life; the harmony and union with nature seem to be fiction, and the mythic way of life a failure. In such a crisis the reunion needs a savior. And one appears.

By its combined will, the reunion "brings" Jack Renfro out of prison (*LB*, 32). No one is really startled when he appears, although he has a day to go on his sentence to Parchman. Jack's character and his reintegration into the circle illustrate several of the characteristics of the mythical consciousness that Welty sees so clearly.

The rite of "forgiveness," which is a high point of the reunion, absolves Jack of his "sin"—not the legal transgression that got him sentenced to Parchman (the reunion does not recognize *that* law) but the withholding of his physical presence, whether voluntary or not (*LB*, 211). The circle is not an idea but a tangible reality to the reunion, in which every "certified" member participates. But the reunion confers special status on Jack as the one who is going to reestablish the harmony with the land: "We're relying on Jack now. He'll haul us out of our misery" (p. 194). In a time when all of the young men have to leave the family to get by, the fact that Jack stays is of monumental importance to the reunion.

Jack's sojourn in the outside world, the chaos, makes his reentry just a little difficult. "But they've all growed old, that's the shock!" (*LB*, 97). A year and a half in the outside world has accustomed Jack to a different view of time—a time that ages and changes people. But his faith, foolish

or saintly, in the rightness of the reunion equips him to put this disjunction behind, even though this leap of faith disturbs Gloria. "'Do you still
think you're going to pick up living where you left off?' she asked fast.
'Did something put the idea in your precious little head I can't?'"
(p. 113). Gloria, a former teacher and a pupil of Julia Mortimer, has a
different conception of time from that of her husband. Jack, in accepting
the authority of the reunion, accepts also its conception of time, in
which the past is not irretrievable, in which the unusual and disturbing
variations from the accepted pattern can be abolished by the ritual of the
reunion. Jack's "forgiveness" and reintegration into the reunion is an example of the power of the mythic clan. The reunion's mastery over time
empowers it to command Jack to reverse his charitable act of extricating
Judge Moody's Buick from a roadside ditch, and even allows Granny to
bridge the gulf of death, as Aunt Cleo learns: "'Hey, don't she know the
difference yet? Who's alive and who's dead?' 'She knows we're all part of
it together, or ought to be!' Miss Beulah cried, turning on her" (p. 346).
At the height of its powers the reunion can hold the past within the
present, erase unwanted time or events that do not fit into the archetypal pattern, free itself from the worry and pressure of the future by making existence the constantly recurring pattern of what has always been.
These are the weapons the mythical consciousness uses against the historical in *Losing Battles*. The other side fights just as steadfastly with its
own weapons.

Gloria Renfro is locked in a hand-to-hand combat with the reunion
in the person of her husband, Jack. Her ideas of family ties, the family
circle, individual rights, and the nature of time reflect a mind heavily
influenced by her teacher, Julia Mortimer, the champion of the historical. Gloria's perspective on life is largely that of the historical mind, and
her "peculiarities" stand out sharply in her mythic surroundings.

Unlike the reunion, Gloria does not rejoice in the security of "home
ties." For her the buffer they provide between self and chaos seems more
like an encumbrance: "'I'm here to tell you Jack Renfro's case in two
words—home ties. Jack Renfro has got family piled all over him.' 'Proud
of it,' said Jack'" (*LB*, 163). Gloria's battle with the reunion, and with
her husband, like Robbie's, is a battle against an oppressive "pile" that
nullifies privacy and individuality. Jack, a true son of the reunion, is willing to deny his will (if, indeed, it can be said that he has one) in favor of
the will of the family. He submits to the expropriation of his truck to pay

for a new roof. He swallows his sorrow at the loss of his horse. But Gloria's constant ambition is to take Jack and Lady May away from the circle. She fights every step of the way, holding herself aloof, protecting her dream of solitude with her own small family. "'Oh, if we just had a little house to ourselves, no bigger than our reach right now,' she whispered. 'And nobody could ever find us! But everybody finds us. Living or dead'" (p. 171). To escape the network of dependencies is Gloria's ambition to the end of the novel. "'If we could stay this way always—build us a little two-room house, where nobody in the world could find us—' He [Jack] drew her close, as if out of sudden danger" (p. 431).

The danger in these ideas is very real to a man of Jack Renfro's mind, in which family means safety, companionship, defense against the chaos. The reunion pities a "human deserted" (*LB*, 35), and cannot understand the willful isolation of Julia Mortimer from the morning yell. Gloria's desire to escape the same net is the stamp of Julia Mortimer's influence.

Gloria's fixation upon the future runs smack into the reunion's indifference to time. For the reunion the future is an unknown concept. The past and the present, interchangeable in the circle of existence, are all they know or care of time. But for Gloria, time is not a circle that eternally turns up the identical pattern, but a road that leads ahead and runs to an end whether people keep up with it or not. Such conflict with the reunion over the nature of time and the place of men within it causes her pique at Jack's apparent obliviousness to the eighteen months he spent away at Parchman. The same conflict still smolders toward the end of the novel. "'I don't see our future, Jack,' she gasped. 'Keep looking, sweetheart.' 'If we can't do any better than we're doing now, what will Lady May think of us when we're old and gray?' 'Just hang onto my heels, honey,' he cried out. 'We're still where we were yesterday. In the balance,' Gloria said" (*LB*, 390). And Gloria cannot live with the idea of movement without progress.

Progress—the idea of man as a creature who answers the challenge of universal chaos by using his brains and will to make some order out of it —is the characteristic response of the historical consciousness. Whereas the mythical mind figuratively draws the wagons into a circle and ignores the chaos by the constant reaffirmation of the archetype of order, the historical mind enters the chaos and tries to make it answer to the dream of order. Enter Judge Oscar Moody, the very name calling up suggestions of the brooding, introspective, abstracting mind.

Judge Moody is the pupil of Julia Mortimer who stayed, to face the chaos and to try to improve it. He is a man of the written word and justice, not of oral communication (hearsay) and family ties. The reunion is appalled that the judge would ignore Jack's home ties and sentence him according to a written law. He, in turn, is appalled by the reunion's rejoicing at the fact (as they accept it) of Gloria's blood relationship to the family. What appears to the man of history as the danger of inbreeding is to the reunion only the happy doubling of family ties.

Moody, while the captive of the reunion, reaches a degree of detachment more meaningful than that of any other character in the novel. Even Julia Mortimer could not laugh at herself. But Judge Moody, after the hilarious rescue of his automobile and a night with the reunion, stands in the cemetery and laughs (LB, 431). Standing back from the battles, responding to the seriousness and hilarity alike with laughter, is usually the stance of the author of Losing Battles.

Julia Mortimer, whose name suggests death for the "primitive men" of Banner, never achieves the perspective of humor. Julia, like Granny Vaughn, the last of her kind (LB, 47), is too deeply dedicated to her cause to admit the relative imperfections of both sides of the battle. Her testament, the written word of her side in the midst of the oral words of the reunion, implies a mind at odds in every particular with the mythical consciousness. The first line, "I have always pretty well known what I was doing," hits right at the heart of the reunion's behavior—rituals performed because they have always been performed, without a breath of curiosity as to why.

Julia Mortimer "always thought if [she] could marshal strength enough of body and spirit and push with it, every ounce, [she] could change the future" (LB, 298). Dedicated to a belief that the condition of man could and should be changed, Julia posthumously espouses heresy in the midst of the reunion; it is no wonder that they protest the reading of her letter. The reunion's cherished patterns are attacked by the teacher's forces; she seeks change, while the reunion gathers to abolish it through ignorance.

Dying, Julia Mortimer is granted the realization that both sides were using the same tactics, fighting for the same thing—survival (LB, 298). And she saw more: "The side that gets licked gets to the truth first" (p. 298). There are grounds to believe, or to hope, that when Julia was wandering in the dusty street in the last minutes of her life, she was seeking some kind of human connection: "'She knew exactly who she was,' [Judge Moody says]. 'And what she was. What she didn't know till she got to it was what would *happen* to what she was'" (p. 306).

Julia Mortimer is the leader of the forces of the historical conscious-ness in the novel, just as Granny Vaughn is the head of the clan. Both sides have their limitations. The fate of the pupils trained by Julia is to flee the backwoods for the places where their knowledge or expertise will be rewarded. If the reunion stifles individual initiative, it also stifles much greed and self-interest. The variety of license plates at Julia's funeral, the shadow reunion of the novel, is effective testimony of the failure of her dream, for "She wanted a doctor and a lawyer and all else we might have to holler for someday, to come right out of Banner" (*LB*, 235). The trouble with introducing the young children to the road in-stead of to the circle is that they just might take it. Willy Trimble, the boy whom Julia had taught to hammer and saw in lieu of reading and writing, said: "'I owed it [a coffin] to her, that's how I figured it,' he went right on. 'After she taught me just about everything I knew. Once I got started, I just never looked back'" (p. 232).

The novel returns to the natural world in the end, for the same earth that holds the bodies of the reunion holds the remains of Julia Mortimer, despite her quixotic dying wish to be buried beneath the front step of the Banner school. Jack Renfro visits the graves of his family and the places reserved for those still upon the earth. With an eloquence not heard in him before, he comments: "There's Mama and all of 'em's mother and dad going by. . . . Yet when you think back on the reunion and count how many him and her managed to leave behind! Like something had whispered to 'em 'Quick!' and they were smart enough to take heed" (*LB*, 426). When the adversary is mortality itself, all battles are losing battles. Neither the defense of the mythic consciousness nor the defense of the historical consciousness avails anything against death. One might respond as Julia Mortimer did: "I haven't spent a lifetime fighting my battle to give up now. I'm ready for all they send me. There's a measure of enjoyment in it" (p. 299). A last, solitary battle cry on the "darkling plain." One might also respond as Jack Renfro does, with a loud song of rejoicing at just being alive to sing. Neither is a whimper.

*Losing Battles* is not confined to the partisan values of either side, though both the reunion and the schoolhouse are given their full say. As a novel it meets the limitations of a specific time and place and draws

from the meeting the aspect of universality that all human activity contains. *Losing Battles* is, finally, much more than the sum of its parts.

Looking at the novel in terms other than strictly literary reveals the
real scope of its achievement. Welty has refined what she acknowledges
as the raw material of fiction—place, character, plot, symbolic meaning,
and feeling—into a novel both delicate and durable.[17] Place is both
concrete and universal in application; it is Banner, Mississippi, and the
whole condition of earthly existence as men try to live it. Characters,
even to the smallest bit part, are finely drawn and patiently watched and
listened to. They are also human examples of the abstractions called
mythical and historical consciousness. Trees and gold rings, both natural, plausible objects, are the agents of symbolic meaning for the story.
And the feeling is the honest judgment of limitations and the praise due
to worthy thought and actions. The result of the refinement is a novel
true to the widest range of human life.

This may not be said so unequivocally of *Delta Wedding*. The triumph
of *Losing Battles* is largely the triumph of the "onlooking" point of view.
Always serene, it is never aloof or condescending. Welty's reverence for
things—to return to the opening of the novel—is the real source of
authority in *Losing Battles*. We are not in a silent world of translucent
consciousness, as in *Delta Wedding*, but in a tactile, substantial, teeming
reality. The world *is*, as every Welty novel and story strives to say, and
to the susceptible it opens with beauty and meaning of which we ourselves are natural parts.

The mythic-minded hill people, here steadfastly treated with a generous yet just impartiality, are part of the world without knowing it. There
is no distance, literal or figurative, between the Beecham and his or her
dead forebear, and no distance between the member of the clan and the
spreading bois d'arc, its totem. But for those of the historical mind,
there is distance, and there is laughter for the judge as he gains the vision
of both sides of the battles.

Deep within the heart and memory of the individual this vision fights
for light. Just as fiercely the individual fights to keep it in the dark, for
the vision requires the leaving of the self and all that defines it. There
was Julia Mortimer wandering the dusty streets lost to herself after so
many years of such certain knowledge.

17. Welty, "Place in Fiction," 57.

## IX

So much depends, she
thought, upon distance:
whether people are near
us or far from us.
Virginia Woolf,
To the Lighthouse

# The Culminating Moment:
# *To the Lighthouse*
# and *The Optimist's Daughter*

One writer's admiration of another may be expressed in many ways—the visible tribute of a borrowed name or style, or a subliminal influence of which the present writer, perhaps, is unaware. The influence of Virginia Woolf in the writing of Eudora Welty has never been manifested in overt imitation. Instead, it is a kind of long-standing excitement about Woolf's achievements that has never diminished. "She was the one who opened the door. When I read *To the Lighthouse*, I felt, Heavens, *what is this*? I was so excited by the experience I couldn't sleep or eat. I've read it many times since."[1]

The deeply engendered excitement is much in evidence in *The Optimist's Daughter*. The "discourse" between these two writers, through these novels, is too intimate for the term *influence*. It is as if the experience of reading Virginia Woolf presented Welty with the images of her own unspoken, as yet unwritten ideas, hopes, and themes.

Both novels, *To the Lighthouse* and *The Optimist's Daughter*, return again and again to an idea of distance, whether the distance is created by the passing of time or by the gulf between the self and the public role, self and society, self and loved one, and self and the truth.

It is not condescension in Woolf to transform Mrs. Ramsay's *daube* into a meal of sacramental union. The mundane is miraculous because,

---

1. Kuehl, "The Art of Fiction XLVII," 75.

to the penetrating eye, the mundane is also the terrible realm of distances. The Ramsay family and their guests are tied by every kind of human connection: marriage, childhood and parenthood, friendship, courtship, discipleship. But beneath a superficial level on which the characters enter into combinations of love or enmity, the self remains isolated and frightened. The distances separating these people are overcome by miracles, and only temporarily. Mrs. Ramsay's heart longs for the miraculous victory over distance and time; Mr. Ramsay's mind devises constructs of permanence to stand outside the human and survive.

The same concerns with time and distance distinguish *The Optimist's Daughter*. The goal is the same, a miracle of unity in justification of a faith in human life. In her longer novel, *Losing Battles*, Welty also faces the enigma of distances, but indirectly. Her characters are separated from our present world by time and from the mainstream of their own era by poverty and uncertain, unmarked roads.

For *The Optimist's Daughter* Welty scales down her cast and locates place and time in the present. Groups hold the field in *Losing Battles*; the possible importance of individual conflict is secondary. In *The Optimist's Daughter* a single individual, Laurel McKelva Hand, is herself the battlefield and the conflicting sides—the self with the McKelva family name, rooted to a place and its people; and the self with the married name Hand, bound by love and memory to an individual life outside the family and place of birth.

Welty focuses on one family—mother, father and only daughter—through the eye and memory of the daughter. The events and images of the novel are simple, homemade, yet charged with the possibility of a miraculous richness, or the threat of tinny emptiness. These are the same kinds of mundane, daily events out of which Virginia Woolf produces miracles.

Laurel contends with the issues of distance in human relationships, with memory, and with faith in human life—issues that concern Virginia Woolf in *To the Lighthouse*. Dr. Courtland's examination instrument, with its "excruciatingly small, brilliant eye" (*OD*, 7) could not detect more finely the intricacies of the condition—the significant distances between what is spoken as truth and what actually *is* the truth about people, the haunting fear that there is an unknowable distance between the truth and the ability of humans to perceive it.

The distances show up clearly, in their full and surprising magnitude. But this short, controlled novel is not complete until the forces that seem to separate have yielded their treasury of connection. However chaotic and potentially destructive those forces may seem, there is a possible unity that can encompass them. The unity is created by the act of seeing, which, faithfully performed, stills the seer so that she, or he, might see the connections that link us to one another and to the world. The object of seeing—a lighthouse, for instance—is the catalyst, as Lily Briscoe discovers.

The "bridesmaids" who meet Laurel at the train station seem almost ageless in their ability to recreate their shared past. The years since Laurel's wedding seem to have been phantoms. But time has opened new distances behind this appearance of permanence.

Tish Bullock, one of the bridesmaids, seems to be at a busy intersection of change. Her parents, Welty says in the novel, have been married so long that they have begun to look like each other. But Tish is divorced. In the *New Yorker* version of the story, which preceded the novel, Welty writes that Tish, like others of Laurel's friends who had raised families, had children "close by in college" (*ODNY*, 95). For the novel, Tish's personal history is revised to include her divorce, and to distance her children "farther away still, off in college now" (*OD*, 123).

The other bridesmaids, too, have put distance between themselves and the past. They now have subdivision homes in the "new part" of Mount Salus. And in the novel Tish's youngest son does not appear. "Tish's youngest son was still at home. 'He won't come out, though,' Tish had said. 'He has company. A girl came in through his bedroom window—to play chess with him. That's what she said. I think she's the same one who came in through his window last night, close to eleven o'clock. I saw car lights in the driveway and went to see. They call him every minute. Girls. He's fifteen'" (*OD*, 123–24).

These small changes and additions to the novel point in the direction of an intentional but muted concern with the distances that are always widening at an alarming, unstoppable rate between people in the tightest groups. What does Tish reveal except her confusion and the pain of estrangement and distance from her own son?

The family, though it tries to be a formidable stronghold in the shifting field of change, is not without its dangers for the individual member.

Welty has always considered the family, in her writing, to be a double-edged weapon. Its conservatism and protectionism stifles as well as shelters. In *The Optimist's Daughter*, the complicated political and personal institution of the family, with its eternal tensions often blazing into open warfare, keeps returning to the fore as a major concern.

The Dalzell and the Chisom families, constantly chattering, seeming so insensitive and impervious to reason and reflection, loom in Laurel's imagination as a warning to the individual of suffocation under the mass of the group. The Dalzells, who occupy the hospital waiting room as the judge lies dying down the corridor, shuttle in and out of the intensive care section, lounge among the scraps and wrappers of their supper, and show no reluctance to talk about the hopeless condition of the dying Dalzell. They are the primal family; they dissolve the mystery and the horror in individual death with their own unhushed pleasure in each other.

Fay runs to them for comfort and is taken in, while Laurel, more suspicious, paces around them, trying in vain to block out their conversation, which is a grim and funny contest to see who can tell the best hospital story. These are elemental people, lovable and frightening in the purity of their physical concern for the dying: "No, if Dad's going to die I ain't going to let him die wanting water!" (*OD*, 39–40). With a blind but true instinct, the family knows that the only service it can render to the dying is the simple alleviation of physical pain and discomfort. For weeks Laurel has kept a useless vigil at her father's bedside, worn out in the futile attempt to reach his mind or his memory by reading his favorite books. But Fay, in the offering of her cigarette, and in her desperate attempt to "take ahold" (p. 32) of her husband the night of his death, comes closer to reaching him than Laurel does.

The family shields its members from the outer horrors by keeping attention focused inward. The family's instinctive defense when death threatens is to talk louder and faster, tell the familiar stories once again, assert that nothing is changing, never let the conversation die (*OD*, 36). Other families in the waiting room join in. The clamor of human voices is contagious and comforting to the family. "The family laughed louder, as if there could be no helping it. Some of the other families joined in" (p. 40).

To Laurel, pacing the perimeter, holding herself aloof and silent, the clan is frightening. The reason for their gathering in the hospital, the stunning, awe-filled approach of death, is ignored. The wake becomes a carnival. Laurel is alone in trying to get through to Fay that the judge is dying, might already be dead. But, inside the compound of the family, Fay is unreachable.

The distance between Laurel and family fluctuates. In the hospital waiting room she could not be farther away. The gulf is wide; differences of education, social class, and upbringing mark it clearly. Back in Mount Salus the distance is not so obvious. The bridesmaids and the community of Laurel's childhood appear to offer her comfort and peace. But their tactics worry Laurel as much as the Dalzells' chattering.

The Mount Salus wake also dissolves in chatter. The mourners have their own contest, to determine who can tell the most laudatory, though apocryphal, story about the late judge, their leader. The community's doctor is the first to venture a tale; he remembers saving the judge's life when they were both boys. And, without criticism from the group, his story enters the public record.

The judge's friend and law partner, Major Bullock, tells the most elaborate tale, an epic confrontation between the judge and a local band of "whitecaps." The teller casts the judge in the role of Gary Cooper in "High Noon": the grim, isolate, virtuous hero standing alone against overwhelming odds, while the community he is sworn to protect cowers behind its frilly curtains.

Laurel protests: "What's happening isn't real" (OD, 82), "They're misrepresenting him" (p. 83), "Father was delicate" (p. 74), "Father knew it wasn't funny" (p. 72). But her objections and corrections are summarily dismissed. The community is not searching for the truth, but for a truth that will cozily fit its corporate image of itself, just as the family in the waiting room ignored the fact of death because it was a threat to them all, the Mount Salus community ignores Laurel's story because it introduces details of private life that will not fit the fixed roles upon which the community depends for continuity.

The Dalzells, the Chisoms, even the bridesmaids and the Mount Salus community, are subdivisions of the great, interrelated family. They are the people for whom distance does not exist because they ignore it. The special case of the individual, the loneliness of the private self, the submerged life that Virginia Woolf's Mrs. Ramsay attends to with every breath—those aspects of life the "brood" ignores. Roscoe Chisom put his head in an oven and turned on the gas. His mother may tell the tale of Roscoe many times, yet she will never recognize the private weight that sent Roscoe, with his troubles, to a friend outside the clustering brood.

Laurel perceives the great distance between what the family demands and accepts from its members as the truth, and the actual, complicated private truth of each individual self. "They might have come out of that night in the hospital waiting room—out of all times of trouble, past or future—the great, interrelated family of those who never know the meaning of what has happened to them" (OD, 84). If the brood has the last word in human relationships, then the outlook is indeed pessimistic. We would perish, like Roscoe, "each alone." But Laurel remains optimistic that there is a state, accessible to the individual, that acknowledges both family and self without denying either one. The climax of To the Lighthouse is Lily Briscoe's discovery of the unifying miracle that had been Mrs. Ramsay's work. Laurel, too, makes her slow way through memory and error until the unifying vision is hers also.

Judge McKelva takes a public role as the embodiment of society's image of itself. He is a descendant of lawyers and missionaries. With the double heritage of public service, he is well suited to his office of leadership. To Laurel, his only child, he is both known and unknown, available and distant, father and judge.

His illness is enough to shock Laurel into the awareness of his vulnerable mortality. In his long decline toward death, the roles and titles drop away, leaving the man. He is almost a stranger to his daughter. Perhaps he always was. Laurel's first sight of him after his eye operation is startling. "Judge McKelva's head was unpillowed, lengthening the elderly, exposed throat. Not only the great dark eyes but their heavy brows and their heavy undershadows were hidden, too, by the opaque gauze. With so much of its dark and bright both taken from it, and with his sleeping mouth as colorless as his cheeks, his face looked quenched" (OD, 14). This moment is a kind of epiphany for Laurel, the more startling because it is natural. The moment in which parents appear naked of their aura of permanence and invincibility is one of the normal shocks of family life.

Each day of Laurel's vigil is filled with renewals of this shock. Her father "lay there unchangeably big and heavy, full of effort yet motionless, while his face looked tireder every morning" (*OD*, 22). Laurel's efforts are not directed toward her father's physical recovery. Instead, she reads aloud his favorite books and authors, trying to reinstate the figure of the father. But the physical decline is irreversible. "Eventually, Laurel saw that her father had accepted her uselessness with her presence all along. What occupied his full mind was time itself; time passing: he was concentrating" (p. 19).

Laurel cannot intervene in his interior battle. None of the public relationships hold any longer; none of the ties of friendship, love, or blood carry their former weight. The fact that approaching death erases all those ties is the one fact that cannot be evaded. So Laurel feels her uselessness, and, in it, a great, yawning distance between herself and her father. This distance demands an explanation. Her father's death presents Laurel with the need to understand her own life in a new light.

She soon learns that her effort to understand her father antagonizes the community for whom he is a paragon. Her objections to the public version of his life are brusquely overridden. Her desire to keep the coffin closed is a privilege the mourners will not allow because to them such privacy seems to scant generosity. "'And I've never forgiven him for that. [The judge had kept his wife's coffin closed.] Nobody ever really got to tell Becky goodbye,' Miss Tennyson was saying at the same time. 'But honey, your father's a Mount Salus man. He's a McKelva. A public figure. You can't deprive the public, can you? Oh, he's lovely'" (*OD*, 63).

Slowly, Laurel begins to realize the distance between her father's public mask and the man behind it. When the Chisoms, Fay's family, arrive for the funeral, the Mount Salus community reacts possessively, as if their figure were being usurped by an alien public. It is even rumored that the Chisoms have come without an invitation. But Major Bullock discloses that Judge McKelva himself, before departing for the hospital, had given him the address of Fay's family. This act, besides putting the nature of the judge's "optimism" in doubt, is also his ultimate deference to the rights of the family he had acquired by marrying Fay. "You can't deprive the public, can you?" Laurel begins to hear the answer her father would give, to realize his involvement with the public.

Notification of the next of kin is a lawyerly formality. But Welty sees meaning in the typical human action. In the *New Yorker* version of the story, Welty has Major Bullock summon the Chisoms on his own initiative (*ODNY*, 61). But, by shifting the responsibility for the summons to the judge himself, she accomplishes, with an economical stroke, a sharp insight into his character and the enrichment of her concern with humans at a distance. The news that the judge had seen to it that the Chisoms would be invited surprises Laurel with a new and unknown facet of her father's character. He becomes, in that moment, the prime conspirator against his own daughter's desire to keep his funeral private.

Laurel pursues her father into his public role. Finding his desk and his papers, she suddenly begins to realize how thoroughly he was the public figure. She finds all his official correspondence but not one of his personal letters. "He'd never kept them [his wife's letters to him]: Laurel knew it and should have known it to start with. He had dispatched all his correspondence promptly, and dropped letters as he answered them straight into the wastebasket; Laurel had seen him do it" (*OD*, 122).

The community and its projects took precedence in his life. Laurel comes across the records of his work on a flood control project for the county. But, she remembers, the mourners would rather have the apocryphal stories of melodramatic heroism. The public figure, it seems, must suffer his public actions to be taken for granted and his private life to be made up.

Welty's portrayal of the judge is an integral part of her concern with the distances that separate all people. Virginia Woolf's understanding of the character of Mr. Ramsay, and of the radical difference between him and Mrs. Ramsay, introduces a similar theme in *To the Lighthouse*. Mr. Ramsay, more thin-skinned than the judge, is, nevertheless, also a man whose self image is founded upon the esteem of his colleagues and students in public, intellectual circles. Also like the judge, Mr. Ramsay faces the world armed with logic and "laws." Virginia Woolf describes Mr. Ramsay as having "a splendid mind. For if thought is like the keyboard of a piano, divided into so many notes, or like the alphabet is ranged in twenty-six letters all in order, then his splendid mind had no sort of difficulty in running over those letters one by one firmly and accurately, until it had reached, say, the letter Q. He reached Q" (*TL*, 53).

Mr. Ramsay thinks rationally, sequentially, logically—the way the judge thinks. To the judge, the law is rational and logical; it separates, defines, "ranges . . . all in order." The judge and Mr. Ramsay both cling to the realm of the abstract concept for meaning and stability in life. And they are both wrung by the horror of reaching some unfinished point, the letter Q, beyond which their powers cannot take them.

Laurel discovers her father's letter Q in the memory of her mother's final illness. In that charged atmosphere her father's public self-image tottered and would have fallen but for an infusion of "optimism." Whenever Becky's demands for understanding became too strong and his power to comfort her became useless, he would return to his work, to bolster his sagging confidence. Then, near the end, he made some innocent, but false, boosting promises to Becky. Laurel remembers her mother's cry, and her father's reaction: "'Lucifer!' she cried. 'Liar!' That was when he started, of course, being what he scowlingly called an optimist; he might have dredged the word up out of his childhood. He loved his wife. Whatever she did that she couldn't help doing was all right. But it was *not* all right! Her trouble was that very desperation. And no one had the power to cause that except the one she desperately loved, who refused to consider that she was desperate. It was betrayal on betrayal" (*OD*, 150).

Laurel's insight into the private lives of her parents comes to her through memory. Her father's optimism was, like his work, his refuge. Just as Mr. Ramsay was dedicated to the spanning of the alphabet of human knowledge with his "splendid mind," the judge was dedicated to the work of his legal mind. The work and the accessibility of the goal were together the essence of this optimism. Phil, Laurel's husband, was not an optimist because he recognized no hope of ever making the object of one's work permanent: "She knew that. Phil had learned everything he could manage to learn, and done as much as he had time for, to design houses to stand, to last, to be lived in; but he had known they could equally well, with the same devotion and tireless effort, be built of cards" (*OD*, 162).

In the field of distances in the novel, the judge stands close to the stability of the public role. He steadfastly upholds traditions as the vessels of meaning. Though he knows little about his wife's roses, and though his pruning technique is clumsy and leaves the bushes looking "like puzzles," he makes the expected appearance on George Washington's Birthday, because that is the time-honored day for the pruning of roses. He is more for the tradition than for the roses.

Deliberately trying to infuse the abstract with meaning by constant reenactment is the judge's way. But it cost him close touch with the private, as Laurel learns. Laurel's mother and father are as opposed, in their receptions of life, as Mr. and Mrs. Ramsay. They might have been closer if they had realized they were fighting the same antagonist—life itself. To rescue something from the flow of time with the permanence of the truth was their common object.

Laurel notes that "there were twenty-six pigeonholes" in the desk where her mother's letters still remain, untouched; "but her mother had stored things according to their time and place, she discovered, not by ABC" (OD, 135). Laurel's discovery is her—our—insight into the polarity that her parents tried to bridge with their marriage. Her father arranged his papers according to an orderly filing system, chronologically and alphabetically. But Becky ignored the alphabet and followed her own order, gathering her letters around the times and places of her memory. This is a small fact about Becky's way with life. But, combining Becky's other domestic habits such as her refusal to detail the exact steps in her recipes, Welty creates a vividly present character who, like Julia Mortimer of Losing Battles, never appears in person.

Becky stands opposite the judge's position of the public figure adhering to his optimistic faith in the power of abstract guides such as the law, tradition, and logic. She is intensely, even ruthlessly, private. Her world is filled with physical sensation—the sounds of her mother and brothers, the feel of the dough when kneading has brought it to the best texture. Her mind is not the thorough, methodical mind that perseveres in conviction from Q to R and on to Z; it works by a kind of inspiration, beginning anywhere and leaping to Z, pulling unity out of the multiplicity of life by the force of her will.

Becky shares her position with Mrs. Ramsay, for Mrs. Ramsay's miracles are similar leaps from many to one. For both women life itself is the major foe, offering none of the challenge and opportunity for progress that it holds up before their husbands. Life, in the eyes of the women, means only dreadful losses. Mrs. Ramsay's poem expresses her constant concern with the transient nature of the lives it is her responsibility to nurture and propel.

> All the lives we ever lived
> And all the lives to be,
> Are full of trees and changing leaves (TL, 178)

All that life shows to her is "changing leaves," changing only to die. Mrs. Ramsay, observing the large family that she loves, is always vulnerable to a despair as deep and difficult to express as her miracles are beyond analysis.

> They [her children] all had their little treasures . . . and so she went down and said to her husband, Why must they grow up and lose it all? Never will they be so happy again. And he was angry. Why take such a gloomy view of life? he said. It is not sensible. For it was odd; and she believed it to be true; that with all his gloom and desperation he was happier, more hopeful on the whole, than she was. Less exposed to human worries—perhaps that was it. He had always his work to fall back on. (p. 91)

The public world is the refuge of both men, as well as their arena. Both fall back on their work when life becomes mysterious or depressing. But the women do not have such a refuge; they are exposed. Mrs. Ramsay regards time as the enemy that transforms her children into adults, with all the suffering, care, and failure of adults. Becky tries to ignore the public world, tries, by retiring "up home" every summer, to keep her past green beyond the time allotted to it.

The women face time differently in trying to arrest it. Laurel, watching her dying father, senses his characteristic attitude toward the time left to him. She realizes that he can no longer push it forward. Becky was always for holding time still. The character of her memories shows this. The events of successive years lose the specificity of dates and collect, like her letters, around a place or a time. There are very few coordinates in Becky's memories. The place is "the mountain," or "up home," and "the river" winds below the mountain. Only the outside, alien places have names—Baltimore, Mount Salus, Chicago. Becky's memory condenses her whole childhood and youth up to her marriage (which meant moving into the outer world) into the pure, timeless present of a mild summer pastoral. On her deathbed, the past is more vivid to her than the present. When she looks at her own hands, she sees, as if they were there before her, the hands of her mother, cracked and bleeding after breaking ice in the water bucket.

Becky's final illness strips away the last of her reserve; and the passionately individual person emerges. She takes on, one at a time, the public figures and their orthodoxies. First, she uses her own wasting condition to attack Dr. Courtland's professional role as the doctor. He is a man in the splendid refuge of his work. It gives Becky satisfaction to penetrate the fortifications.

Then she requests the help of the minister, Dr. Bolt. But the match is uneven. Becky can recite the psalms from her tenacious memory faster than he can read them. And to his orthodox counsels of faith in the hereafter, Becky replies with a parable of the white strawberries. Her parable says that to live in this world demands a kind of adamant courage and stamina rooted deep within the private self. You must have the strength to get there, alone, and the courage and presence of mind to eat the berries on the spot. The minister, she says, would line his hat with leaves and take every precaution in bringing back the berries for another time. But they would spoil and never have the same sweetness.

Becky's credo is heresy to the "clusterers"; it is private and secular, but still reverent. She is oceans apart from Mrs. Chisom and the other mother hens whose role society depends upon. There is no protective cushion, no role, no matriarchal wing to use for shelter. Becky is exposed in her decline, as she willfully lived her life. She has courage, Laurel knows, but she cannot give comfort, not even to herself.

The judge's optimism is his comfort, the deliberate belief that everything will come out all right in the end. Becky and Mrs. Ramsay, with their tendencies to pessimism, cannot accept that belief. As Mrs. Ramsay sees the issue: "How could any Lord have made this world? She asked. With her mind she had always seized the fact that there is no reason, order, justice: but suffering, death, the poor. There was no treachery too base for the world to commit; she knew that. No happiness lasted; she knew that" (*TL*, 98). Laurel remembers her mother with a similar superstition. "'Mother had a superstitious streak underneath,' Laurel said protectively. 'She might have had a notion it was unlucky to make too much of your happiness'" (*OD*, 124). The differences between her parents always come back, Laurel realizes, to time. Her father was aggressive, tried to be, in pushing time forward. "As he lay without moving in the hospital he had concentrated utterly on time passing, indeed he had. But which way had it been going for him? When he could no longer get up and encourage it, push it, forward, had it turned on him, started moving back the other way?" (pp. 151–52). There is the suggestion of Sisyphus in Laurel's vision. She pictures her father losing a futile struggle against an irreversible process. The judge's strategy against time, Laurel imagines, had been to take control of it, or seem to, making a line of progress out of random moments. His optimism was his manifesto and his creed, his public message and his private meditation.

But Becky was always different. Her energies were devoted to isolating the timeless essence of things and people. Mrs. Ramsay's day is crowned with the dinner in which she coaxes the restless egos around her into a single, almost sanctified body. Becky's life, as Laurel revives it in her memory, was the vain but admirable effort to do a similar thing. But she was defeated.

In her mother's crusade to sanctify "up home," Laurel sees a life that deserves a tribute and a criticism. In Becky's proud isolation she found the strength to make the trip with her dying father to Baltimore, to face the strange world without blinking. That earns Laurel's tribute: "But Becky had known herself" (*OD*, 144). But the same pride in her self-knowledge distanced Becky from others. "How darling and vain she [Becky] was when she was young! Laurel thought now. She'd made the blouse—and developed the pictures too, for why couldn't she? And very likely she had made the paste that held them" (pp. 136–37).

As Becky lies on her back, blind, weak, and dying, time finally routs that self-sufficiency. The real distances that she had declared between herself and others echo with her desperate cries, "Lucifer! Liar!" and her recriminations, accusations, disputes, and protestations against defeat. Out of her schoolgirl's memory, Becky seizes a recitation exercise from McGuffey, "The Cataract of Lodore." With its dozens of present participles, this verse is Becky's last desperate effort to arrest time, to hold off the end until the last possible moment. "With her voice she was saying that the more she could call back of 'The Cataract of Lodore,' the better she could defend her case in some trial that seemed to be going on against her life" (*OD*, 147). Welty places this verse as the last message of a fiercely proud woman whose strength, whether rooted in herself or in her attachment to a group, proves only human after all. In this moment, Laurel uses the language of distance, placing her mother opposite her father, as the defendant in a trial over which death presides.

"She had died without speaking a word, keeping everything to herself, in exile and humiliation" (*OD*, 151). This is the same end that enveloped the judge, and Becky's own father in the Baltimore hospital, and Laurel's husband in the Pacific in World War II, and Roscoe, and everyone everywhere. Laurel is faced with the end and with two ways of preparing for it, contrasted in her parents. Her father had worked to squeeze as much use out of his time as possible. In the process he fell away from the private and personal. Having trained his eye in the reading of legal documents, he became blind to much of the human. He must have looked out of his study window a thousand times, Laurel thinks, and never once seen Adele Courtland waiting for him in her own stubborn, proud loneliness. And Becky could not avert her attention from the end, fighting more heatedly, fiercely, ruthlessly, the closer it came. She ignored the relationships that might have comforted. (With this vision of life, how much more important than public success are the single things —the beam of light, the sound of the waves lapping against the side of a boat, the memory of a mountain, a brother scraping on a banjo—around which separate moments cluster. These are the things in *To the Lighthouse* and in *The Optimist's Daughter* that allow the vision to sharpen, usually away from the center of the action, and discover the path to unity that the larger human drama obscures.

Laurel is between these two poles, compelled by her allegiance to answer both father and mother. She needs the insight into the truth that unifies both ways, not the sign that confirms one and outlaws the other. She is like Lily Briscoe in many ways—introspective, sensitive to the bustling and fighting around her, yet reluctant to leap out of herself and into the ring. She is like Lily also in a way that is significant for the novel; Laurel's discovery of the unifying stroke that coaxes contradictions into harmony, the gift of an inspired moment of her heart's attention, fulfills and climaxes the book.

The problem of distance confronts Laurel in the fullest reach and twist of its complexity. She has, alone in the novel, the sharpness of eye, the depth and sensitivity of awareness, to see and to feel each turn and gulf. Though she never admits it, the distance between Chicago and Mount Salus, home and home, has changed her. She has never lost the vivid memory of her excitement and promise when she and Phil rode the train south to their wedding. Everything seemed possible for her then. Time seemed to be a blessed companion. Birds, like watchful attendants, followed the couple south, and the confluence of rivers welcomed them as a sign and a guarantee of hope and happiness.

Now Laurel makes the journey on a jet. The years of her widowhood lie behind the novel; so do the symbols, birds, and rivers, now to be re-encountered. In the foreground are the bridesmaids and the lure of Mount Salus. Laurel feels the great distance that has grown between them and herself. Finally, overwhelming these intermediate distances is the strange distance she finds where she expected the most familiar territory—between herself and her parents.

The same concern for the real binding strength of the closest human ties figures importantly in *To the Lighthouse*. Mrs. Ramsay, looking for solace in human closeness, is pessimistic. "A shadow was on the page . . . precisely now, at the very moment when it was painful to be reminded of the inadequacy of human relationships, that the most perfect was flawed, and could not bear the examination which, loving her husband, with her instinct for truth, she turned upon it" (*TL*, 62).

Laurel, with her instinct for truth, and loving her parents, is uniquely suited to pierce the distortions of social, sexual, family, and personal roles that hide the truth of human intercourse and veil the answer to whether any real touch takes place between self and other. The question is similar to Virginia Woolf's: does the flaw invalidate "the most perfect" relationship, and, therefore, all relationships? Must we live *and* perish, each alone? So many protective and defensive screens move in and out between us and the world of experience we share with others, both novelists say, that success in touching the real and true of the world is life's consuming challenge.

Laurel's return to New Orleans, to be with her father for his eye surgery, is a reentry behind a familiar set of screens. In Dr. Courtland's office, the opening scene of the novel, Laurel is given asylum from the immediate truth. The discussion of her father's condition skirts the medical facts. Before the data, a lifetime of shared experience must be read into the record to preface the here and now. The judge has chosen Dr. Courtland because, he says, "I know his whole family." The shared memory of Becky's death envelopes Laurel and Dr. Courtland without a word from either one. He thinks, "This girl knows," and nods toward Laurel—a sufficient explanation of medical history and diagnosis. The impersonal medical vocabulary is used, finally, to explain to Fay, the alien. And its use seals her exclusion. Laurel is already implicated in the automatic conspiracy to keep Fay at a distance.

From the outset we have a clear outline of the obstacle Laurel faces—a network of time-honored relationships and shared pasts that is substituted, in whole or in part, for the unpleasant facts of the present. This system cushions—for the straight language of facts is painful—and it also excludes. Fay has no hope of acceptance. The protection works two ways; if Fay cannot get in, Laurel cannot escape.

Laurel's sad homecoming with her father's coffin, the rites of the community, the ragged encounters with Fay and her clan are temptations to renege on her nascent pledge to live, to go on with it (one of the simple values of *Losing Battles*). The goal, which Laurel gradually clarifies, is the truth above the babel of things and people. Laurel, named for the evergreen, believes in continuity in life and must face these temptations to divorce herself from life's less virtuous and happy encounters. Hers is a true optimism.

The pursuit of objectivity is not achieved simply by disavowing all obstacles, denying antecedents, and declaring personal autonomy. Fay's charge carries no weight: "Oh, *I* wouldn't have run off and left anybody that needed me. Just to call myself an artist and make a lot of money" (*OD*, 28). Laurel is not so selfish. Her goodness comes from her unselfish and patient allowance for the people around her, their legends, needs, beliefs. Although at times her patience is tried, she knows that life is shared. Laurel, as Reynolds Price has written, is an "onlooker" by nature, patiently sorting out the truth from a tangle of error, memory, and observation in "their" apocrypha and her own blind spots.[2]

Laurel, on her way to the truth, must confront and correct her own weaknesses. It is not all "their" fault. Perhaps Laurel's basic weakness is her natural reticence about personal contact, which amounts almost to outright fear of others not as reserved and sensitive as herself. This could be interpreted, by someone on the insecure end of a relationship with Laurel, as a snobbish distaste.

Fay must believe that Laurel disapproves of her in such a way. In the New Orleans rooming house, with Fay separated from her only by a "landlord's strip of wallboard," Laurel's insecurity grows. "Where there was no intimacy, Laurel shrank from contact; she shrank from that thin board and from the vague apprehension that some night she might hear Fay cry or laugh like a stranger at something she herself would rather not

2. Price, "The Onlooker Smiling," 116.

know" (*OD*, 18). In the rooming house the protective circle of familiar people with common, interlocking life stories is unavailable; Laurel faces in her own fastidiousness something close to treason against life.

Laurel's timidity about human contact goes deeper than her apprehension about Fay. It can be traced back to the childhood visits with her mother "up home." One summer her grandmother's pigeons seemed, to a child's uncontrolled fears, to threaten her.

But Laurel had kept the pigeons under eye in their pigeon house and had already seen a pair of them sticking their beaks down each other's throats, gagging each other, eating out of each other's craws swallowing down all over again what had been swallowed before: they were taking turns. The first time, she hoped they might never do it again, but they did it again next day while the other pigeons copied them. They convinced her that they could not escape each other and could not themselves be escaped from. So when the pigeons flew down, she tried to position herself behind her grandmother's skirt, which was long and black, but her grandmother said again, "They're just hungry, like we are." (*OD*, 140–41)

The heart of the novel might be located in this passage. In facing this memory Laurel faces the tight knot of contradictions that challenges her growth. The pigeons depend upon each other for nourishment, each member of the brood contributing his share to the digestion that is essential for the survival of the group. The cost to the individual is plain; each member gives up its individual freedom and allows the other members free access to its body for digestion and warmth. Nothing is surprising; there are no secrets. Each one is known to the others.

Sexual themes in the novel have the same tension. The negative aspects of sex as a weapon underlie portions of the novel. The rivalry of Edna Earle and Bonnie Dee goes underground. Fay is nearly the same age as Laurel and is obviously a creature of high, if strident, sexual presence. This aura is not lost on Laurel or on the other women of Mount Salus, who would have liked to arrange a match for the judge. Their feeling of being cheated is evident when they congregate in Becky's garden for a catty session of gossip, with Fay as the subject. Fay is not domestic; they have seen her and the judge taking Sunday breakfast in a restaurant. Fay would rather go to Mardi Gras and sleep in a peach satin bower (that contraption is not really a bed), than perform the duties of a loyal, domestic wife. The women believe they have a valid indictment of Fay as the cheap seductress. Adele Courtland participates in the session only with her dry, satiric comments; the mockingbird showers the whole conversation with his "mocking" notes. To close the scene a band of narcissistic cardinals, all cocks, swoop at their reflections in tin "bird frighteners." Adele has the last word, "nothing but a game."

But Laurel, coming to her new awareness, abstains from the condemnation of Fay. Human relations, including the sexual, are a shifting ground. Her memory has revealed much to her about her parents' marriage. Laurel remembers her own brief marriage with a stiffly checked tenderness. "'If Phil could have lived—' But Phil was lost. Nothing of their life together remained. Except in her own memory; love was sealed away into its perfection and had remained there" (OD, 154). Her tenderness is controlled by her objectivity. She admits that her marriage had been one of "magical ease" and "brevity" (p. 121). It was never susceptible to change, to decay, to the flaws that Mrs. Ramsay feared and suspected in the most perfect of relationships. But Laurel has outlived that perfect marriage. Survival, she realizes, means change for the living. "Even if you have kept silent for the sake of the dead, you cannot rest in your silence, as the dead rest" (p. 130). Though her memory blesses her with "firelight and warmth" (p. 133), and with "the character of spring" (p. 115), Laurel knows that the blessing means ever greater distance between the survivor and the dead.

As Laurel moves closer to the unifying point, her memory blooms more richly. Forced ever deeper into her house by the swift that is trapped inside with her, Laurel delves more deeply into the memories she had once felt too sacred for fresh appraisal. In the light shed by time and her own growth, these events seem to take on a different aspect. Becky's splendid self-sufficiency might have been self-satisfaction and unfair aloofness. The judge's enviable public career might have been the robes covering certain personal inadequacies.

After the harrowing of her memory, Laurel is near the brink of the miracle. Between the New Yorker story and the novel, Welty made significant changes in the climax. These changes show the author's increased awareness of the nature of Laurel's discovery.

In the New Yorker, Laurel spends the long night reading her mother's letters in the small sewing room, when she cowers in fear of the bird that occupies the rest of the house. She then takes the stone that her father had carved for her mother and "presumes" to give it to Adele Courtland. Thus she trespasses on a privacy she should have respected. Adele declines the memento. Laurel keeps it for herself: "It was stolen from this house; she was a thief now. At the same time, having it there in her bag was a way to go back to Chicago. It was one of her ways to live—storing up to remember, putting aside to forget, then to find again—hiding and finding. Laurel thought it a modest game that people could play by themselves, and, of course, when that's too easy, against themselves. It was a game for the bereaved, and there wasn't much end to it" (*ODNY*, 126).

Taking one small memento to save for the future is the way to an artificial memory—as if Laurel were a person of uncertain memory who needed a charm to pull it all back. Welty removed the above passage from the novel; she made other small changes that contribute to the depth of Laurel's Mount Salus experience. One of these smaller changes is the removal of Laurel's Chicago friend. In the story, Laurel makes two calls from the hospital, one to her office and one to a friend (*ODNY*, 40). In the novel, Laurel makes only one call, to her place of business, thus leaving her less sheltered in the challenge to her new faith. Without the protection of "games" or of friends who might, just by their existence, offer refuge, Laurel is on her own in the novel.

Laurel's climactic encounter with Fay undergoes drastic changes from story to novel. In the story version, Fay returns from her visit to Texas with the intention to "forgive" Laurel: "And *I* came back to part friends. *I* was ready to kiss and make up. DeWitt talked me into it. DeWitt says in this old world we all need to make some allowances for all the cranks in it" (*ODNY*, 128). The creaking clichés, "part friends," "kiss and make up," "this old world," though they mark Fay as a simple-minded woman, also relieve her of some opprobrium. At least she *says* she is willing to forget, however hackneyed her reasons. Laurel feels a pang of shame at this moment in the story. Her own behavior seems to verge upon snobbishness. Whatever ordeal Laurel has endured in the story, this late encounter puts a crease in the nobility of it.

Then, in the *New Yorker* story, Laurel rushes together her own apocryphal, half-imaginary picture of the events. She thinks that there might have been a "Fay" long before Becky had become ill and died. The judge might have taken one for solace during his wife's long absences "up home" in the summers, or during his long trips as a circuit judge. Again Laurel is caught with shame. The discovery of her mother's breadboard, made by Phil, then causes her self-esteem to curdle. "As she held it there, all the pride she had felt in the cleaning, the polishing, the burning of the evidence, in all she had driven herself to do, changed suddenly and wholly into shame. Shame beat inside her, thudded against her chest" (*ODNY*, 127).

At the end of the *New Yorker* story Laurel is, at best, in a static position. She realizes how devious are the ways she fools herself. She is embarrassed by her own tactics of evasion and falsification in trying to alter the past—burning evidence, blaming Fay, scheming to correct the past by giving the carved stone to Adele Courtland. Laurel leaves Mount Salus, in the story, without affirming the continuity in life.

Changes for the novel show that Welty decided that this ending was unsatisfactory. Her changes transform Laurel from a woman caught in a web of self-deception and gaming into a woman whose growth has assumed the past, with its contradictions and mysteries, and made it part of her own unity. Love, not shame, is the emotion the new Laurel discovers. "For her life, any life, she had to believe, was nothing but the continuity of its love" (*OD*, 160). And again, "For there is hate as well as love, she supposed, in the coming together and continuing of our lives" (p. 177). Laurel's slow ascent to this point, like Lily Briscoe's long contest with her own unfinished picture, must take its own time. The summit is composed of memory and love and joy; there is no need for physical possession of the past. "Memory lived not in initial possession but in the freed hands, pardoned and freed, and in the heart that can empty but fill again, in the patterns restored by dreams" (p. 179).

So Fay clacks in, strident as a jay to the end of the novel, with not even parroted sentiments of forgive-and-forget. Fay is as impervious, functional, and predictable as the modern push-button kitchen she has installed in Becky's house. She is Laurel's final obstacle, a temptation to retribution that must be resisted.

The breadboard is still the pivot of this crucial scene. Laurel raises it above her head as if to smite Fay in righteous, heaven-condoned vengeance for her callous spoiling of it, her unwitting desecration of the hands that made it and the hands that used it. But no violence is needed. "'What do you see in that thing?' asked Fay. 'The whole story, Fay. The whole solid past,' said Laurel" (*OD*, 178).

Touch is, in the novel, an index of a person's response to life. Dr. Courtland's hands, Laurel imagines, could read the time through the crystal of his watch. Becky's hands, sewing, weeding, kneading bread, are printed in Laurel's memory more vividly than the features of her face. And her own dead husband, Philip Hand, has become in memory a condensation of the work of his hands—his architectural designs, his home repairs, his breadboard. Now these memories pour through Laurel's hands and make a genius of her heart. In a moment of inspiration she discovers, in the snug, hand-fitted unity of the breadboard, the continuity of life beyond the sketchy sense her own memory and knowledge can make of it. "Experience did, finally, get set into its right order, which is not always the order of other people's time" (*OD*, 174). Nor is it the order of her own time either, but of a time as serene and untouchable as the time in the Chinese prints that hang on the wall near the McKelva clock (p. 73).

Lily Briscoe discovers unity in her art; the stroke of her brush separates her from her completed picture. Laurel also discovers unity; her discovery also confirms her separation from the past, its sufferings, dead ends, mysteries, and joys. But she has her approachable, evergreen, heart. At the end of the *New Yorker* story Laurel is significantly short of this rebirth, detoured by a temptation to fix the past to her own terms and her own less than impartial judgment of Fay.

Reynolds Price, writing about the *New Yorker* version, says that Laurel's final emotion is joy.[3] If so, it is the qualified joy, perhaps relief, of one who has not been compelled to face the deepest mysteries and secrets in herself. The major revisions in the Random House novel dwell, I think, on this vital area of Laurel's condition as a family member who is not yet fully aware of what that family embraces. The continuity of life—the essential need of others for the presence and survival of the self in life and after death—is much more deeply realized in the novel.

Laurel, in the novel, strikes deeper roots. She faces her weaknesses and mistakes, and leaves them behind her. She leaves her house to Fay, not in shame and surrender, for she has burned everything of value. She leaves it, not as a temple deconsecrated and left to the vandals, but as a real place, a house, where real lives were lived and will be lived, the site of errors, love, faith, and treason. She leaves the house in Mount Salus and goes on to live the rest of her life, believing in its continuity without the need for palpable symbols.

3. *Ibid.*, 134.

# Afterword:
# Reading Welty

Has there ever been a writer so concerned about the act of reading? Many authors complain when their works are read ignorantly, esoterically, or too seldom. For Welty, however, concern with being read is not so egotistic. Her concern for the reader—a strong and consistent concern that has filled her own literary tastes and criticism—comes from the same wellspring of reverence for people and the world that feeds her fiction.

For Welty the reader is a partner in imagination, working toward the same moment of communication for which the author strives.[1] The writer works by craft and sensitivity; the reader, it is hoped, responds with love and imagination, so that author and reader find each other by the slow synchronizing of their voices. For Welty, the writer—the artist in general—is not a single voice that proclaims its own existence whether anyone hears or not; the artist's voice always calls for meeting, for the completed act of communication.

Welty's constant theme is communication itself, the state of human existence in which individuals, because of some connection with each other in the natural world, become more than the simple integers they might seem. Every hero and heroine, from Mrs. Larkin to Laurel McKelva Hand, leaving the private, silent world of memory, grief, or dream,

1. Welty, *Short Stories*, 53.

crosses a threshold into a real world that is enriched by that very entry, by that self so long withheld.

Also part of this passage is the reader of Welty's fiction. He must be attentive to the totally and artistically synthesized vision of the world that sustains her work.[2] The moment of vision is built upon the particular world each fiction summons into existence. The climactic experience of each of Welty's fictions is not only the resolution of a plot but a denouement of the form, in which the world appears in its integrity before the reader, allowing him to realize how and when the parts become whole.

This world is naturally rich in nuance and allusion, suggestion and mystery; it possesses the coherence and the integrity of a living thing. Centuries of mythology confirm that man's needs for stories to order phenomena have never been desperate or consciously artificial means of pretending there is order. Each individual in his or her time—like Virgie Rainey—sees the world through eyes bequeathed by seers far back, and the relays are successful because the world seen by each human is the same.

It is the thing made, the work of art in the act of being made that discovers this integrity of seer and the world. Literature requests of its readers an alertness of the imagination, a sensitivity so sharp that incident, setting, and character (the basic elements of fiction) may be appreciated as unique elements and as pieces of a whole. Sometimes one might almost think that Welty writes with the hope of frustrating the literary critic, for the integrity of her vision stays beyond the reach of analysis. The act of reading Welty, then, harbors the vision, the meaning. The analytic statement is the bare outline of an already completed itinerary.

Welty has often expressed the opinion that literary analysis may not, in fact, be the true response to the "world-surround" of a particular author. "Story writing and an independently operating power of critical analysis are separate gifts, like spelling and playing the flute, and one person proficient in both has been doubly endowed. But even he can't rise and do both at the same time."[3] "Literary analytics," in her view, is not the most advantageous approach for her reader because it sacrifices the experience of discovering the "thing made" to the convenience of

2. Welty, "How I Write," 245.
3. *Ibid.*, 240.

having it presented by a previous reader who has tagged and judged each part. Instead, the reader should work toward the essential vision of the fiction from the outside while the author strives through style to escape the self and to objectify experience in the act of communicating it.[4] Success is meeting, and meeting, in various forms, is a frequent theme and motif of Welty's fiction. Thus, making a story is only one part of the artistic act; there must be a mind and heart striving from another direction to complete it. That is reading.

Imagination, sensitivity, vision (words closely synonymous in Welty's essays on writing and writers) must be the essential possessions of writer, reader, and critic. Criticism, when it becomes too analytical and dissective, often destroys the imagination because it takes away some or all of the suggestion inherent in things themselves. Fiction depends on the natural suggestive and connective power of experiences rising into language, for communication comes in "degrees and degrees and degrees."[5] Welty reads fiction this way, following degree after degree of communication to the irreducible heart of the artist's vision of himself in the world. Her essays on Bowen, Cather, Austen, Chekhov, and Faulkner, among others, bear witness to the consistency of her view. Her own work must be read in the same spirit. Her fiction, like all great fiction and all (for lack of a better cliché) great art, teaches each beholder how to read it, how to see it. In her essay on Willa Cather's fiction, Welty alludes to this enriching effect: "A work of art is a work: something made, which in the making follows an idea that comes out of human life and leads back into human life. It is an achievement of order, passionately conceived and passionately carried out."[6] I have been learning the process, the concerted action of intellect and imagination, from Welty's fiction; this study is my attempt to record what I have learned. Each work builds upon passion and order, heart and head, love and knowledge. To pay close attention to how the writing is made is to be drawn into this rhythm and ultimately to a point of unity.

In the fiction of a writer who has said, "We start from scratch, and words don't" and who has also called for such respect for the imagination as to name it both the process and the end of writing, one must pay

4. Eudora Welty, "Words into Fiction," *Southern Review,* I (Summer, 1965), 551.
5. *Ibid.,* 543.
6. Eudora Welty, "The Physical World of Willa Cather," *New York Times Book Review,* January 27, 1974, p. 22.

close attention to each detail, must never expect the work to be finished, must never expect that its meaning is hiding in one circumscribed and definable reservation within a given story or novel.[7] In Welty's work the *how* is the *what*. Technique in its most fundamental aspect—its unique way of responding to the world and of expressing the impact of the world it meets—is what is given to the reader.

Welty has given, and will continue to give (for these works are soundly made and will stand), a literature that reaches great stature in its theme of love. Few writers understand that the most complex human emotion, love, is also the most simple, and that a true treatment of the theme is both discussable and not. As John Bayley has written, "The world, the theme, the meaning [of love] exist and yet do not exist: they are both inside us and outside."[8] Bayley's study of the characters and theme of love in works by Shakespeare, James, and Tolstoi provides a surprising illumination for Welty's fiction. His statements, "Art has chosen the theme of love both to indicate human separation and to unite humanity again" and "Love may sometimes give us a marvellous degree of mutual consciousness but it also reinforces our most intractable solipsism," present beautifully apt descriptions of the themes and characters in Welty—Jenny and Billy Floyd in "At the Landing" and the cumulative theme of *The Bride of the Innisfallen*, for example.[9] And Bayley's comments further illuminate the technical difficulty faced by the writer who desires to respond to the imperative of love as topic, the writer who loves his characters treats them, and indeed his whole work, as both a private creation and something ultimately separate and beyond his power to render.[10]

Welty's achievement is exactly this. The world she creates in her fiction is unmistakably hers, and also irresistibly the world itself. One approaches Welty's fiction with humility and imagination, which needs order to "survive": "We come to terms as well as we can with our life-long exposure to the world, and we use whatever devices we may need to survive."[11] In Welty's fiction the reader must not expect or depend upon

7. Welty, "Words into Fiction," 543.
8. John Bayley, *The Characters of Love: A Study in the Literature of Personality* (London, 1960), 33.
9. *Ibid.*, 7, 5.
10. *Ibid.*, 5.
11. Welty, *One Time, One Place*, 8.

the infallible key, for meanings shift and "doubleness" (as Clement Musgrove painfully discovers) abounds in all things. The hero, the writer,
and the reader—each is expected to try to "come to terms" with a pro-
tean existence that flows and metamorphoses before the eye a thousand
times between reach and touch. In such a world, then, the writer must
keep eye and heart open to the vital movement in which beholder and
beheld merge, in which Perseus, slaying Medusa, becomes his own victim. Reading fiction that is rooted in such an intricate sense of the inter-
connectedness of time, gesture, and identity, the reader must not be
anxious for the definitive slogan, the point of the story. "The mystery
lies in the use of language to express human life." [12] From Welty's earliest
stories her use of language and style attempts to find expression for the
life and the mystery, to communicate the thing without omitting its
mystery.

A kind of passion is necessary in the reader as well as the writer.
Welty herself frequently uses the word *passion* in her own critical writing
to describe the state of extraordinary consciousness during which a writer
makes a completed thing, realizes all of the "capacity" in a certain experience and form. "Literary analytics" might discover the chips and
strands of that beginning but will not recover the essential, unique spirit,
the passion that was present in the creation. If a reader sees the parts
working toward the whole, he may partake of the passion of the writer
and gain greater pleasure and communication from the work the writer
has made, and from his own act of reading. That is the experience of
literary art, according to Welty—the joy of reading:

Yes, I think we write stories in the ultimate hope of communication, but so do
we make jelly in that hope. Communication and hope of it are conditions of
life itself. Let's take that for granted and not get sidetracked by excitement. We
hope somebody will taste our jelly and eat it with even more pleasure than it
deserves and ask for another helping—no more can we hope for in writing a
story. Always in the back of our heads and in our hearts are such hopes, and
attendant fears that we may fail—we do everything out of the energy of some
form of love or desire to please. [13]

It is clear that this passionate hope of communication and love better
suits the reader of Welty's fiction than does, say, the apparatus of a cer-

12. Welty, "Words into Fiction," 545.
13. Welty, *Short Stories*, 5.

tain critical theory. I have made some choices in my reading of Welty's fiction in order not to be caught passive before the fiction. These choices —angles of vision, analogies, comparisons with other works of literature —might not, in all cases, do the fiction full justice. But, in the end it is not any writing *about* Welty's fiction, but the work itself, that will last or have the final word.

Reviewing the *Selected Letters of William Faulkner*, Welty made a quick tour of the major scholarly approaches to her fellow writer. In the end, however, she wrote that his fiction is still the best and truest voice of the writer: "Read that," she said.[14] A writer's life—his work—is in the care of his readers.

14. Eudora Welty, review of *Selected Letters of William Faulkner*, in *New York Times Book Review*, February 6, 1977, p. 30.

# Bibliography

WORKS BY EUDORA WELTY

*Books*

*The Bride of the Innisfallen and Other Stories.* New York: Harcourt, Brace, 1955.
*Delta Wedding.* New York: Harcourt, Brace, 1946.
*The Eye of the Story: Selected Essays and Reviews.* New York: Random House, 1978.
*Fairy Tale of the Natchez Trace.* Jackson: Mississippi Historical Society, 1975.
*The Golden Apples.* New York: Harcourt, Brace, 1949.
*Losing Battles.* New York: Random House, 1970.
*Music From Spain.* Greenville, Miss.: Levee Press, 1948.
*One Time, One Place.* New York: Random House, 1971.
*The Optimist's Daughter.* New York: Random House, 1972.
*The Ponder Heart.* New York: Harcourt, Brace, 1954.
*The Robber Bridegroom.* Garden City, N. Y.: Doubleday, Doran, 1942. Also adapted for the stage by Alfred Uhry and Robert Waldman. Performed by the Acting Company, Saratoga Summer Theatre, August 2, 1975.
*Selected Stories of Eudora Welty.* Introduction by Katherine Anne Porter. New York: Modern Library, 1954.
*Short Stories.* New York: Harcourt, Brace, 1949.

*Short Stories*

"Golden Apples." *Harper's Bazaar* (September, 1947), 216–320.
"The Hummingbirds." *Harper's Bazaar* (March, 1949), 195–252.

"The Optimist's Daughter." *New Yorker*, March 15, 1969, pp. 37–128.

"Shower of Gold." *Atlantic Monthly*, CLXXXI (May, 1948), 37–42.

"The Whole World Knows." *Harper's Bazaar* (March, 1947), 198–338.

*Essays and Reviews*

"The House of Willa Cather," in Bernice Slote and Virginia Faulkner, eds., *The Art of Willa Cather.* Lincoln: University of Nebraska Press, 1974, pp. 3–20.

"How I Write." *Virginia Quarterly Review*, XXXI (Spring, 1955), 240–251.

"The Physical World of Willa Cather." *New York Times Book Review*, January 27, 1974, pp. 19–22.

"Place in Fiction." *South Atlantic Quarterly*, LV (January, 1956), 57–72.

"Some Notes on River Country." *Harper's Bazaar* (February, 1944), 86–156.

"Words into Fiction." *Southern Review*, I (Summer, 1965), 543–53.

"In Yoknapatawpha." *Hudson Review*, I (Winter, 1949), 596–98.

Review of Elizabeth Bowen's *Pictures and Conversations*, in *New York Times Book Review*, January 5, 1975, pp. 4, 20.

Review of *Selected Letters of William Faulkner*, in *New York Times Book Review*, February 6, 1977, pp. 1, 28–30.

*Unpublished Writing*

"The Bride of the Innisfallen," short stories. Carbon copy of typescript, with author's revisions. Humanities Research Center, University of Texas at Austin.

"The Delta Cousins," short story. Typescript. Department of Archives and History, Jackson, Mississippi.

"The Robber Bridegroom," synopsis and fragments of screenplay. Typescript. Department of Archives and History, Jackson, Mississippi.

"The Wide Net," short stories. Carbon copy of typescript, with author's revisions. Humanities Research Center, University of Texas at Austin.

Letter to Joseph Fields and Jerome Chodorov, March 28, 1955. Department of Archives and History, Jackson, Mississippi.

OTHER SOURCES

*Bibliographies*

Polk, Noel. "A Eudora Welty Checklist." *Mississippi Quarterly*, XXVI (Fall, 1973), 663–93.

Thompson, Victor H. *Eudora Welty: A Reference Guide.* Reference Guides in Literature, No. 11. Boston: G. K. Hall, 1976.

*Books and Parts of Books*

Appel, Alfred, Jr. *A Season of Dreams: The Fiction of Eudora Welty.* Baton Rouge: Louisiana State University Press, 1965.

Bayley, John. *The Characters of Love: A Study in the Literature of Personality.* London: Constable, 1960.

Bogan, Louise. "The Gothic South," in *Selected Criticism*. New York: Noonday Press, 1955, 207–209.

Bowen, Elizabeth. *The Death of the Heart*. New York: Alfred A. Knopf, 1939.

———. Review of Eudora Welty's *The Golden Apples*, in *Seven Winters and Afterthoughts*. New York: Alfred A. Knopf, 1962, 215–18.

Bryant, J. A., Jr. *Eudora Welty*. University of Minnesota Pamphlets on American Writers, No. 66. Minneapolis: University of Minnesota Press, 1968.

Charity, A. C. *Events and Their Afterlife*. Cambridge, England: Cambridge University Press, 1966.

Eisinger, Chester. "Eudora Welty and the Triumph of the Imagination," in *Fiction of the Forties*. Chicago: University of Chicago Press, 1965, pp. 258–83.

Fields, Joseph and Jerome Chodorov. *The Ponder Heart: Adapted from the Story by Eudora Welty*. New York: Random House, 1956.

Forster, E. M. *Aspects of the Novel*. New York: Harcourt, Brace & World, 1955.

Glenn, Eunice. "Fantasy in the Fiction of Eudora Welty," in Allen Tate, ed., *Southern Vanguard*. New York: Prentice Hall, 1947, pp. 78–91.

Gray, Richard. *The Literature of Memory: Modern Writers of the American South*. Baltimore: Johns Hopkins University Press, 1977.

Hardy, John Edward. "*Delta Wedding*: Region and Symbol," in *Man in the Modern Novel*. Seattle: University of Washington Press, 1964.

Hawthorne, Nathaniel. *The Blithedale Romance*. New York: W. W. Norton, 1958.

Hohenberg, John. *The Pulitzer Prizes*. New York: Columbia University Press, 1974.

Howard, Zelma Turner. *The Rhetoric of Eudora Welty's Short Stories*. Jackson: University and College Press of Mississippi, 1973.

Isaacs, Neil D. *Eudora Welty*. Steck-Vaughn Southern Writers Series, No. 8. Austin: Tex.: Steck-Vaughn, 1969.

Kenner, Hugh. *A Homemade World: The American Modernist Writers*. New York: Alfred A. Knopf, 1975.

Langbaum, Robert W. *The Poetry of Experience: The Dramatic Monologue in Modern Literary Tradition*. New York: Random House, 1957.

Manz-Kunz, Marie-Antoinette. *Eudora Welty: Aspects of Reality in Her Short Fiction*. Swiss Studies in English. Bern, Switzerland: Francke Verlag, 1971.

Marx, Leo. *The Machine in the Garden*. New York: Oxford University Press, 1964.

Price, Reynolds. *Things Themselves: Essays and Scenes*. New York: Atheneum, 1972.

Ransom, John Crowe. "Reconstructed but Unregenerate," in Twelve Southerners, *I'll Take My Stand: The South and the Agrarian Tradition*. Baton Rouge: Louisiana State University Press, 1977, pp. 1–27. Originally published in 1930.

Rubin, Louis D., Jr. *The Faraway Country.* Seattle: University of Washington Press, 1963, pp. 131–54.

Simpson, Lewis P. *The Man of Letters in New England and the South: Essays on the History of the Literary Vocation in America.* Baton Rouge: Louisiana State University Press, 1973.

Stapleton, Laurence. *The Elected Circle: Studies in the Art of Prose.* Princeton, N.J.: Princeton University Press, 1973.

Utley, Francis Lee. Introduction to Max Lüthi, *Once Upon a Time: On the Nature of Fairy Tales.* Translated by Lee Chadeayne and Paul Gottwald. New York: Frederick Ungar, 1970.

Vande Kieft, Ruth M. *Eudora Welty.* New York: Twayne, 1962.

Woolf, Virginia. *To the Lighthouse.* New York: Harcourt, Brace & World, 1955.

*Periodicals*

Aldridge, John W. "Eudora Welty: Metamorphosis of a Southern Lady Writer." *Saturday Review*, April 11, 1970, pp. 21–22, 35–36.

Allen, John A. "Eudora Welty: The Three Moments." *Virginia Quarterly Review*, LI (Autumn, 1975), 605–27.

Bishop, John Peale. "The Violent Country." *New Republic*, November 16, 1942, pp. 646–47.

Blackwell, Louise. "Eudora Welty: Proverbs and Proverbial Phrases in *The Golden Apples.*" *Southern Folklore Quarterly*, XXX (December, 1966), 332–41.

Bradford, M. E. "Looking Down From A High Place: The Serenity of Miss Welty's *Losing Battles.*" *Recherches Anglaises et Américaines*, IV (1971), 92–97.

Bunting, Charles T. "'The Interior World': An Interview With Eudora Welty." *Southern Review*, VIII (October, 1972), 711–35.

Carson, Franklin D. "Recurring Metaphors: An Aspect of Unity in *The Golden Apples.*" *Notes on Contemporary Literature*, V (September, 1975), 4–7.

Curley, Daniel. "Eudora Welty and the Quondam Obstruction." *Studies in Short Fiction*, V (Spring, 1968), 209–24.

Devlin, Albert J. "Eudora Welty's Historicism: Method and Vision." *Mississippi Quarterly*, XXX (Spring, 1977), 213–34.

Farwell-Brown, Abbie. "The Lucky Stone." *St. Nicholas Magazine*, XLI (January–July, 1914), 215–814.

Fleischauer, John F. "The Focus of Mystery: Eudora Welty's Prose Style." *Southern Literary Journal*, V (Spring, 1973), 64–79.

Glaser, Jean. "Reviews." *Ephemera*, V (Winter, 1942), 29.

Kuehl, Linda. "The Art of Fiction XLVII: Eudora Welty." *Paris Review*, LV (Fall, 1972), 72–97.

McHaney, Thomas L. "Eudora Welty and the Multitudinous Golden Apples." *Mississippi Quarterly*, XXVI (Fall, 1973), 589–625.

Morris, Harry C. "Eudora Welty's Use of Mythology." *Shenandoah*, VI (Spring, 1955), 34–40.

Oates, Joyce Carol. "Eudora's Web." *Atlantic Monthly*, CCXXV (April, 1970), 118–120, 122.

Peden, William. "The Incomparable Welty." *Saturday Review*, April 9, 1955, p. 18.

Ransom, John Crowe. "Delta Fiction." *Kenyon Review*, VIII (Summer, 1946), 503–507.

Rosenfeld, Isaac. "Double Standard." *New Republic*, April 29, 1946, pp. 633–34.

Rubin, Louis. "Two Ladies of the South." *Sewanee Review*, LXIII (Autumn, 1955), 671.

Schorer, Mark. "Technique as Discovery," in James Calderwood and Harold Toliver, eds., *Perspectives on Fiction*. New York: Oxford University Press, 1968, 200–16.

Slethaug, Gordon E. "Initiation in Eudora Welty's *The Robber Bridegroom*." *Southern Humanities Review*, VII (Winter, 1973), 77–87.

Thompson, Victor H. "The Natchez Trace in Eudora Welty's 'A Still Moment.'" *Southern Literary Journal*, VI (Fall, 1973), 59–69.

Trilling, Diana. "Fiction in Review." *Nation*, May 11, 1946, p. 578.

Trilling, Lionel. "American Fairy Tale." *Nation*, December 19, 1942, p. 687.

Vande Kieft, Ruth M. "The Vision of Eudora Welty." *Mississippi Quarterly*, XXVI (Fall, 1973), 517–42.

Warren, Robert Penn. "The Love and Separateness in Miss Welty." *Kenyon Review*, VI·(Spring, 1944), 246–59.

Yardley, Jonathan. "The Last Good One?" *New Republic*, May 9, 1970, pp. 33–36.

*Newspaper Articles*

Boatwright, James, Review of Eudora Welty's *Losing Battles*, in *New York Times Book Review*, April 12, 1970, pp. 1, 32–34.

Breit, Harvey. "Books of the Times." *New York Times*, August 18, 1949, p. 19.

Brookhouser, Frank. "Miss Welty's New Talent in Short Stories." *Philadelphia Inquirer*, December 3, 1941.

Bunn, Frances, "Short Stories." Raleigh (N.C.) *Observer*, April 19, 1942.

Cournos, John. Review of Eudora Welty's *Delta Wedding*, in *New York Sun*, April 15, 1946, p. 21.

Douglas, Louise. "Genuine Artistry." Nashville *Banner*, December 20, 1941.

Engle, Paul. "Miss Welty's Full Charm in First Novel." Chicago *Tribune*, April 14, 1946, pp. 3, 12.

Gilman, Richard. Review of Reynolds Price's *The Surface of Earth*, in *New York Times Book Review*, June 29, 1975, pp. 1–2.

Hauser, Marianne. "Miss Welty's Fairy Tale." *New York Times Book Review*, November 1, 1942, p. 6.

Hutchens, John K. "Miss Welty's Somewhat Puzzling Art." New York *Herald Tribune*, April 10, 1955, p. 2.

———. "Books and Things." New York *Herald Tribune*, August 18, 1949, p. 13.

Kane, Harnett T. "Eudora Welty's Authentic and Vital Talent." New York *Herald Tribune Weekly Book Review*, April 14, 1946, p. 3.

Kazin, Alfred. "An Enchanted World in America." New York *Herald Tribune Books*, October 25, 1942, p. 19.

Lehmann-Haupt, Christopher. "Books of the Times." New York *Times*, April 10, 1970, p. 37.

North, Sterling. Review of Eudora Welty's *The Bride of the Innisfallen*, in New York *World Telegram*, April 7, 1955, p. 22.

Price, Reynolds. "Frightening Gift." Washington *Post*, April 17, 1970, Sec. C, pp. 1, 4.

Pryce-Jones, Alan. "Almost a Winner." *Newsday*, June 2, 1970.

Ruffin, Carolyn R. "Sensitivity Runs a Poor Second." *Christian Science Monitor*, June 11, 1970, p. 13.

Schiff, Sarah. "Stories Too Green To Burn." Springfield (Mass.) *Republican*, January 11, 1942, Sec. E, p. 7.

Schmucker, Walter. "A Visit With Eudora Welty in Mississippi." Dallas *News*, December 24, 1950.

Steegmuller, Francis. "Small-Town Life." *New York Times Book Review*, August 21, 1949, p. 5.

*Theses and Dissertations*

Carson, Franklin D. "Eudora Welty's *The Golden Apples* and the Problem of the Collection-Novel." Ph.D. dissertation, University of Chicago, 1971.

Hinds, Katherine Powell. "The Life and Works of Eudora Welty." M.A. thesis, Duke University, 1954.

Hochberg, Mark Robert. "Narrative Forms in the Modern Southern Novel." Ph.D. dissertation, Cornell University, 1970.

Thompson, Victor H. "'Life's Impact Is Oblique': A Study of Obscurantism in the Writings of Eudora Welty." Ph.D. dissertation, Rutgers University, 1972.

Wild, Rebecca Smith. "Studies in the Shorter Fiction of Elizabeth Bowen and Eudora Welty." Ph.D. dissertation, University of Michigan, 1965.

# Index

This brief index is chiefly an aid to the reader in locating information on books and short stories in places not indicated in the table of contents.